The Makeup of
RuPaul's Drag Race

The Makeup of *RuPaul's Drag Race*

Essays on the Queen of Reality Shows

EDITED BY JIM DAEMS

McFarland & Company, Inc., Publishers
Jefferson, North Carolina

LIBRARY OF CONGRESS CATALOGUING-IN-PUBLICATION DATA

The makeup of RuPaul's drag race : essays on the queen of reality
shows / edited by Jim Daems.
    p.   cm.
Includes bibliographical references and index.

ISBN 978-0-7864-9507-8 (softcover : acid free paper) ⬭
ISBN 978-1-4766-1886-9 (ebook)

1. RuPaul's drag race (Television program : 2009–)
2. RuPaul's drag U (Television program : 2010–)   3. Female
impersonators on television.   4. Sexual minorities on
television.   I. Daems, Jim, 1966– editor.

PN1992.77.R87M35 2014
791.45'75—dc23   2014034052

BRITISH LIBRARY CATALOGUING DATA ARE AVAILABLE

Front cover images © 2014 iStock/Thinkstock

Printed in the United States of America

McFarland & Company, Inc., Publishers
  Box 611, Jefferson, North Carolina 28640
  www.mcfarlandpub.com

Table of Contents

Preface

This book is a critical examination of *RuPaul's Drag Race* (with some attention paid to its spin-offs, *Drag U* and *Untucked!*). Although the essays collected here approach this reality TV show from a variety of academic perspectives, I do believe that the book is accessible to a wider popular readership. The RuPaul franchise is important both in terms of putting drag on TV and the wider socio-political contexts that it engages with. Certainly, we can see the program as a sign of wider tolerance of LGBTQ people in North America, even if it runs on specialty channels aimed at an LGBTQ audience (Logo in the U.S., OUTtv in Canada). However, we cannot avoid the more negative socio-political aspects that still impact the program and the lives of LGBTQ people, particularly the ongoing struggle for equal civil rights such as same-sex marriage, the violence faced by trans people, and day-to-day trans- and homophobia. We also cannot ignore the larger world picture in which homosexuality continues to be or is being criminalized and LGBTQ people are actively hunted and terrorized in countries such as Uganda and Russia. The program is, then, a progressive step in terms of visibility and engagement with some of the important issues faced by its LGBTQ audience and its allies.

This project began with my interest as a fan of *RuPaul's Drag Race*—and not only from a queer perspective, but also because the show continues to be a fabulous camping of tired reality TV genres. Even when we are, as academics, critical of aspects of the program, I believe that for all the contributors gathered here, an underlying enjoyment as fans of *RuPaul's Drag Race* motivates our readings of the program.

Introduction
RuPaul's Ambivalent Appropriation of Pop Culture

JIM DAEMS

Premiering in February 2009, *RuPaul's Drag Race* quickly became Logo TV's biggest hit and revitalized RuPaul's career. Currently in its sixth season, and renewed for a seventh, *Drag Race* has been nominated for a number of television awards and has won, for example, "Most Addictive Reality Star" (Ongina in 2009 at the NewNowNext Awards), "Outstanding Reality Program" (2009 GLAAD Media Awards), "Best Reality Competition Series" and "Best Reality Show Judge" (2012 TV.com Awards). In a 2008 pre-series publicity interview with Perez Hilton, RuPaul jokingly stated of the show,

> Tell Tyra [Banks] that the Queen has returned, and while you're at it have Heidi [Klum] clear the runway. I'm going to pump some "realness" into reality. To be a winner on this show the contestants need to be a fashion designer, an American Idol, and a top model all rolled up into one. And they definitely have to be smarter than a fifth grader.[1]

This statement neatly encapsulates *Drag Race* as a mix of "reality TV" subgenres that have so effectively contributed to the program's success. Writing in *The New Yorker*, Emily Nussbaum, for example, recognized that *Drag Race* effectively parodies and explicitly queers *Project Runway* "which was already the gayest thing in town."[2]

The premise of *Drag Race* is to find "America's Next Drag Superstar." At the beginning of each episode, contestants face a mini-challenge (an assigned task with little or no preparation time). Winning the mini-challenge often gains a contestant an advantage in the main challenge (such as first pick of teammates or of wardrobe items). The main challenge is followed by the contestants facing a more elaborate task with a longer preparation time. During the two challenges, RuPaul appears in a man's suit, "male drag," chats with contestants, and gives them advice on what they are planning for the main challenge. Like RuPaul in the first two segments, the contestants are seen primarily in male clothing or in various stages of drag transition preparing for the challenges. This very explicitly presents their transformations from male to queen for viewers and can be seen as highlighting the way gender works in our culture. But it can also highlight the way in which those very gender constructs can be subverted. In addition, when he announces the first mini-challenge, RuPaul tells the contestants, "'Gentlemen, start your engines. And may the best woman win!' Examining this phrase helps us understand that the audience (and the contestants) should view the participants' gender as both male and female depending on the situation or context."[3] Eir-Anne Edgar adds that the judging criteria RuPaul announces before the first challenge begins further destabilize gender binaries:

> Judges will be looking for their [the contestants'] "Charisma, Uniqueness, Nerve and Talent," their C.U.N.Ts, if you will. While on stage, the Queens need to make sure that their C.U.N.Ts are present for the judges to rate. The articulation of femininities (and the contestants' metaphorical cunts) helps us see that gender is situational; its display in the context of this show spills over socially constructed demarcated binaries that separate man from woman.[4]

While this catchphrase, one of many on *Drag Race*, does destabilize gender binaries, it has been seen by some as misogynistic. Others have noted that the video "She Mail" announcement to the contestants at the beginning of the program, in conjunction with the above catchphrase, can also be read as misogynistic and transphobic. Indeed, a recent mini-challenge where the contestants were shown a picture of part of a body and asked to decide whether the person was "female" or "she-male" prompted a significant amount of criticism. This led to the following apology on the *RuPaul's Drag Race* Facebook page:

> We wanted to thank the community for sharing their concerns around a recent segment and the use of the term "she-mail" on Drag Race. Logo has pulled the episode from all of our platforms and that challenge will not appear again. Furthermore, we are removing the "You've Got She-Mail" intro from new episodes of the series. We did not intend to cause any offense, but in retrospect we realize that it was insensitive. We sincerely apologize.[5]

A number of essays collected here will address these issues.

The program then culminates in a runway presentation judged by RuPaul, now in female drag, and a celebrity panel of judges that include regulars Michelle Visage and Santino Rice and two guest judges (these range, for example, from Lady Bunny to Chaz Bono and LaToya Jackson to Henry Rollins). The winner of the week is announced, and the two queens that are judged to have performed the most poorly through the challenges and the runway presentation are put head-to-head in a "Lip Sync for Your Life" performance. The loser is then eliminated and "sashays away." This continues until there are three remaining contestants of which one will be judged "America's Next Drag Superstar." In addition, each episode is interspersed with candid comments by contestants about themselves and their competitors.

Ideally, then, *RuPaul's Drag Race* brings drag to a wider audience. However, this is still essentially a queer audience as defined by the specialty channels that air the program. Edgar notes,

> It seems unlikely that a viewer would stumble across *Drag Race* accidently while channel surfing. While audience exclusivity may impede gaining new viewership, it also legitimates and authenticates the show through its close proximity to a queer audience. Significantly, *Drag Race* is positioned as the official reality television show for queer America, demonstrating the permissible forms of drag and gender performance.[6]

Yet despite audience limitations, there are positive consequences to a wider exposure of drag within the LGBTQ community. RuPaul has stated that

> for many contestants—young queens learning the ropes of the art, gay men estranged from or reuniting with their families, trans women in various stages of transition—the show is a visible step on their journeys of emotional growth. It sounds trite, but for each queen who allows a chapter of her life story to be featured on *Drag Race*, there's an opportunity for a teachable moment in the audience. With weekly recaps and regular coverage in mainstream media outlets like *Entertainment Weekly* and *Television Without Pity*, the Polari, or slang, of drag culture—as well as the everyday lives of gay men and trans women—serve to educate the audience and humanize the show's contestants in a subversive way.[7]

The show does, indeed, reveal the human beings beneath the drag. This can be beneficial beyond the individual contestants' "journeys of emotional growth" to those journeys for LGBTQ viewers, but, as Edgar notes, *RuPaul's Drag Race* does, arguably, delimit "permissible forms of drag and gender performance."

In this collection, for example, Mary Marcel argues that viewers of the program are afforded access to a "wide and non-traditional representation of sex, gender and sexual orientations," which, combined with the racial and ethnic diversity of the contestants, can provide a space for such journeys. This aspect of *RuPaul's Drag Race* is furthered significantly by the fact that the program is created and performed by drag queens. In this way, *Drag Race* is a form of self-representation which counters a long history of negative representations of drag in popular culture. But, as Marcel notes, this is potentially challenged by the pressures of commercial television and product placement within the show, as well as the treatment, within its diversity of drag queens, of trans contestants.

Laurie Norris notes, however, that the earlier diversity of queens has, by season five of *Drag Race*, been replaced by a predominance of Fishy queens. From this realization, Norris interrogates the notion of homonormativity as the mirror image of heteronormativity on the show and how this contributes to both misogyny and transphobia. She focuses primarily on three queens (Tatianna, Carmen Carrera, and Monica Beverly Hillz) to trace the effects of this on the program and, along with Marcel, engage with *Drag Race*'s handling of trans issues.

Focusing on another aspect of diversity, Libby Anthony questions the notion of the program's purpose to find "*America's* Next Drag Superstar" by doing a "translingual" reading of *Drag Race*. Many of the contestants on the show are from Puerto Rico, an unincorporated territory of the United States. Anthony argues that while *Drag Race* may push against gender and sexuality boundaries, by analyzing the assumptions made by the other contestants, judges, and the show's producers regarding multilingual contestants, one can assess the significant role that the English language, or "Standard English," plays in a contestant's quest to become "America's Next Drag Superstar." For Anthony, this adds one more level to the diversity presented audiences of *Drag Race*.

Hence, while the program brings drag into mainstream pop culture packaged as "reality TV," a number of the essays collected here question the consequences of what can be seen, through heavy product-placement, as a commodification of drag. In a sense, each essay engages with Judith Butler's assertion that

> drag is an example that is meant to establish that "reality" is not as fixed as we generally assume it to be. The purpose of the example is to expose the tenuousness of gender "reality" in order to counter the violence performed by gender norms.[8]

Viewing the transformations of the queens in each episode, juxtaposed with personal comments about their experiences that often include homo- or transphobia, does demonstrate the performativity of gender and the "violence" of gender norms. But presenting drag within a context reliant on product placement may well undercut this. One approach to this concern centers on RuPaul's judging choices (he makes the ultimate decision of who wins the week and who is eliminated) which can be seen as motivated by a desire to choose "America's Next Drag Superstar" in his own image of glam drag. What is notable here, however, is the way that RuPaul in "male drag" is separated from RuPaul in female drag:

> With *RuPaul's Drag Race*, he [RuPaul] has found his calling: extolling the virtues of personal empowerment. He spends most of each episode in funky tailored suits (what he calls "male drag"), doling out advice on everything from beauty to relationships. Ending each episode of *Drag Race* with an Oprahfied affirmation ("If you can't love yourself, how in the hell you gonna love anybody else? Can I get an amen!") he reveals his own philosophy of love and self-worth. Drag was the door RuPaul walked through to reach stardom, but it's what he does with his public platform that defines him.[9]

This is similar to what Elizabeth Schewe notes of the rags-to-riches narrative of RuPaul's autobiography, *Lettin' It All Hang Out*:

> At this narrative level, RuPaul analyzes his relationship with his distant father as the foundation for later dysfunctional relationships, and the final chapter (before the Diana Ross afterword) posits as the story's resolution his ability to forgive his father and begin to love himself.[10]

As the Oprah of drag, RuPaul extends his own "journeys of emotional growth" into the advice given to contestants and the very format of the show—challenges such as roasting RuPaul and performing a ballet based on his life. His response to criticism of a preference for glam contestants is illustrative of this: "What we're looking for is someone who can really follow in my footsteps: Someone who can be hired by a company to represent their product, someone who can put together a sentence on television and present themselves in the most incredible way."[11]

A few points are significant in this statement. Similar to how contestants manage certain challenges in which they are coupled with either a male or a female to do up in drag, often choosing a "mini-me" approach, RuPaul himself can be seen as taking this "mini-me" approach in judging. In terms of the goal of being a product spokesperson, this highlights the significance of product placement on *Drag Race*. Kai Kohlsdorf argues that product placement on the program undercuts any potential for gender and/or sexual subversions. Like Norris, Kohlsdorf believes that making drag into a mainstream format of reality TV plays into normative expectations: "The queens on the show are policed to become RuPaul replicas in order to sell products." RuPaul's stress on commercialization in the quotation above can also be seen as influencing a performance art that has traditionally, with some exceptions, including RuPaul himself, been marginalized, even at times within queer culture. Arguably, then, in *Drag*

Race, the legitimacy of the queens is gauged by their ability to represent products—to become a part of mainstream society. For Fernando Gabriel Pagnoni Berns, the "reality" format and mainstream commodification calls into question just what a drag queen is because *Drag Race* "reveals both the complexity of the figure of the drag queen and the arbitrariness of reality shows." He argues that the nature of the challenges bears little relation to the concepts of "real" femininity and the "prettiness" that is stressed on the show and favored by RuPaul's judging. Interestingly, for Berns, the program embraces a ludic freedom amidst its commodifying tendencies.

Similarly, both R. Gabriel Mayora and Josh Morrison examine the consequences of mainstreaming drag, arguing that the show plays into assimilationist strategies. Mayora looks at *Drag Race* "as a mirror of the current relationship between mainstream gay culture and queer Latino/a masculinity." He argues that locas challenge the "normativity" of current LGBTQ politics in the U.S. while also emphasizing the marginalized status of queer Latino/a masculinities in the white mainstream. Mayora believes that *Drag Race* offers a key site, through the interactions of the queens and the program's popularity, from which to analyze the relationships between U.S. LGBTQ communities. Whereas Mayora focuses on Latino/a queens, Morrison uses critical camp studies to examine how *Drag Race* promotes "particular gender roles and homonormative political causes." Drawing on Caryl Flinn's concept of "loving assassination," he argues that both *Drag Race* and *Drag U* commodify drag, thereby incorporating queer males into "normative regimes of power." The most surprising example of this process is Morrison's reading of the season two challenge where contestants were paired with Stonewall-era men for a drag makeover, subverting, to a degree, the significant role of drag queens in the riots. In such readings, *Drag Race* and *Drag U* are seen as complex negotiations of both drag history and the development of LGBTQ political activism. The drag transformation of these Stonewall-era men is especially interesting because

> while the drag queens of Stonewall and the less publicized uprisings that preceded it have been lionized by a new generation (and some might argue, revisionist generation) of queer historians, their very presence at a rally after the first San Francisco gay pride parade in 1972 was enough to prompt feminists and their gay male supporters to refuse to participate in future parades in which drag queens were permitted to "mock" women.[12]

The Stonewall challenge on *Drag Race*, then, partakes in a revisionist reading that mainstreams a "lionized" past in order to align it with a more acceptable, less politicized view of drag. In effect, it drags a significant moment in North American LGBTQ history.

These essays, then, suggest that the commodification of drag challenges any notion of its potentially transgressive nature to lay bare gender as a social construct in both *Drag Race* and *Drag U*. However, others in this collection argue that there still is a predominantly subversive element present in these programs. Carolyn Chernoff begins with the "charm school" episode of *Drag Race*, season one, before turning to *Drag U*. She argues that the "Pygmalion formula" of the makeover of women by drag queens destabilizes the performance of femininity and binary notions of gender. The "mini-me" approach here, Chernoff contends, by bringing together queens and cis-gendered women in a collaborative partnership, highlights the social construction of gender and allows for its critique.

To round out the essays collected here, and their critiques of positive and negative aspects of mainstream drag as represented by *RuPaul's Drag Race* and *Drag U*, David J. Fine and Emily Shreve examine the significance of allusions to *The Prime of Miss Jean Brodie* in the RuPaul franchise. These allusions allow them to interrogate the relationship between RuPaul, the contestants, fans, and critics of the programs. RuPaul's interaction as mentor to the contestants on *Drag Race*, as well as his role of Dean on *Drag U* can be seen, Fine and Shreve argue, to parallel Miss Jean Brodie's teaching career:

> RuPaul's school for girls is prone to the tensions that threaten all forms of education: to maintain tradition is oftentimes to stifle the new; to engender her story is already to circumscribe it; to teach with charisma, uniqueness, nerve, and talent truly is to open oneself to unflattering readings.

We can recall here RuPaul's assertion cited earlier that "for each queen who allows a chapter of her life story to be featured on *Drag Race*, there's an opportunity for a teachable moment in the audience." Fine and Shreve argue that the analogy between Brodie and RuPaul allows us to comprehend fully the programs' radical potentials and their fundamental legacies for drag.

Thus, this collection of essays provides profound insights into making drag a reality TV program and the possible ways of reading the relationship between the two. That relationship is clearly a contested one, leaving viewers and critics a variety of interpretations of the significance of both *RuPaul's Drag Race* and *Drag U*. In *Television Culture*, John Fiske comments on the polysemic nature of television and argues that

> the preferred meanings in television are generally those that serve the interests of the dominant classes: other meanings are structured in relations of

dominance-subordination to those preferred ones as the social groups that activate them are structured in a power relationship within the social system. The textual attempt to contain meaning is the semiotic equivalent of the exercise of social power over the diversity of subordinate social groups, and the semiotic power of the subordinate to make their own meanings is the equivalent of their ability to evade, oppose, or negotiate with this social power.[13]

RuPaul's Drag Race and *Drag U* are, as part of the larger LGBTQ community, located within the dominance-subordination relations that Fiske alerts us to. Within that negotiation of social power, there may be the same "deep ambivalence" that Schewe sees in *Lettin' It All Hang Out*:

> In spite of RuPaul's celebration of pop culture, his observation that "all we learn about in school is about shopping, about going to the mall. We learn about how to enslave the soul and how to enslave our brothers, by buying and selling things, buying and selling each other" suggests a deep ambivalence about his beloved popculture market.[14]

Each contributor critically engages with this negotiation and deep ambivalence in their own ways, making their own readings by evading, opposing, and negotiating with RuPaul's pop culture commodities.

Notes

1. Perez Hilton, "The Search for America's Next Tranny," Perezhilton.com, May 14, 2008. http://perezhilton.com/2008–05-14-ru-paul#sthash.sYrZ4VSe.dpuf (accessed November 10, 2013).

2. Emily Nussbaum, "Camptown Races," *The New Yorker*, April 23, 2012. http://www.newyorker.com/arts/critics/notebook/2012/04/23/120423gonb_GOAT_notebook_nussbaum (accessed November 15, 2013).

3. Eir-Anne Edgar, "*Xtravaganza!* Representation and Articulation in *RuPaul's Drag Race*," *Studies in Popular Culture* 34, no. 1 (2011): 139. http://ehis.ebscohost.com.proxy.ufv.ca:2048/eds/pdfviewer/pdfviewer?vid=4&sid=f349708e-25fc-4cfa-94df-ec9e4ed4a148%40sessionmgrll3&hid=102 (accessed November 2, 2013).

4. Edgar, 140.

5. *RuPaul's Drag Race*, Facebook, posted April 14, 2014.

6. Edgar, 135.

7. Sharmin Kent, "How 'Drag Race' Gave RuPaul a Comeback—and Made Him a Next-Generation Oprah," *Thinkprogress*, October 11, 2013. http://thinkprogress.org/alyssa/2013/10/11/2771461/rupaul-drag-race/ (accessed November 2, 2013).

8. Judith Butler, *Gender Trouble: Feminism and the Subversion of Identity* (New York: Routledge, 1999), xxii–iii. http://site.ebrary.com/lib/ucfv/Doc?id=10054731 (accessed November 2, 2013).

9. Kent.

10. Elizabeth Schewe, "Serious Play: Drag, Transgender, and the Relationship

Between Performance and Identity in the Life Writing of RuPaul and Kate Bornstein," *Biography: An Interdisciplinary Quarterly* 32, no. 4 (2009): 678. http://ehis.ebscohost.com.proxy.ufv.ca:2048/eds/detail?vid=5&sid=8f223ff9-1c4b-4020-ac04-369dc9ac3829%40sessionmgr112&hid=102&bdata=JnNpdGU9ZWRzLWxpdmU%3d#db=aph&AN=47903518 (accessed November 2, 2013).

11. Kyle Buchanan, "RuPaul on *Drag Race*, Hannah Montana, and 'Those Bitches' Who Stole Annette Bening's Oscar," *Vulture*, April 4, 2011. http://www.vulture.com/2011/04/rupaul_on_drag_race_hannah_mon.html (accessed November 9, 2013).

12. Bruce Drushel, "Performing Race, Class, and Gender: The Tangled History of Drag," *Reconstruction: Studies in Contemporary Culture* 13, no. 2 (2013). http://ehis.ebscohost.com.proxy.ufv.ca:2048/eds/detail?vid=11&sid=1c89b3de-6284-4a2c-bf9b-9cd1afe2a9e8%40sessionmgr110&hid=16&bdata=JnNpdGU9ZWRzLWxpdmU%3d#db=hus&AN=90487034) (accessed November 2, 2013).

13. John Fiske, *Television Culture* (rpt.: London: Routledge, 1990), 126–7.

14. Schewe, 678.

Representing Gender, Race and Realness

The Television World of America's Next Drag Superstars

MARY MARCEL

In the non-mediated, non-televised and generally not fabulous world, November 20 is Transgender Day of Remembrance. In November 1995, a transgender woman named Chanelle Pickett was strangled to death by her date, William Palmer, in Watertown, Massachusetts, allegedly because he was unaware that she had a penis, and needed to quiet her down after he made this "discovery."[1] Palmer received a two-year prison sentence. A group of activists in Boston started the event after the murder of a second transgender woman, Rita Hester, in Allston, Massachusetts, in November 1998. These two murder victims were transgender women of color.

Every day transgender and cross dressing people around the world, including drag queens, are verbally and physically harassed, robbed, beaten and killed, despite their own best efforts to protect themselves.[2] Few of these cases are prosecuted and many murders remain unsolved. Advocates and allies of the community, though, often miss the mark. Even the estimable Lady Gaga can sing her hit song "Born This Way" and breezily erase the irony and hyperbole, the danger and pain which fuel drag fierceness, while claiming its aesthetic valences as her biological own.[3] By suggesting that the performative acts of a drag queen are simply "a drag" for the cisgendered suggests that drag queens are to blame for their own oppression. The seminal 1991 documentary *Paris Is Burning*, about drag ball performers in New York, captured in similar manner the voguing Madonna coopted from gay and transgender people early in her career; while Madonna danced her way to a lucrative career, the young dancers whose moves she mass-marketed remained culturally, economically and socially marginalized.[4] The cisgendered, even women who should know better, can well be accused of projecting their privilege as if the queer among us already enjoyed it.

It seems reasonable to think that it will be a long time before the majority of Americans will have attended a live drag show, in the way that a vast number of Americans can say they have attended a professional sporting event or a Broadway show. Into the breach sail television and online video, which do for current generations what books did for those without direct access to live performance in past centuries. Television shows and videos give access to lives and possibilities beyond the scope of immediate experience. In the best-case scenario, the shows and videos depict insiders documenting, creating, revealing and expressing their own lives from their own standpoint. They escape the symbolic annihilation of others coopting their forms of expression, and appear themselves, claiming voice and presence. As RuPaul put it,

> I have a ranch in Wyoming that I go to constantly and on the television in the middle of nowhere, our little show comes on and I can imagine some of the kids in the area flipping around and landing on our show and getting an education, a real education. Not just gay kids, but anybody who wants to go out in this world and face their cross to bear. Whatever that cross may be.[5]

Thus the relevance and importance of drag queen—created and—performed drag on television.

Ten years after the establishment of Transgender Day of Remembrance, RuPaul debuted the first season of *RuPaul's Drag Race*. In an interview with *The Hollywood Reporter*, RuPaul discussed the show's timing:

> I worked with [*Drag Race* producers] for like 300 years. Probably in '98, they said, "Let's go out and do some reality stuff." And I said, "I cannot." I thought the climate was too hostile and reality TV seemed too mean-spirited. I finally relented because it seemed like the timing was right and it seemed like the hostility towards people who dance to the beat of a different drummer had lifted a bit. The Bush Administration was over, and there seemed to be this easiness in the air. The fear-mongering from 9/11 had died down, and so we took this show out.[6]

Its sixth season is about to start, and it has been a success on many levels. It has claimed a devoted if modest viewership; fan sites and blogs abound; and it has generated buzz and revenues for RuPaul's career, the show's sponsors, and many of the contestants.[7] I want to explore *RuPaul's Drag Race* as a site where, in theory, drag queens can use their own voices and claim their own visual and discursive space through the medium of television.

Extravaganza Meets the Small Screen

After the appearance of drag queens as characters on several prime-time scripted dramas—most frequently as the victims of crime—reality TV also discovered the appeal of characters who defy, but also trade on, traditional gender binaries.[8] Chaz Bono, the female-to-male and fully transitioned son of Cher and Sonny Bono, appeared on *Dancing with the Stars*. Chris March, drag queen and costumier to the drag-inclined, finished third on season four of *Project Runway*, but turned his over-the-top fashion viewpoint into a show called *Mad Fashion*, which premiered in October 2011. And Patti Stanger, the *Millionaire Matchmaker*, tried to match Frank Marino, a Las Vegas headliner and drag performer, on episode eleven of season five of her reality TV show in November 2011.

All these shows have begun to bring transgender lives and drag sensibilities to ever-wider audiences. But the most fully-realized showcasing of dragtastic performers to date remains *RuPaul's Drag Race* on the Logo network—though in my local Boston cable market, I have been able to watch many episodes on VH1, which is included in my basic cable package.[9] With perhaps half a million regular viewers and as many as a million for season premiers, the show has too low a viewership to be rated by Nielsen. So while about 48 million viewers get Logo, the show attracts far fewer regular viewers.

RuPaul's Drag Race presents both the male bodies and female personas created by its host and contestants. While RuPaul is an iconic and beautiful drag queen, the show consistently presents RuPaul both in and out of drag. Likewise, contestants' comments to the camera are always done out of drag. This results in visual and discursive tension, and underscores the dual gender personas of many drag performers. However, as the seasons progress and talented contestants must be found, the reality of differences among performers with multiple gender personas has begun to reveal itself. Not all drag performers are gay (or straight) men creating female personas.[10] Some are transsexual women, born with male bodies but certain of their feminine natures and desirous of completing a full corporeal alignment with their self-experienced gender. Thus, RuPaul's famous provocation that "we are all born naked, and the rest is drag" will be put to the test.

It was perhaps only a matter of time in the development of the reality television genre that a series would be created by people who routinely judge each other's "realness," a criterion drawn from the world of drag balls, and which has mostly to do with the success of an illusion which passes itself unremarkably as the "real."[11] Whatever naïve early notions the public may have had about the "realness" of reality television, many years in, we know that reality TV programs are cast, edited, and often scripted to within seconds of their airtime, removing "amateur" cast members' spontaneity almost entirely. If in the beginning reality television was a way to save money, by cutting out rooms full of script writers and eliminating professional, unionized actors, it seems clear that once the formula started to succeed and there was also money to be made, the forces of show business moved in to eliminate as much risk as possible from the emerging formulas of its show-genres.

So, perhaps, a reality television show about a group of drag queens vying to become America's Next Drag Superstar was tailor-made, both for the contestant demographic and for the viewership the show could draw. After all, drag performers are *performers*, and their success is at entertaining. And who better than a group of drag queens to bring along the most fabulous wardrobes, wigs, and makeup in the entire reality television world—all at no cost to the producers.

In another sense, *RuPaul's Drag Race* combines elements of almost every other reality contest show and genre that focus on femininity and women. Many have observed the close resemblances to the glamour and modeling aspects of *America's Top Model*.[12] *RuPaul's Drag Race* embodies the runway attitude of its creator, RuPaul, including the Supermodel Lunch of a single breath mint, which she serves to contestants in their one-on-one interviews. It includes lip syncing and choreography, thus scooping up the singing and dancing career-making elements of *American Idol, So You Think You Can Dance, The Voice, America's Got Talent*, and all their kin. There are the design and dressmaking-on-the-fly elements of *Project Runway* and other fashion design-making shows. There is the catty dish of all the *Real Housewives* franchises as well as Joan Rivers' *Fashion Police*. There is no actual sex, however, which distances the show from the *Jersey Shore*, Kardashian, Bethenny Frankel, *Millionaire Matchmaker*, and *Bachelor/Bachelorette* franchises. The one instance of a contestant, Willam Belli, who had sex with her husband during the quarantine period of taping the show, resulted in her being disqualified.[13] There are a few elements of *The Apprentice*, in that RuPaul's word rules the day and despite the input of other judges, her word is final. Of course, we would all prefer to be told to "Sashay away" than "You're fired." There was the wedding episode in season two, so contestants got to say yes both to a dress and to a tux (and facial hair). There is almost no cooking, unlike many shows in that genre; occasionally, however, contestants have been required to use fruit in their challenge costumes.[14] And of course, there is a nod to *The Great Race*, in the show's title and Indy 500–sounding tagline.

But *RuPaul's Drag Race* also does many things that none of the aforementioned shows tackle. The series presents both the male bodies and female personas created by its host and contestants in every episode—in some cases, male guests are also transformed into female drag performers.[15] More than scripted television shows, in which drag characters are often the victims of crimes, and thus seen in extreme and upsetting states, or comedies, where men in dresses are often comedic precisely because they fail to achieve female "realness," *RuPaul's Drag Race* depicts a great deal of the process of transformation that its contestants work at, to achieve their feminine, or in some cases androgynous, personas.[16] Apart from actually showing a drag queen tucking her genitalia (although the outtakes show is called *Untucked!*), most other stages of visual drag preparation and transformation are fairly lovingly depicted, except the transformation of RuPaul herself.

The feminist critiques, however, remain. *RuPaul's Drag Race*, like much drag in general, does hyperbolically reinforce many looksist, skinny, and hyper-feminine, Barbie Doll–proportioned versions of what a female identity means.[17] Bodacious drag queens like Victoria Parker of season one and Stacy Layne Matthews are often among those eliminated in the first half of the season, although in season four, the self-described "large, in charge, chunky, yet funky" Latrice Royale, a fan favorite, was eliminated only in the eleventh of fourteen episodes.[18] Still, being judged for "charisma, uniqueness, nerve and talent," in RuPaul's criteria for success, add up, no matter how wittily, to a misogynist synecdoche.

The show also commodifies and thereby alters drag performance and performers. The drag show scene is frequently performed as a local benefit for members of the LGBTQ community and their service organizations. Many of the show's contestants do have careers as recording artists, actors, and drag performers prior to coming on the show. But *RuPaul's Drag Race* clearly uses contestants to develop advertising and marketing for commercial sponsors and products like Absolut Vodka and M.A.C. makeup, among others. And of course, it seems to be a strong desire of most contestants that participation in *RuPaul's Drag Race* will make it easier for them to have a well-paying career as a drag performer. As RuPaul put it in a 2011 interview, "What we're looking for is someone who can really follow in my footsteps: Someone who can be hired by a company to represent their product, someone who can put together a sentence on television and present themselves in the most incredible way."[19] I would argue that

that is quite a small part of what has made RuPaul the most successful drag queen in multimedia history, but it certainly serves to put into context the objectives of the show.

By the same token, the format of the show means that the double *entendres* and subversive humor of practicing drag queens that function as pointed social, sexual, and political commentary are frequently pushed to the background, in favor of visual and non-verbal aspects of drag performance. When participants do speak on camera, more commercially acceptable and middle-of-the-road observations tend to be the norm, with RuPaul herself offering the most (and sometimes the only) old-school drag commentary during the judging period of each episode. In the same 2011 interview, RuPaul stated that being on the show teaches contestants to "understand television. In fact, even on *Drag U*, which we just finished shooting the second season of, I continue to train them on how to speak fluent television: how to speak in sound bites, how to think about what to say first, how to incorporate the question into the answer, all of those things."[20] What she doesn't teach is how to develop the political insight and verbal repartee of old school drag, which at other times she does valorize. Throwing shade and reading—the drag queen's unladylike verbal arts of nastily critiquing others[21]—are, of course, very much in evidence, because reality television, like all television, loves to show girls fighting.

Likewise, the transgender community has offered its own critiques. The rules of the show require contestants to appear half the time on camera as "boys."[22] This directly restricts fully transitioned transsexual male-to-female drag performers from participating in the show, a requirement which is at odds with the range of people who perform female drag in the non-televised world. In an interview with Nico Lang, Precious Jewel, a transgender woman who auditioned for the show but was not cast, had this to say about the season five episode in which Monica Beverly Hillz comes out as a transgender woman:

> The episode also shows us a loving and affirming RuPaul who dotes on Monica and proclaims, "I brought you here because you are fierce," although she deftly sidesteps the actual word transgender. This shows that Ru has an understanding that at times the intersections of gender and performance meet at drag's doorstep in an undeniable package, but that she may not yet be ready to fully come to terms with the repercussions those commonalities could have on her show. It had to be the right time for a transgender contestant to come out on *Drag Race*.[23]

Hillz was eliminated in the third episode.

Nevertheless, I believe *RuPaul's Drag Race* makes a significant contribution to television and its viewers in three important ways. The show mainstreams cross gender and bisexual lives to viewers who otherwise might have no access to these depictions in their own life world. It mainstreams approaches to gender personas which both reinforce and disrupt gender binarism. And it sometimes disrupts racial and ethnic notions of beauty using drag.

Mainstreaming Cross Gender and Bisexual Lives

While RuPaul is an iconic and conventionally beautiful drag queen, the show consistently presents RuPaul both in and out of drag. This repeated visual act forces all viewers to confront the possibility that such a beautiful woman started the day as a gentleman. Given the history of violence and murder committed against men who wear dresses and date other men, often rationalized as the "gay panic defense," *RuPaul's Drag Race* does perhaps more than any show on U.S. television before it to denaturalize and de-center feminine beauty as the unique property and potential of female bodies. We all have lived in times when a heterosexual man could go to a cross-dresser/transgender bar looking for a date, murder his date when he "discovered" s/he had a penis, and effectively be judicially exonerated for this criminal act, because his date's penis "induced" his own homophobia and transphobia.[24] Those who wanted to live in a world in which there was plausible deniability that a beautiful woman could ever be a man are directly challenged in their willful ignorance by the very existence of six seasons of this television show, and its wide dissemination both via cable television and the Internet.

The show also offers access to drag queens who serve as role models to young ones who may have inclinations toward gender play and performance, but have no encouragement or safe space to express their feelings where they live. Precious Jewel herself offers this reflection on the influence RuPaul has had on her life:

> Ru was the closest thing I could identify with on television growing up and all through adolescence. It's almost like how you love your family even though you disagree with some of the things they do. So no matter what, Ru will always be an icon to me. Ru has made it very clear that she is not interested in discussing the semantic meanings of words like "tranny," or for that matter, whether she is referred to as he or she, but at the end of the day I do believe in her eternal message of love, energy and life. We as a community need to do less crucifying and more identifying with the gifts that the universe has placed within each of us.[25]

The painful side of throwing shade,[26] in other words, is the internalized self-hatred that feminists, out gays and lesbians, transgender people, and bisexuals reject and seek to heal through many means. The motto most frequently uttered by RuPaul, besides "You got to work" and "Don't f*** it up," is "If you can't love yourself, how the hell you gonna love somebody else? Can I get an amen up in here?" This is the sort of spirit and affirmation which RuPaul offers, in a world where many people will never hear such words spoken to them, and where losing support and even contact with family members is often the price of coming out.[27]

While many contestants identify as gay men, some have discussed the children they have fathered. The winner of season two, Tyra Sanchez, spoke frequently on camera about her son, underscoring a biological male sex coupled with an at least part-time feminine gender identity and a primarily gay sexual orientation.[28] Thus I would argue that the reality format, as well the show's editorial choices, have enabled a wide and nontraditional representation of sex, gender, and sexual orientations to be shown in every episode, spoken about in the first person by drag queens themselves. Bisexuality is the orientation most likely to either drop out of the discourse, or to be subsumed under the gay or straight heading. And yet Tyra Sanchez, for however brief a time, engaged in sex with a biological woman and became a biological father, thus keeping that space open in the wider imagination.

The series also attempts to include the wide range of drag queens' many shared experiences, including in some cases commercial sex work. Latrice Royale talked about turning to crime because of her extreme poverty.[29] And it includes connections to and difficulties with their parents and siblings, and being young boys who started doing drag, in some cases as early as middle school. A frequent on-camera question answered while not in drag is how and when the contestant first got interested in doing drag. All this results in what I consider the most drag-safe space within television—and, I would argue, the first of its kind in U.S. television history. And thus for all the ways in which the show does not very often reproduce the range of political and social commentary for which the most brilliant drag queens are well known, I would argue that there is a different kind of value created by this consistent, self-defined depiction of drag queens and their performances in this extremely visual medium. Anyone who has ever unexpectedly gotten explicitly sexual visual content in a Web search in which one was not seeking it has also probably been made aware of the dehumanizing and reductive images of drag queens and transgender women which can turn up online. In a media world where this is the case, I think we can take it as a progressive development that *RuPaul's Drag Race* offers alternative, drag-positive visual representations of drag performers, and self-created verbal descriptions of their upbringings, experiences, and aspirations. And while these are obviously edited, I am hard-pressed to think of any other television series which routinely gives as much airtime to voicing any aspect of the actual lived lives of drag queens.

Approaches to Gender Expression

Through the participants' self-naming language, the show also represents some of the sex and gender dynamics of the drag queen contest and drag ball scenes, along with interactions with other reality television genres. I would like to note here, though, that the contest rules for *RuPaul's Drag Race* go some way to limiting the categories of gender expression which are seen on the show. Marlon Bailey, whose brilliant and important work on the drag ball scene, largely the province of African American and Latina/o drag performers, observes a six-part gender system, which takes into account surgical, medical and wardrobe/cosmetic ways of altering the body:

(1) butch queens, who are biologically born male who identify as gay or bisexual men and are and can be masculine, hypermasculine, or feminine; (2) femme queens (MTF), who are transgender women or people at various stages of gender reassignment-through hormonal and/or surgical processes; (3) butch queens up in drag, who are gay men who perform drag but who do not take hormones and who do not live as women; (4) butches (FTM), who are transgender men or people at various stages of gender reassignment or masculine lesbians or women appearing as men regardless of sexual orientation (some butches use hormones and have surgical procedures to modify their bodies); (5) women, who are biologically born females who identify as lesbian, straight, or queer; and (6) men/trade, who are biologically born males who are straight-identified men.[30]

The world of *RuPaul's Drag Race*, in terms of contestants and contest rules, is much more circumscribed than this.

The male contestants do represent a range of gender identities: from the four who after the show decided to complete a full medical transition to becoming women, to contestants who have had some surgical interventions such as breast augmentations or facial surgeries, to gay men who use drag as gender performance.[31] The first transgender woman to reveal her status was Sonique in the twelfth episode of season two, during the reunion special. In season five in the first episode, Monica Beverly Hillz became the first contestant to reveal her status as a transgender woman during the regular season. Two other contestants, Carmen Carerra in season three and Kenya Michaels in season four, made known their transition after their stint on the show ended.

Earlier in RuPaul's own career, the female persona was the only one s/he revealed. In the show, however, RuPaul consistently starts the show in male drag and subsequently appears in the judging segments in female drag. I would argue that this marks one limit of the show's range of acceptable gender identities, contra transsexuals, for example, for whom gender identity is more fixed and gender identity disorder is a risk. To the extent that the "women" must appear on camera a significant amount of the time as "boys"[32] means, in effect, that a fully transitioned female drag performer would not be cast. This rule supports the frisson of the boy-to-girl-to-boy transformation that gay (and straight) male drag performers create. But as Precious Jewel Davis points out,

> Some of the most respected individuals in the business are transgender women as well as drag queens: Mimi Marks, Candis Cayne, Sasha Colby, and Carmen Carrera. All of those women have broken through glass ceilings. We need trans* women as drag superstars to show the world that we are no longer going to hide or question who we are or accept the slandering of our character for mainstream culture. We need trans* women as drag superstars to model that we as transgender women are more than just the victims of crude humor and murder. We are women who deserve to occupy positions of power and leadership, and we will be the ones to define our own expectations surrounding our individual gender identities.[33]

This sense of drag is excluded by the very premise of *RuPaul's Drag Race*: "Gentlemen, start your engines, and may the best woman win." RuPaul's version of drag is that the biologically male self is proximate, in time and body, to the act of female drag performance. Bailey's delineation of the gender system within the drag ball scene is much more expansive than this. RuPaul's discussions of "fishy queens" in season five refers to drag queens who may lack, not sufficient feminine realness, but sufficient *masculine* or *male* realness under the costume to qualify as doing drag, in the show's delimitation of drag. To that extent, one can decry the narrowness of the show's definition of drag vis-à-vis drag practice, especially in many communities of color and the drag ball scene.[34] At the same time, the show trades on the frisson of the boy-to-girl-to-boy traffic that each contestant engages in during each episode. Presumably, the show's producers believe that viewers are not interested in the personal journeys of identity construction undertaken by many drag performers, for whom fierceness is a necessity for survival, and thus would find transgender women less intriguing than gay male drag queens.

As I discussed earlier in this essay, it is certainly the case that the drag depictions of feminine personas on *RuPaul's Drag Race* are frequently of the old school, hyperbolically femme variety. Nipped-in waists, large breasts, lots of long legs, and overt and dramatic makeup are de rigeur. However, Raja Gemini, winner of season three, was praised by RuPaul and rewarded for a less "high femme," more gender-blended drag. Raja's drag had much more to do with David Bowie, in many ways, than the other two finalists in her season. Alexis Mateo presented a largely unironic and traditionally feminine persona. Manila Luzon, while much more playful and adept at ironic sendups in her personas, nevertheless remained within the lines of a consistently female persona, albeit with a good dose of comedy and self-deprecation in her drag repertoire.

Showing contestants in many stages of getting into drag, and using the reality television convention of having contestants speak directly to the camera and giving commentary while not in drag, create visual and discursive tensions. But over time, as with all representations, these, too, may lose some of the power of surprise and disruption regarding gender expression, and morph into interest in what the contestants will create for each challenge: what they will wear and how they will perform. Because the show takes place in the very unreal world of television, over time, it may become less about the sharp and ironic distance between a gay man in a baseball cap becoming Cher, and more about the creativity, artistry, glamour, and realness of the drag performance alone. For infrequent viewers unfamiliar with the drag scene, of course, the contrast will be fresh.

And yet, if it becomes more routinized, I am not entirely sure that that is a bad thing. As Marlon Bailey points out, the reality for many drag performers of color means, for every moment spent outside the ball, also having to perform a gender role that the non-drag world finds acceptable, because it appears congruent with one's biological body.[35] And unlike "reality" television, the communities in which many drag performers of color live and work often *do* believe in rigid gender binaries and assigned social roles for men and women, and are willing to aggressively enforce them. This probably could be said for most white-majority communities as well. As such, the success of those off-stage gender performances is a day-to-day matter of life and death, and not merely a foil for an extravagant drag performance. *RuPaul's Drag Race* is a televised, but also aspirational, safe space.

Race and Ethnicity

Producers for the first six seasons of *RuPaul's Drag Race* selected casts of contestants who come from a wide range of ethnically and racially diverse backgrounds. More than half of each season's cast, and in general closer to three-quarters, have been Latina, African American and Asian American performers. The winner of season one was a native of Cameroon, BeBe Zahara Benet. She valorized her dark skin and facial features, and in some episodes wore beautifully big and kinky Afro wigs, affirming as beautiful much of what we never see on magazine covers. Season two winner Tyra Sanchez and season three winner Raja Gemini also represent as persons of color. In fact, it was not until season four that a white drag queen, Sharon Needles, won the contest.

Given RuPaul's high intelligence and adherence to many of the conventions of old school drag, I have to believe that, as an African American himself, it was with some intention that he decided to put the race into *Drag Race*. While drag by itself is frequently a sendup of conventional femininity, glamour, and heterosexual norms, the contestants also have sent up their own and others' racial and ethnic identities. Just as RuPaul's blond wig against her brown skin reconfigures whiteness as glamour available to all races, and her white Afro against her brown skin reconstructs African American hair and skin as glamour that others should emulate, race has sometimes been a theme of both homage and parody by contestants.

In season three's final episode, Manila Luzon and Raja Gemini in particular played with race and ethnicity in their performance pieces. Raja appeared in a kind of post-modern Native American–inspired runway look, while Manila Luzon created a much more campy and comedic sendup of certain stereotypes of Asian women held by non–Asians. By contrast, Alexis Mateo, for all her strengths, seemed to lack a sense of irony toward her own Latina heritage, and arguably affirmed rather than critiqued a certain kind of glamour and womanliness that she so well personified.

I suspect, however, that given the desire of RuPaul and her sponsors to teach drag queens how to speak as well as dress "television," the risk involved in presenting very much that is satirical or ironic commentary on racial or ethnic stereotypes would be viewed as too great. There have been no Chris Rocks or even Margaret Chos in *RuPaul's Drag Race*, and given its embrace of commercial sponsors, we may doubt that there will be.

Given my earlier arguments in support of the visual contributions the show makes in terms of drag queens' self-created gender expressions and performances, including performances of beauty, the contribution to my mind will be weakened if the racial and ethnic diversity of the cast decreases over time. Since its inception, television has served as a powerful vehicle to reinforce not only social gender roles, but notions of beauty and acceptable expressions of femininity as well. Given the enormous importance of the largely African American and Latina/o ball scene to the world of drag, we would hope that RuPaul would continue to recruit and cast drag queens who do more than reinforce the desirability of white skin, narrow noses, and straight hair in a still-racist society. Perhaps the greatest kind of subversiveness that *RuPaul's Drag Race* could achieve would be valorizing much more racially- and size-diverse visions of feminine beauty and play.

Room for Realness?

Reality television is, after all, just television. By this I mean that it is no more real than a painting of a haystack is a pile of hay. For *RuPaul's Drag Race*, one extremely unreal aspect of the show is the quarantine under which contestants are put once the show starts taping, a standard practice in reality TV production. This means that the distractions and threats and messiness of non–TV life are, for about six weeks, put aside, and drag contestants can focus solely upon being drag queens full time, albeit in a setting where they will be constantly scrutinized and judged by other drag queens.

This directly contrasts with the experience of many drag performers living in their home communities. Marlon Bailey reminds us of the dual life-performances that African American drag performers whom he studies must carry out, as strategies and practices for survival:

Ballroom members refashion themselves by manipulating their embodiments and performances in ways that render them visible and remarkable within the ballroom scene but invisible and unmarked in the world outside of it. Former ballroom member and cultural critic Tim'm West, a butch queen who is also a former member of the House of Ninja in New York City […] describes how some ballroom kids in the city develop a broader range of performance because of the world in which they live; "A boy rides up to the Bronx on the D train every day and after a certain street he gotta act like a boy. He turns it on. But after 14th Street, girl it came right back off!" […] [B]allroom community members understand that they are seen through a racist and homophobic lens propagated and internalized by various sectors of society. Therefore, members seek greater agency in shaping how they are viewed by altering and performing their bodies in ways that disguise their gender and sexual nonconformity.[36]

Bailey's conclusion, that only inside the ball scene can participants escape biological sex, gender role, and relational binaries, suggests that these are both imposed upon them, but also accepted and enforced by all other members of society, including their own racial and ethnic communities. To the extent that this is true for the drag artists whose performances and lives Bailey describes, it seems clear that 2009 is not very far from 1999 after all. Television can be a very self-congratulatory enterprise, and it would be very easy to hope that *RuPaul's Drag Race* would be the fluoride in the media water supply that would keep the decay of corrosive hatreds from breaking out over and over again. It is easy to hope that the very existence of the Logo television network, which many LGBTQ viewers simply refer to as the gay channel, would mean that social progress has been made, and lives are both safer and more secure because of it. But if a drag ball is the only safe space to be, the symbolic work of *RuPaul's Drag Race* to widen the social space for non-binary expressions of sex and gender will be hollow, unless attitudes and actions change.

I would like to believe that *RuPaul's Drag Race* has moved the television depiction of drag queens forward, along the four stages of TV's representation of minorities first outlined by Cedric Clark.[37] The first stage is non-representation, with no media appearances. The second involves some inclusion, but with the group in question being ridiculed, disrespected, and represented in stereotypical ways. In the third stage, the group is represented but regulated. I would argue that this is where we are with *RuPaul's Drag Race*. The formulaic nature of the maturing reality television genre of contest shows almost requires the reduction or elimination of elements which producers (including RuPaul) would consider not "commercial," such as the kind of drag queen commentary and humor which non-televised drag thrives on. Likewise, the fact that the show airs on the Logo network and not, say, Lifetime, HBO, or even BBC America, suggests that the presence of drag queens on TV, especially so many all up in one place together, has to be contained, at least for the time being, by the network/channeling system, to keep its content from spilling over onto audiences who would reject it.

In Clark's final stage, the group is presented in a range of positive and negative roles that members occupy in real life. Stereotypical characterizations still appear, but in a context of other representations. Given that stereotypes abound in drag, and are the synecdoches which make the irony possible, we would expect that, even in this drag nirvana world, the stereotypes, such as they appear, don't become the basis for disrespecting, dismissing, or demeaning the drag queen as less-than.

And then there is the reality of non-gay drag. *RuPaul's Drag Race* hits against the limits of Butler's social constructivist, gender-as-performance claims which, if they were universally valid, would mean that no one ever felt the overwhelming need to go beyond clothes and makeup, and physically remodel one's body to align with one's self-experienced gender, as Sonique Love, Monica Beverly Hillz, Carmen Carerra, and Kenya Michaels did. It may all be performance; but the fact of the matter is that people still make choices about which performances they wish to undertake. And the fact that they also fiercely resist engaging in some kinds of gender performances suggests, not simply that access to social power is involved in those choices, but that a sense of selfhood, of personhood is involved. Some have referred to this as desire, as if that would circumvent the seemingly dangerous possibility that we might actually be made differently, and that that difference could matter to us. The danger in accepting social constructivist versions of gender is that the same rationale can be used to justify "gay reeducation" camps and psychotherapy. If gender is seen as a choice, because it is merely performative, then sexuality can be seen in the same light, and it would be reasonable to expect people, then, to choose certain "performances" over others.

We no longer routinely speak about "sexual preferences"; the term sexual orientation has, I think, taken on the more accurate valence or understanding that people have some kind of core sexual orientation. Pace Kinsey, that may mean that something like 40 percent of the population is bisexual; there, the question of seeking, from the basis of desire, to pursue a same-sex or different-sex partner may be considered a choice. But the baseline desire to pursue that choice comes from something beyond a rational calculus of social conformity or disruption. For the remaining parts of the population, one's sexual orientation, like one's gender, seems more clearly that: something which feels aligned and stable. I would argue that in all cases, from the standpoint of human rights, we are on safer ground to treat all orientations and all expressions of gender as equal under the law, and offer them the same treatment and the same protections. Social constructivist arguments perform an important function, in levering apart the majoritarian and often patriarchal ideology of subordinating the sex of our brains to the sex manifested by our bodies, and further subordinating femininity and femaleness to masculinity and maleness. But they hit against a more trenchant human reality: that if we do learn how to perform genders, our sense of which gender(s) we choose to perform come(s) from within us. Judith Butler should have known better; the experiment had already been tried by John Money at Johns Hopkins University, and with disastrous and tragic results for David Reimer, whose male genitalia Money had surgically removed at birth and whom he forced to be raised as a girl.[38] It does a terrible disservice to every transsexual person, whose self-understanding was that her or his brain knew her or his body was out of line, and that s/he had to do something to change the physical self in order to complete her or his gendered humanity. If a change of clothes were all it took, no one would ever crave a different body. But some of us do. And some of us who do also do drag.

Audre Lorde, fierce African American lesbian poet, tried to teach us that it isn't differences which matter, but what we make of them. From the standpoint of a sometime activist and perpetual ally of the LGBTQ community, I do believe that *RuPaul's Drag Race* gives us good reasons to make something different of the differences. And there are many differences within the world of drag, including non-gay male bodies, and the visual characteristics and embodiments of beauty which RuPaul's own subtle commitment in her title seems to promise. *RuPaul's Drag Race* is a commercial product that nevertheless could embrace the possibilities of Gordene MacKenzie's "Fifty Billion Galaxies of Gender," at least one episode at a time. Avoiding—and perhaps averting—the racial white-out of feminine beauty on television may prove to be an even greater achievement.

Notes

1. Mary Marcel and Gordene MacKenzie, "From Sensationalism to Education: Media Coverage of Murder of US Transgender Women of Color," in *Local Violence, Global Media: Feminist Analyses of Gendered Representations,* ed. Lisa Cuklanz and Sujata Moorti (New York: Peter Lang, 2009), 79; Tim Murphy, Ryan Wenzel, and Andrea James, "Gay vs. Trans in America," *The Advocate,* December 18, 2007, 39, http://www.proquest.com/ (accessed February 17, 2014).

2. Marlon M. Bailey, "Gender/Racial Realness: Theorizing the Gender System in Ballroom Culture," *Feminist Studies* 37 (2011): 365–367; Katie J. M. Baker, "'A Graveyard for Homosexuals,'" *Newsweek,* December 13, 2013; Thaddeus Russell, "The Color of Discipline: Civil Rights and Black Sexuality," *American Quarterly* 60, no. 1 (March 2008): 101–128, http://www.proquest.com/ (accessed February 17, 2014); Koritha Mitchell, "Love in Action: Noting Similarities Between Lynching Then and Anti-LGBT Violence Now," *Callaloo* 36, no. 3 (Summer 2013): 688–717, http://www.proquest.com/ (accessed February 16, 2014); E. J. Graff, "What's Next?" *Newsweek,* September 27, 2013, 1, http://www.proquest.com/ (accessed February 16, 2014).

3. Lisa Robinson, "Lady Gaga's Cultural Revolution," *Vanity Fair,* September 2010, 280, http://www.proquest.com/ (accessed February 18, 2014).

4. Isaac Jackson, "Reading Madonna: The Lessons of Truth or Dare Offer a Challenge to the Lesbian and Gay Community," *Gay Community News*, June 1, 1991, 20, http://www.proquest.com/ (accessed February 18, 2014).

5. Seth Abramovitch, "RuPaul, Inc.: Advice from a Business-Savvy Drag Queen," hollywoodreporterwww, April 3, 2013, n.p., http://www.lexis.com (accessed February 19, 2014).

6. Abramovitch.

7. There are dozens of articles in the trade press about the show starting in the months before the first season. Examples include Alison Brower and Stacey Wilson, "The Reality Heat List," *Hollywood Reporter* 419 (April 12, 2013): 44–51, http://www.proquest.com/ (accessed February 16, 2014); Joshua Gamson, "Reality Queens," *Contexts*, Spring 2013, 54, http://www.proquest.com (accessed February 16, 2014); and Keith Caulfield, "'Drag' Divas Make Splash," *Billboard* 125, no. 6 (February 16, 2013): 73, http://www.proquest.com/ (accessed February 16, 2014).

8. Tanner Stransky, "Kings of Queens," *Entertainment Weekly*, December 15, 2006. 28, http://www.proquest.com/ (accessed February 16, 2014); Hugh Ryan, "TV's Transformative Moment," *Newsweek*, Global Edition, July 17, 2013, 1, http://www.proquest.com/ (accessed February 16, 2014).

9. Thomas Pardee, "Is Gay Too Mainstream for Its Own Media?" *Advertising Age* 83, no. 11 (March 12, 2012): 1, http://www.proquest.com/ (accessed February 16, 2014).

10. Bailey; Judith Halberstam,"Drag Queens at the 801 Cabaret," *Journal of the History of Sexuality* 13, no. 1 (2004): 124–126, http://www.proquest.com/ (accessed February 19, 2014).

11. Bailey, 377–379.

12. For example, Gamson, 54.

13. Tanner Stransky, "Controversial 'RuPaul's Drag Race' Queen Willam Explains Disqualification: 'My Husband Was Coming to Bang Me Out,'" *Entertainment Weekly*, May 1, 2012, http://popwatch.ew.com/2012/05/01/rupauls-drag-race-willam-disqualified-banged-out/ (accessed December 31, 2013).

14. Ken Wheaton, "Adages," *Advertising Age* 80, no. 3 (2009): 38, http://www.proquest.com/ (accessed February 17, 2014).

15. Gamson, 54.

16. "How Are Gays Being Represented on TV?" *National Public Radio*, Morning Edition, January 2, 2013, http://www.proquest.com/ (accessed February 17, 2014).

17. See, for example, Elizabeth Schewe, "Serious Play: Drag, Transgender, and the Relationship Between Performance and Identity in the Life Writing of RuPaul and Kate Bornstein," *Biography: An Interdisciplinary Quarterly* 32, no. 4 (Fall 2009): 672, Academic Source Premier (accessed February 17, 2014); Michele D. Dunbar, "Dennis Rodman—'Barbie Doll Gone Horribly Wrong': Marginalized Masculinity, Cross-Dressing, and the Limitations of Commodity Culture," *Journal of Men's Studies* 7, no. 3 (April 30, 1999): 328, http://www.proquest.com/ (accessed February 19, 2014).

18. Lew Whittington, "Latrice's Secret Weapon," *Huffington Post The Blog*, posted 11/27/2012, 2:13 p.m., http://www.huffingtonpost.com/lew-whittington/latrices-secret-weapon_b_2184520.html (accessed February 19, 2014).

19. Kyle Buchanan, "RuPaul on Drag Race, Hannah Montana, and 'Those

Bitches' Who Stole Annette Bening's Oscar," *Vulture*, April 4, 2011, http://www.vulture.com/2011/04/rupaul_on_drag_race_hannah_mon.html (accessed January 30, 2014).

20. Buchanan.

21. For definitions of these traditional terms, see Jaimie Etkin, "RuPaul's Drag Race Dictionary," *Newsweek Web Exclusives*, April 24, 2011, http://www.proquest.com/ (accessed February 16, 2014).

22. Nico Lang, "Breaking Ground: An Interview with Precious Jewel on RuPaul's Drag Race," *WBEZ 91.5 Chicago*, February 22, 2013, http://www.wbez.org/blogs/nico-lang/2013-02/breaking-ground-interview-precious-jewel-rupauls-drag-race-105658 (accessed January 30, 2014).

23. Lang.

24. MacKenzie and Marcel, 78.

25. Lang.

26. Etkin.

27. Katy Chance, "He Ain't Heavy—She's My Sister," *Business Day* (South Africa), February 7, 2013, Arts, Culture and Entertainment Section, http://www.proquest.com/ (accessed February 16, 2014).

28. Björn Flóki, "Drag Dad," http://www.dragdad.com/about-the-film/ (accessed January 30, 2014).

29. Lauren Levitt, "Reality Realness: Paris Is Burning and RuPaul's Drag Race," *Interventions Journal*, November 7, 2013, http://interventionsjournal.net/2013/11/07/reality-realness-paris-is-burning-and-rupauls-drag-race/ (accessed February 19, 2014).

30. Bailey, 370–371.

31. Precious Davis, "What I Learned Auditioning for RuPaul's Drag Race," *We Happy Trans*, February 13, 2013, http://wehappytrans.com/news-media/rupaulsdragrace/ (accessed February 21, 2014); Maria Sciullo, "Shrimp Toss Ward for Loss in Semifinals of 'Cook-Off,'" *Pittsburgh Post-Gazette*, February 9, 2013, http://www.lexisnexis.com (accessed February 21, 2014). All information relating to shows and casts was taken from http://www.logotv.com/shows/rupauls_drag_race.

32. Lang; Levitt; Davis.

33. Lang.

34. See Bailey, 371; Ivan Monforte, "House and Ball Culture Goes Wide," *The Gay & Lesbian Review Worldwide* 17, no. 5 (September 2010): 28–30, http://www.proquest.com/ (accessed February 17, 2014); Amy Herzog and Joe Rollins, "Editors' Note," *Women's Studies Quarterly* 41: 1 & 2 (2013): 9–10; Gregory Phillips II, James Peterson, Diane Binson, Julia Hidalgo and Manya Magnus, "House/Ball Culture and Adolescent African American Transgender Persons and Men Who Have Sex with Men: A Synthesis of the Literature," *AIDS Care*, 23, no. 4 (April 2011): 515–520.

35. Bailey, 373–374, for example.

36. Bailey, 380.

37. Cedric Clark, "Television and Social Control: Some Observations of the Portrayal of Ethnic Minorities," *Television Quarterly* 9, no. 2 (1969): 18–22.

38. Graff, 1.

Of Fish and Feminists
Homonormative Misogyny
and the Trans*Queen

LAURIE NORRIS

Heteronormativity has become something of a mainstay in critical theory over the last twenty years with the rise of gender and queer theories. A bulwark of patriarchy, critics align the privileging of heterosexuality and gender roles fixed to biological sex with phallologocentric hegemony. In recent years, though, a counterpart to heteronormativity has gained increasing focus. Homonormativity, a term often associated with critic Lisa Duggan,[1] also makes assumptions about sexual identity in terms of cultural power structures. Homonormativity privileges the stereotypical "homosexual," eliding many of the so-called letters of the Alphabet Soup of sexual and gender identity. It positions individuals who identify as sexually attracted to members of their same biological sex as culturally visible[2]; it hides any and all queer identified people who locate themselves elsewhere on the sexual orientation and gender spectrums, such as bisexual, asexual, intersex, or transgender people, and so on.[3]

Additionally, both heteronormativity and homonormativity privilege stereotypical masculinity at the direct expense of other forms of gender identity, specifically feminine identities. Whereas the heteronormative positions straight white men[4] as the default, homonormativity marks as Other anyone outside of a fairly strict definition of gay white men. Left out in the proverbial cold by both of these systems, regardless of sexual orientation, are white women and peoples of color. Ironically, while these social systems position white masculinity as invisible, as the default against which every other type of identity is negatively defined as "Not White Masculinity," they also render those other identities as socially and politically unseen and unheard. Stripping them of voice and power, hetero-normativity and homonormativity subjugate the Other in similar, mirror-image ways. As Susan Stryker notes, homonormativity "aim[s] at securing privilege for gender-normative gays and lesbians based on adherence to dominant cultural constructions of gender, and it diminish[es] the scope of potential resistance to oppression."[5] It is simply heteronormativity refashioned for the LGBTQ community.

We can see these echoes play out across popular culture media. José Esteban Muñoz has called for a reexamination of queerness in the media, in that popular culture helps transmit staid notions of who is, and is not, appropriately queer. He sought a methetic media, one that takes the larger experience of the queer community in mind. He believed that

> queer media must call for participation, vivification, and an expanded sense of a queer commons that is not quite present but altogether attainable. It is urgent that the lulling sound of the laugh track be put aside so we can engage in the production of a vitally methetic queer media that is equally turbulent and productive.[6]

Such a stance would allow the voices silenced by both hetero- and homo-normative standards room to speak. Sadly, his call has been left mostly unanswered. Queer representations in media, both mainstream and those targeted at an LGBTQ demographic, remain intensely normalized. In fact, as Ben Aslinger[7] and Eve Ng[8] have pointed out, in an era of microbroad-casting, even the cable network ostensibly dedicated to LGBTQ issues and viewers has begun "gaystreaming" its content in order to attract a wider, generally heterosexual cis*female, audience. Ng notes the way that Logo, the cable network that hosts *RuPaul's Drag Race*, uses the show to both placate LGBTQ activist groups' demand for more queer representation in the media while simultaneously reaching out beyond the LGBTQ community for straight audiences. She writes that on

> *RuPaul's Drag Race* [...] the host is a queer African American man who oversees a competition of contestants transgressing gender expression. At the same time, *RuPaul* also provides Logo with a convenient go-to program for its diversity quotient, even as the shift to gaystreaming means that programming with people of color has decreased.[9]

Working from a similar angle, Aslinger also writes that

> continued attention to who counts in industrial definitions of the audience and the conditions under which various audiences matter is necessary to understand shifts in media economics and organizational structures and how various forms of alterity are constructed by the culture industries.[10]

This echoes Muñoz's demand that queer media engage with the relationship between hetero- and homonormative expectations and provide a voice for the full spectrum of LGBTQ experiences.

Professional Fish versus Simply Pretty Girls: Glamour Fish and Real Fish Queens

We can see this ironic alignment of paradigms play out in *RuPaul's Drag Race*. A hierarchy exists, if unofficially, within the show that privileges certain types of drag queens over others. Before she even joins the cast, contestant Chad Michaels' oft-repeated refrain of "I'm a professional" haunts the show. The seasoned and established performers, often those who also participate in the pageant circuit, sit atop the *Drag Race* power structure. Contestants whose style falls outside of the narrow bounds of the fashionable pageant queens are often dismissed as not being "real" competition. What's more, the least-experienced performers frequently end up the brunt of bullying from the other, more powerful queens in the cast. Intriguingly, these younger performers are also often more fishy.[11] According to the logic of the show, there are two types of fishy queens: those performers who look like dazzlingly hyperfeminine impersonations of women, and those who could essentially pass as cis*women. Often called out for not costuming themselves as flamboyantly and exaggeratedly as the other queens, these "Real Fish"[12] performers end up lower in the pecking order amongst the contestants.

The show favors "Glamour Fish" more connected to high fashion and exaggerated runway performances than those who present a less professionally polished character. The Real Fish queens are derided by the other cast members, and often by the very structure of the show, for not taking their performances seriously. They are "read for filth,"[13] or verbally mocked by other queens, for not being professional enough, when in fact their performances simply deviate from the established homonormative hierarchy.

This is not to say that the show itself always echoes such privileging and positioning. Watching how the show evolves from season to season, paying particular attention to the storylines created around Real Fish queens, as well as those cast members who now identify as women, we can witness change. I will tease out some of the ways that *Drag Race* establishes the rules of homonormativity and has begun to break them.

Art Imitates Life, Life Imitates TV: RuPaul's Drag Race *and* America's Next Top Model

Much of the way sex and gender hierarchies function within the show actually stem from its structure. As a parodic version of American-style reality competition shows, *Drag Race* has always relied on its metanarrative and paratextual features to provide subtext. Modeled after the long running *America's Next Top Model* (hereafter referred to as *ANTM*), *Drag Race* emulates many of the defining characteristics of the other series.[14] RuPaul takes the place of Tyra Banks, a panel of judges surrounding her on stage just as Tyra's does her. *Drag Race* cast members are introduced and fit into storylines just as the model hopefuls are on *ANTM*, with RuPaul cheekily proclaiming in-episode challenges as based off aspects of her early career just as Tyra does. Even the narrative action within individual episodes of *Drag Race* mirrors those of *ANTM*. *Drag Race* imitates *ANTM* in high camp fashion, proverbial tongue firmly in cheek. The series' playful skewering of the other show provides satirical bedrock from which RuPaul and her gaggle of contestants can build humor and drama. Crucially, though, not every echo of *ANTM* appears intentional, nor are they all so funny.

One of *ANTM*'s lingering influences on *Drag Race* is the way both shows manipulate their contestants and mold them into conforming to established standards of beauty. *ANTM*'s machinations are much more explicit; each season of the series features an episode dedicated to makeovers, often revolving around storylines of models inevitably hating their new, Tyra-approved looks. On *Drag Race*, the judges maneuverings are more subtle, typically reserved for main stage critiques during the last act of each episode; queens are called out for lack of fashion sense (generally by judge and fashion designer, Santino Rice) or poor make-up technique (often by judge Michelle Visage, one of RuPaul's oldest friends). For both series, however, the end result is the same. Contestants either adapt to the expectations of the series or get sent home. Given that significant prizes are at stake, the cast members have equally significant motivation to reform themselves in the image the judges demand.

On *Drag Race*, that image is of the glamorous, professional, fish. With big wigs, haute couture inspired costumes, flamboyant but sexy make-up, the queens are expected to give both face and body. The beauty ideals from *ANTM* are exaggerated to become the hyperfeminine expectations of *Drag Race*. These Glamour Fish reify the sort of power dynamics that critic Steven Schacht has noticed. His "Lesbian Drag Kings and the Feminine Embodiment of the Masculine"[15] details some of the power dynamics of the drag scene that result from privileging Glamour Fish, though Schacht approaches this issue by way of the lesbian experience within the drag world. His study of the Imperial Sovereign Court of Spokane, a chapter of the Imperial Court System, demonstrates the sex and gender hierarchy of the LGBTQ organization. He finds the community to be deeply homonormative, with the gay drag queens dominating the group. The established pecking order then follows: gay drag queens, gay drag kings, lesbian drag kings, lesbian drag queens.[16] Note that order. The men performing femininity take precedence over everyone else, but, more interesting for me, notice that women performing femininity are at the bottom of the social order. What Schacht observes is a similar pattern in the ICS world as that found in *Drag Race*. The further away from real gender expression a performance is, the more cultural cache that performance merits within the community.[17] Just as in the heteronormative mainstream world, within the homonormative LGBTQ communities of *Drag Race* and the ICS, women are again relegated to subservient positions and their experiences devalued. One wonders if the irony of duplicating such pernicious heteronormative aspects of *ANTM* simply escaped the *Drag Race* production team in the beginning or if, as is usually the case with issues of privilege, they ignored it willfully.

A third option might be in play, too. While *Drag Race* has mimicked *ANTM* from its start, *ANTM* has only recently begun to show signs that its producers recognize and are responding to *Drag Race*'s influence on their show. Those signs, in turn, might also be influencing changes in the underlying logic of *Drag Race*, most notably in the power afforded homonormative standards amongst cast members. Because the changes to *ANTM* seem merely superficial (the casting of a transgender woman as a stunt, a season with both female and male contestants) and do not point to significant structural reorganization, I will leave off reading closely that series for now.[18] More recent seasons of *Drag Race*, however, suggest a seismic, if at first subtle, shift in the sociopolitical implications of the show. I believe we can trace this shift through the way three different queens have been treated by the show and other contestants. Building from Tatianna's villain edit in season two, to Carmen Carrera's role as mean girl known for body in season three, to Monica Beverly Hillz dramatic personal revelation on the main stage during season five, *Drag Race* has attempted to evolve away from the strict homonormative standards that privilege Glamour Fish performances of hyperfemininity over those of Real Fish and transgender women in the casts.

The Lost Season(s), or Why I Ignore Your Favorite Contestants

You will notice that I have not selected exemplars from all five seasons of *Drag Race*.[19] Season one, now referred to as the "Lost Season" in Logo promotions, featured a cast typically comprised of Glamour Fish, Show-girls, Pageant Queens, and the like. Rather than countering those contestants, like Shannel, BeBe Zahara Benet, or Rebecca Glasscock, with Real Fish, this first season cast Genderfuck and Camp Queens, like Nina Flowers, Ongina, and Tammie Brown. Jade is the only performer who approaches what I term Real Fish, but she avoids many of the pitfalls the show associates with that type of performer by also avoiding appearing unprofessional. The only point in her storyline that questions her professionalism while also brushing against her Real Fish tendencies comes in her final episode.[20] She breaks down and all but gives up on the challenge to create a commercial for M.A.C. Cosmetics. Even here, however, the connection between unprofessionalism and Real Fish aesthetic is merely tenuous; her excuse for her behavior is couched in terms of concern for her HIV positive best friend. Though Jade's exit from the show was built up through emotional terms, her storyline paved the way for Ongina's HIV-status confession in the next episode.[21] It is not difficult to imagine the show's editors playing up Jade's seemingly out of nowhere hysterics in order to build to a payoff for another, more popular contest down the line.

Similarly, I am not spending much time on season four. Kenya Michaels certainly deserves mentioning. A Glamour Fish, and the season's requisite Puerto Rican queen with the strongest accent, Kenya was most notable on the show for her tiny stature and her atrocious impersonation of singer Beyoncé during "The Snatch Game."[22] Since appearing on *Drag Race*, Kenya has come out as a transgender woman. The show never explicitly addresses this, and so her transition is not included in the series' overall treatment of (cis* or trans*) women's experience; Kenya's storylines tended rather to focus on language barriers more than the aesthetics of her performance style. Also, while Dida Ritz is an excellent example of Real Fish, her storyline never makes much of her professional status. Instead, the judges would call her out for ashy skin or flat wigs, but her second episode lip sync against The Princess convinced RuPaul of her professionalism and drive.[23] Likewise, the other contestants all seem to embrace and enjoy working with this charming and pleasant performer.

Getting the Villain's Cut: Tatianna's Experience in Season Two

Dida's season two Real Fish counterpart, however, is not treated so well. Tatianna, arguably the series' first real Real Fish, is immediately given the Villain Edit, meaning that her lines and scenes were shot and cut in such a way as to create a storyline for her in which she acts as the antagonist on the show. Though she clearly says things that could annoy or offend the other contestants (which, to be fair, all of the contestants do at some point), the show inserts reaction shots from other cast members that we cannot always verify were captured in the moments that the episodes suggest. The portrait created of Tatianna thus makes her appear like a somewhat flighty, perhaps a bit too vacuous, mall-pretty girl. Any sense of professionalism given to the other contestants is continuously undercut for her. The season two contestants challenge her place on the show outright; the series does so more subtly.

Tatianna's villain edit, interestingly, actually builds out of another contestant's. Raven describes Nicole Paige Brooks, a gawky Atlanta queen, as "wet sand in your underwear"[24] and says she is "not really impressed with her too much. She has acrylic toenails with white French Tips."[25] Nicole is edited to seem daft and out of touch, saying offensive things while appearing utterly unaware of their impact. In the first episode of the companion series, *Untucked!*,[26] many of Nicole's comments are directed toward Tatianna. Pointedly, those comments all stem from Tatianna's admission that she went to homecoming dressed in drag, which lead to this exchange:

NICOLE: "That's tranny-like, though, I think, right? [...] I just find it odd that you're dressing up like a girl in high school but you don't think you're a tranny."

TATIANNA: "I'm not a tranny because I don't want a vagina. I don't want boobs. I..."

NICOLE, cutting Tatianna off: "I want her tested for hormones, bitch!"

Nicole's last line was delivered with a laugh, indicating that she intended it as a joke, but the reaction shots inserted of other contestants mark the moment as serious.[27] Following the reaction shots to Nicole's awkward laugh, the episode cuts to a talking head interview with Tatianna. She proclaims that "I'm a man. I have to wear fake boobs. I have to tuck my dick between my legs. I'm a drag queen."[28] This moment begins Tatianna's overall storyline battle to prove she is professional enough to deserve to be on the show. The bitter sarcasm of her lines also contributes to her overall

persona and is a key element to the show establishing her as an antagonist.

The episode, however, does not entirely side with Nicole and her
misguided attacks. After Tatianna's interview insert, the show returns to
the Interior Illusions Lounge and picks up right after Nicole's laugh.
Jujubee responds with a playful "You a bitch" retort to Nicole before
launching into a mini-speech about femininity and empowerment.[29] She
says, "People don't hate gay guys 'cause they're gay; they hate anything
that's feminine [...]. We do drag because we want to empower."[30] The editing beats for the rest of this *Untucked!* episode, trends that mimic those
in the original series as well, align the show with Jujubee's perspective.

Including this statement allows the show to boast about its inclusive
and empowering stance, but the way Jujubee casually tosses out the word
"bitch" and then frames her statement as a response against mainstream
society's treatment of gay men actually underlines the misogyny inherent
in the show. At least in these early stages. The show seems to think, or
tries to suggest, that "bitch" has been reclaimed by the LGBTQ community
much the same way that "queer" has been without ever addressing the
misogyny inherent in the word and its use. While some feminist critics
have also attempted to examine the impact of and reclaim "bitch" as a
term for women, such as cultural studies critics like Janice Haaken[31] or
the editors behind *Bitch* magazine,[32] *Drag Race* is not interested in nor
attempts to engage with the critical implications of the term.

Contestants in every season frequently use "bitch," sometime play-
fully, sometimes mean-spiritedly, but they do not consider the weight of
its insult and how demeaning the term is for women watching the show
and the trans*women in the casts. As journalist Rohin Guha notes, gay-
streamed media portrayals have allowed

> gay men a liberal margin of misogyny, allowing them to write such behavior
> off as part of their identity. Gay men were allowed to say things like, "I find
> vaginas so alien" or more reductively, "Ew!" at the mention of female anatomy
> because such responses were viewed as hilarious, because the negative impli-
> cations of such humor wasn't ever really dissected.[33]

He later concludes that

> somehow being gay has become a coded way for many men to assume there's
> no wrongdoing when they talk about women's bodies, when they jokingly use
> "ho," "slut," or "bitch" as a synonym for "lady" or "woman"—and the spriteness
> [*sic*] with which they get defensive when called out for this kind of impropri-
> ety.[34]

Guha ties this unselfconscious use of derogatory language back to the issues of privilege at the heart of homonormativity by citing Peggy McIntosh's important piece on the power dynamics of race, "White Privilege: Unpacking the Invisible Knapsack," where she observes that it is

> the silences and denials surrounding privilege [that] are the key political tool here. They keep the thinking about equality or equity incomplete, protecting unearned advantage and conferred dominance by making these taboo subjects.[35]

Early seasons of *Drag Race* seem complicit in these "silences and denials," as the encounter between Tatianna, Nicole, and Jujubee highlight.

Flipping the Script with the Paratextual: Carmen Carrera's Experience After the Show

However, though the show continues to rely on terms like "bitch" or "hunty,"[36] the way contestants in later seasons are treated and the sort of storylines allowed for them reveal an evolution in how the show itself engages with such misogyny. Neither a straight line nor a politically innocent path to be sure, but we can see the show evolving from Tatianna's mistreatment through to Carmen Carrera's depiction on the show and ultimately on to Monica Beverly Hillz's coming out on the main stage. For Carmen, though, her role in this evolution is actually more paratextual than it is on-screen. During her season, Carmen was known as a "body" queen, even to the point of wandering the workroom completely naked on numerous occasions and infamously removing her already barely-there skirt on stage in a lip-sync against Raja.[37] She was a member of the "Heathers" clique, a group of contestants who considered themselves the pretty ones in comparison with the rest of their competition, queens they dubbed "Boogers." Carmen came off as a bit flighty but nowhere near as conniving or biting as some of the other members of her clique. Many of the other contestants, however, dismissed her as relying on her beauty too much and not putting in the sort of effort expected of "professional" drag queens. Inclusion of comments like that from cast members, and judge Michelle Visage's infamous admonition that Carmen should "stop relying on that body!"[38] demonstrate the subtle way the show tries to position Carmen alongside Real Fish; her inclusion in the "Heathers," however, rubs up against those sort of labels. She resists them, realigns herself with the Glamourous Fish traditionally favored by the show, and forces the series to start treating her that way as well. Raja and Manila Luzon's success on the show, and membership in the clique, do a lot to reify Carmen's self-selected alignment with Glamourous Fish over Real Fish.

Carmen's glamorous on-stage persona, though, has less impact on the homonormative politics of the series than her off-stage coming out has. Since leaving the show and then announcing her transition, the *Drag Race* community has used her in many ways as a sort of spokesperson for transgender acceptance. Carmen, who now goes by her stage name even off-stage, is one of the most high-profile former contestants from the show, appearing in nationally broadcast TV shows like the ABC news program *Primetime: What Would You Do?*[39] and Katie Couric's syndicated daytime talk show, *Katie*.[40] Her appearance on the latter generated controversy just as her appearance on TLC's *Cake Boss* did in 2012.[41] Essentially tricked into appearing on what ended up being intensely transphobic episodes, hounded with inappropriately personal questions about her physical transition by the former and then made the butt of jokes by the latter, Carmen and her fans sparked outrage on the internet over her mistreatment. She has turned the controversy into an opportunity to discuss trans* issues with the public, often using her Facebook fan page as an outlet. In the months following the *Cake Boss* and *Katie* fiascos, Carmen has posted updates like

> So Jerry Springer called my manager looking for transgender performers… Like really????????? These people are still making TV, exploiting trans people??? WTF why hasn't this been put to an end??? Do I need to go on there and set them straight? I don't get why these producers enjoy making fun of trans people.[42]

Moreover, she later adds, "I was the body beautiful before I became a female, no surgery needed, haters fall back."[43]

Perhaps more importantly, certainly more important in relationship to ongoing seasons of *Drag Race*, Carmen has been a mainstay of recent *Drag Race* themed promotional tours. She has used this added exposure to be a voice for trans* advocacy, and World of Wonder Productions has used her success to reposition their flagship series as more and more trans* friendly. However, posts such as the following reveal the subtle misogyny that still rests at the heart of the show:

> Being transgender doesn't make me less of a queen. Performing in drag is an art. Who says I need to conform to what YOU think a drag queen should look like? […] "Drag Queen" doesn't mean you are a man who dresses in womans clothing. A drag queen is someone who was born male and performs as a female for entertainment. Simple as that. You cant take me off that list because I have

transitioned. That's like saying every drag who has had facial or body work to enhance their look is not a drag queen anymore (i.e., Raven & Chad).[44]

Carmen, even though now self-identifying as female, still relies on biological determinism to at least some extent to define how she sees and interacts with the world. While Carmen's pushback against some of her detractors highlights some aspects of the unexamined misogyny of homonormativity, the sense of inclusivity intended by her posts, and amplified through *Drag Race*'s positioning of her through its nationwide tours, is a step in the right direction. One can trace a direct through line running from Carmen's advocacy to Monica's storyline in her subsequent season.

So You've Decided to Come Out on National Television...: Monica Beverly Hillz

Though perhaps not readily apparent upon an initial viewing, we can easily see *Drag Race* building towards Monica's announcement throughout the pivotal episode "Lip Sync Extravaganza Eleganza."[45] Very early on in the episode, Monica reveals in a talking-head spot that she feels "different from these girls."[46] Later, in her own interview, Coco Montrese says, "Monica is acting different today."[47] An inserted cut-away shot then catches Monica in an especially low-energy moment. During the episode challenge, where teams of queens recreate infamous moments from past seasons of the show, Monica reveals that she is "fuckin' it up. [She's] not focused and [doesn't have her] 100 percent in this competition because [she has] so much going on in [her] head."[48] The show manages to find moment after moment of Monica looking forlorn or concerned. The act concludes with another talking head interview with her, where she now reveals, "I have so much on my mind. I don't want to be here. I'm petrified to tell these girls my huge secret. I don't know how they're gonna take it."[49] Now well-worn tropes of reality television tell us that many of these interview segments were likely initiated by the production staff, guiding Monica toward a storyline revelation. Her discomfort and anxiety, though, highlight the tenuous position of the trans*woman in a gay male hierarchy. She is nervous about whether or not the other contestants will reject her because of her gender identity, and the show's own history suggests she has reason to be worried (i.e., the dismissive way Nicole's cruelty towards Tatianna was ignored by the show structurally).

The series, at this point, seems aware of such history and tries to position Monica's coming out as an example of its evolving attitude towards misogyny and homonormativity. Everything building up to her runway breakdown is tinged with irony, from RuPaul's comment during Monica's main stage walk—"and it's not padded. Natural born thrillah!"— to guest judge Kristen Johnston's critique that "on your runway as well, I don't know, maybe you're sad today or it's a hard day. You're disconnected." Monica begins to cry, and RuPaul questions her. With those words, somber music fades in on the soundtrack, and the scene cuts back and forth between taken aback yet supportive reaction shots of the other contestants like Detox and Alyssa Edwards, Monica breaking down and knelling down on the stage, and RuPaul nodding in an understanding way. RuPaul then calls Monica out for not maintaining professionalism, the cardinal sin of Real Fish, but tells her that she was chosen for a reason and deserves to be on the show. After Monica acknowledges that she feels better, the show cuts to a talking head interview with Jinkx Monsoon, so that the contestant can call Monica the "strongest girl in this competition. She's my hero."[50] The episode moves on, and the judges continue to critique the other contestants.

The scene climaxes in RuPaul's announcement that Monica, alongside Serena ChaCha, is up for elimination. The episode itself seems built around this final act, a moment where Monica is allowed to shine after admitting her fears and being honest about her off-stage gender identity. What's more, much of the success of Monica's lip sync to Rhianna's "Only Girl (in the World)" rests on her persona as a Real Fish. She looks like the pop singer, dances on the stage like a real woman instead of a showgirl, and carries the emotion of the song through in her performance. That the episode has been gearing up for said performance suggests that the show wants us to read it as accepting of this Real Fish, just so long as she takes to heart RuPaul's advice to focus more on her professionalism.

This trajectory is echoed in the episode's accompanying *Untucked!* edition.[51] The contestants' backstage conversations form a sort of microcosm of what the larger series has been doing as a whole. The winning team, Ivy Winters, Vivienne Pinay, Honey Mahogany, and Lineysha Sparx, head backstage before Monica's big reveal. These contestants engage in the now standard practice of commenting on their fellow contestants, focusing primarily on those whom they feel should be sent home. Serena Cha-Cha is their target. They tear apart her performance, her lack of panache, and nitpick over her physical form, all the while ignoring the Monica-driven storyline created by producers. The team is then quickly ushered into the Gold Room where a "surprise awaits [them] in [their] big, pink, furry box,"[52] a crude yet literal pun for female genitalia used by *Untucked!*

since Carmen Carrera's season to refer to surprise activities for the back-stage contestants. The show's producers use this box to manipulate sto-rylines during this behind-the-scenes series just as they use editing to do so in the original series. In this episode, Team Ivy is prompted to play a game of 20 Questions about the other contestants still on stage. The scene is cut so as to start with the queens mocking Serena following the trajec-tory of the pervious scene, but leads to the following exchange between Ivy and Vivienne about Monica. Ivy draws a name from the box:

> VIVIENNE: "Is she pretty?"
> IVY : "No."
> HONEY: "I got it. It's Detox."
> IVY : "No."
> VIVIENNE: "Is she banji?"
> IVY: "What's that mean?"
> VIVIENNE: "Is she ghetto?" snaps her fingers
> IVY: laughing "Yes."
> Everyone laughs.
> VIVIENNE: "Well, c'mon. Miss Monica."[53]

This game, little more than sanctioned gossip, continues for a while before being cut off by a commercial break. When the show returns, the other contestants have headed backstage, and the overall conversation alternates between loving support for Monica and vicious attacks on a not entirely undeserving Serena. Jinkx Monsoon tells the group, during one of the Monica-focused moments, "This is the last place for close mindedness when it comes to gender expression."[54] The cast then turns on Serena once more, resisting the storyline favored by the show. The producer's manip-ulation once again shows its hand when Monica's mother skypes in to tell her daughter that she loves her. Monica's reply? Through a veil of happy tears, she says, "This is real fucking life."[55] The contestants, again, turn their attention back on Serena, with Coco Montrese getting an insert inter-view telling Serena, "oh, no. Little boy, exit stage left,"[56] dismissing Serena so utterly that she no longer warrants following the drag queen convention of using the female pronoun while in character.

This transition, interestingly enough, comes on the heels of the other cast members lifting up Monica as a deserving competitor in contrast to Serena. The younger queen attempts to shift focus back on the percep-tion of Monica as ghetto, exclaiming, "at this point, the ghetto-lexican is done."[57] Her maneuver backfires. The contestants pounce on Serena for her comment. Meanwhile, the show tries to keep its focus on Monica's storyline via a slow motion zoom in on Monica and slow motion cuts to the other contestants looking aghast but also waiting for Monica's reaction. The bottom left portion of the screen is then filled with a suggested Twitter hashtag: "#NoSheBetterDont."[58] The tide has turned. Serena is now marked out as the unprofessional queen, and Monica is accepted into the heart of the show as a Glamour Fish who just happens to be a woman off screen as well.

Conclusion: Drag Race *Is Never Finished, It Is Only Abandoned*

Over its first five seasons, *RuPaul's Drag Race* has begun the transition from a purveyor of homonormative misogyny and trans*phobia into a safer and more accepting space for LGBTQ identity expression. By no means perfect, the show has come a long way from institutionally sanctioned bigotry (as witnessed through the early treatment of Real Fish contestants like Tatianna). The acknowledgement of transgender women in the casts of the show has forced *Drag Race* as a whole to engage in the pernicious practices associated with homonormative hegemony. The unexamined privileging of the gay male experience and denigration of both cis* and trans* femininity has begun to fade. Rather than always associating Real Fish femininity with unprofessionalism and forcing queens into prescribed storylines, the show has taken steps to begin positioning these contestants as individuals capable of generating comedy and pathos on their own, distinct from their off-stage gender identities. Through the way the show has paratextually-embraced performers like Carmen Carrera, the *Drag Race* world has expanded what it accepts as professional femininity. And the way that the season five contestants refused to play along with a pre-set "shock and awe" coming out storyline for Monica Beverly Hillz demonstrates that, while there is still room for improvement, the *Drag Race* community has had it, officially, with some of the more insidious misogynistic micro-aggressions associated with both hetero- and homonormativity.

Notes

1. L. Duggan, "The New Homonormativity: The Sexual Politics of Neoliberalism," in *Materializing Democracy: Towards a Revitalized Cultural Politics*, ed. Russ

Castronovo and Dana D. Nelson (Durham: Duke University Press, 2002), 175–94. See also Duggan's *The Twilight of Equality? Neoliberalism, Cultural Politics, and the Attack on Democracy* (Boston: Beacon Press, 2003).

2. Gavin Brown, "Homonormativity: A Metropolitan Concept That Denigrates 'Ordinary' Gay Lives," *Journal of Homosexuality* 59, no. 7 (August 2012): 1065–1072. *PsycINFO, EBSCOhost*.

Brown takes issue with academic use of "homonormativity," but does so for the very same reasons that critics like Duggan use the term. He claims that its treatment in current academic conversations elides other possible queer experiences by lumping all queer representations under the homonormative umbrella. His misreading of homonormative theory in fact elucidates all of the reasons why such norming is dangerous, both in society and in academia.

3. The Alphabet Soup seems to be in constant flux, which is perhaps appropriate given that it attempts to put names to many of the fluid identities grouped into "queerness." Right now, the acronym tends to run LGBTTQQIT-SAA, for lesbian, gay, bisexual, transgender, transsexual, queer, questioning, intersex, Two-Spirit, androgyne, and asexual.

4. Zine Magubane, "Black Skins, Black Masks or 'The Return of the White Negro': Race, Masculinity, and the Public Personas of Denis Rodman and RuPaul," *Men and Masculinities* 4, no. 3 (January 2002): 233; Ragan Rhyne, "Racializing White Drag," *Journal of Homosexuality* 46, no. 3/4 (February 2004): 181–194, *EBSCOhost*.

Both heteronormativity and homonormativity are highly raced. In these paradigms, white experience is empowered to the detriment of that of people of color. My focus here is more on gender performance than race, but for an interesting take on the issue see Magubane's treatment of black experience and Rhyne's examination of the performance of whiteness as drag. See also José Esteban Muñoz's extensive work with Latino queerness.

5. Susan Stryker, "Transgender History, Homonormativity, and Disciplinarity," *Radical History Review* no. 100 (Winter 2008): 144–157. *International Security and Counter Terrorism Reference Center, EBSCOhost*.

6. José Esteban Muñoz, "Toward a Methexic Queer Media," *GLQ: A Journal of Lesbian and Gay Studies* 4 (2013): 564. *Project MUSE, EBSCOhost*.

7. Ben Aslinger, "Creating a Network for Queer Audiences at Logo TV," *Popular Communication* 7, no. 2 (April 2009): 107–121. *Communication and Mass Media Complete, EBSCOhost*.

8. Eve Ng, "A 'Post-Gay' Era? Media Gaystreaming, Homonormativity, and the Politics of LGBT Integration," *Communication, Culture and Critique* 6, no. 2 (June 2013): 258–283. *Communication and Mass Media Complete, EBSCOhost*.

9. Ng, 267.

10. Aslinger, "Creating a Network," 120.

11. The origins of the term are as hazy as the origins of most current slang, but "fish" is rooted in name-calling. In Jamaica, it's an offensive word for gay men. In the U.S., the term is somewhat less stigmatized, though some people trace its roots to a derogatory and misogynistic way of describing the smell of women's genitalia. Others trace is back to prison slang for new inmates. No matter where the word comes from, its use is never politically innocent.

12. This is my own phrase. I have not yet run across any other critics who delineate between styles of fishy performance like this and feel "Real Fish" best suggests the distinctions I am trying to make here.

13. "Reading" is slang for the sort of verbal barbs tossed off by one drag queen at another. While by definition insults, the goal of "reading" another queen is to be as funny as possible. Vindictive reads are the exception and are often a sign that the queen is letting her emotions get the better of her.

14. I'd like to thank Robby Nadler for his help as a sounding board for this discussion. He reminded me of the connection between *Drag Race* and *ANTM* and pointed out the transgender contestant on the latter for me.

15. Steven P. Schacht, "Lesbian Drag Kings and the Feminine Embodiment of the Masculine," *Journal of Homosexuality* 43, no. 3/4 (May 2002): 75. *LGBT Life with Full Text*, EBSCOhost.

16. Schacht, 7–8.

17. Verta Taylor and Leila J. Rupp, "When the Girls Are Men: Negotiating Gender and Sexual Dynamics in a Study of Drag Queens," *Signs: Journal of Women in Culture and Society* 30, no. 4 (Summer 2005): 2115–2139. *Literary Reference Center*; Eve Shapiro, "Drag Kinging and the Transformation of Gender Identities," *Gender and Society* 21, no. 2 (April 2007): 250–271. *SocINDEX with Full Text*.

For an interesting take and different perspective on this sort of research, read Taylor and Rupp's study of the 801 Girls in Key West, Florida. They approach a drag community (here made up just of gay men performing as women) as observers, much the way Schacht does the ICS. Their study even includes a discussion of one particular queen, Sushi, who has in the past "passed" as a woman but finally decided that her out-of-drag gender identity is male. Taylor and Rupp's work with this performance troupe has convinced them that, at least for this group of drag queens, "the drag shows at the 801 affirm gay, lesbian, bisexual, transgendered, and transsexual identities; empower participants and audience members; and educate heterosexuals in attendance about gay life" (2119).

Likewise, Eve Shapiro's piece on the feminist drag king and queen troupe, Disposable Boy Toys, builds off the kinds of research performed by Taylor and Rupp. She demonstrates that "drag is not simply an expression of performers' preformed oppositional gender politics or preexisting counter-hegemonic gender identities; rather, the process of participating in drag communities may also function as a form of consciousness raising and a site of identity transformation for performers" (251).

18. Tracey Owens Patton and Julie Snyder-Yuly, "Roles, Rules, and Rebellions: Creating the Carnivalesque Through the Judges' Behaviors on *America's Next Top Model*," *Communication Studies* 63, no. 3 (July 2012): 364–384. *Communication and Mass Media Complete*, EBSCOhost; Sarah Cefai and Maria Elena Indelicato, "No Such Thing as Standard Beauty: Intersectionality and Embodied Feeling on *America's Next Top Model*," *Outskirts: Feminisms Along the Edge* 24 (May 2011): 10. *LGBT Life with Full Text*, EBSCOhost.

Patton and Snyder-Yuly offer a take on *ANTM*, reading the judging panel as a way of obtaining power and control for persons typically denied those things in mainstream society. Though approaching the issue from a considerably different angle than I do, Patton and Snyder-Yuly's work makes an intriguing counterpart to my own observations. Likewise, Cefai and Indelicato's examination of race and beauty is an excellent starting point for anyone interested in how heteronormativity is raced in shows like *ANTM* and *Drag Race*.

19. For the purposes of this project, I am treating the "All-Stars" season as a separate series. Comprised of returning contestants, this series tended rather to rehash old character beats rather than reveal new, significant data with regards to the *RuPaul* umbrella's approach toward misogyny and homonormativity displayed in the regular series.

20. "M.A.C/Viva Glam Challenge," *RuPaul's Drag Race*, World of Wonder, Logo, Los Angeles, February 23, 2009.

21. "Drag School of Charm," *RuPaul's Drag Race*, World of Wonder, Logo, Los Angeles, March 2, 2009.

22. "Snatch Game," *RuPaul's Drag Race*, World of Wonder, Logo, Los Angeles, February 27, 2012.

23. "WTF! Wrestling's Trashiest Fighters," *RuPaul's Drag Race*, World of Wonder, Logo, Los Angeles, February 2, 2012.

24. "Gone with the Window," *RuPaul's Drag Race*, World of Wonder, Logo, Los Angeles, February 1, 2010.

25. "Gone with the Window."

26. "Gone with the Window," *RuPaul's Drag Race: Untucked!*, World of Wonder, Logo, Los Angeles, February 1, 2010.

27. While the producers could not have been aware of the irony beforehand, their cutting to Sonique with a serious (and, in context, upset) expression on her face following Nicole's line about hormones becomes both biting and humorous in hindsight. Sonique comes out as a trans*woman during the season two reunion show. This hindsight makes Sonique and her storyline, both of which otherwise faded into the background in the presence of other louder and flashier performers, much more interesting. Sadly, though, her relatively forgettable presence on the show does little to inform how the series engages with homonormativity.

28. "Gone with the Window," *Untucked!*

29. "Gone with the Window," *Untucked!*

30. "Gone with the Window," *Untucked!*

31. Janice Haaken, "Bitch and Femme Psychology: Women, Aggression, and Psychoanalytic Social Theory," *JPCS: Journal for the Psychoanalysis of Culture and Society* 7, no. 2 (Fall 2002): 202–215. *MLA International Bibliography*, EBSCOhost.

32. Andi Zeisler, "Letter from the HQ," Bitch Magazine: Feminist Response to Pop Culture 55 (Summer 2012): 3. Academic Search Complete, EBSCOhost.

"Bitch will always have to answer for and explain our title—that's a bargain we tacitly agreed to 16 years ago when we chose it. Trying to reclaim and reframe language is tricky, and what's been most clear in these years of being asked the shock-or-reclamation question is this: As long as society continues to gender everything from political power to athletic ability to toy preference, 'bitch' will never lose its particular force as an epithet. And as long as 'feminist' remains a word that people are scared to claim and validate, 'bitch' will continue to be leveled at those who identify with it—and not in a coy, sassy, ready-for-prime-time way."

33. Rohin Guha, "On Gay Male Privilege: Excuse Me Sir, Your Privilege Is

Showing," *Medium: Gender, Justice, Feminism*, January 18, 2014, https://medium.com/gender-justice-feminism/59fc5490b223.

34. Guha.

35. Guha.

36. A portmanteau of "honey" (as a type of pet name for a loved one) and "cunt."

37. "Jocks in Frocks," *RuPaul's Drag Race*, World of Wonder, Logo, Los Angles, April 4, 2011.

38. "The Queen Who Mopped X-mas," *RuPaul's Drag Race*, World of Wonder, Logo, Los Angeles, January 24, 2011.

39. "Transgender Waitress Harassed by Diner," *Primetime: What Would You Do?*, ABC News Network, New York, May 4, 2012.

40. "Carmen Carrera's Quest to Become a Victoria's Secret Angel," *Katie*, Disney-ABC Domestic Television, New York, January 6, 2014.

41. "Bar Mitzvahs, Beads, and Oh Baby!" *Cake Boss*, High Noon Entertainment, TLC, Hoboken, NJ, June 11, 2012.

42. Carmen Carrera's Facebook fan page, posted October 12, 2012. All punctuation original.

43. Carmen Carrera's Facebook fan page, posted July 21, 2013.

44. Carmen Carrera's Facebook fan page, posted July 7, 2012.

45. "Lip Sync Extravaganza Eleganza," *RuPaul's Drag Race*, World of Wonder, Nick Murray, dir., Logo, February 4, 2013.

46. "Lip Sync Extravaganza Eleganza."

47. "Lip Sync Extravaganza Eleganza."

48. "Lip Sync Extravaganza Eleganza."

49. "Lip Sync Extravaganza Eleganza."

50. "Lip Sync Extravaganza Eleganza."

51. "Lip Sync Extravaganza Eleganza." *RuPaul's Drag Race: Untucked!*, World of Wonder, Logo, February 4, 2013.

52. "Lip Sync Extravaganza Eleganza," *Untucked!*

53. "Lip Sync Extravaganza Eleganza," *Untucked!*

54. "Lip Sync Extravaganza Eleganza," *Untucked!*

55. "Lip Sync Extravaganza Eleganza," *Untucked!*

56. "Lip Sync Extravaganza Eleganza," *Untucked!* Coco persists in referring to Serena as "he" for the rest of the episode despite using the feminine pronoun to refer to the other contestants. This is a subtle slight that the show does not make much hay of, but Coco's returning to the well, so to speak, is significant within the politics of the show. Professional queens, worthy of respect, are referred to as female; those deemed beneath contempt get the masculine pronoun.

57. "Lip Sync Extravaganza Eleganza," *Untucked!*

58. "Lip Sync Extravaganza Eleganza," *Untucked!*

Dragging with an Accent
Linguistic Stereotypes, Language Barriers and Translingualism

Libby Anthony

In "Why Don't We Speak with an Accent? Practicing Interdependence-in-Difference," LuMing Mao discusses the case of a truck driver, Mr. Manuel Castillo, who was pulled over in Alabama for a routine inspection and written a citation for $500 for "speaking with an accent."[1] While Mr. Castillo did not commit any vehicular violations, it seems that his accented English was difficult enough for the officer to understand that the officer warranted a citation necessary. Mr. Castillo was cited, very literally, as Mao points out, for driving with an accent. Regarding this situation, Mao asks, "Why is it that people continue to be hung up on the notion that some do and some don't 'speak with an accent' and that some accent is more privileged than other accents? [...] What, if anything, does speaking English 'with an accent' have to do with safety on the road?"[2]

Conversations about the use of the English language in the public sphere have increasingly begun to question the role of language in national identity. And we can apply Mao's questions to many other areas of the national public sphere. What, for example, does speaking English "with an accent" have to do with professional sports? What does speaking English "with an accent" have to do with one's ability to function as part of the American public? What assumptions are made about people who "speak with an accent?" And what does speaking English "with an accent" have to do with competing in a drag competition like *RuPaul's Drag Race*? Indeed, does the presence of an accent help or hinder the contestants? How are accents viewed to be useful or acceptable, or how are they detrimental to the contestants? If a permanent U.S. resident can be cited for driving with an accent, what does it mean for drag queens—an already marginalized and disenfranchised group—to do drag with an accent?

This essay will discuss contestants on *RuPaul's Drag Race*[3] who are from countries outside the U.S. and those who make a point of using and/ or negotiating the competition through the use of multiple languages.[4] Linguistic difference, ethnicity, culture, and race often are conflated in discussions of diversity. And this seems justifiable; often, one's cultural and ethnic backgrounds influence one's language(s) and vice versa. With this diversity, however, often come assumptions or stereotypes about one's abilities and identities.

Stereotypes in drag are nothing new, and stereotypes regarding linguistic patterns of speech are especially common in drag communities. And sometimes, these stereotypes serve a function in drag. In discussing the performative aspects of drag, Stephen L. Mann calls on Barrett[5] to highlight the fact that drag queens often play with the linguistic stereotypes of different cultural groups, and "by drawing on these stereotypes, drag queens highlight, provide commentary on, and often challenge prevailing ideologies."[6] Mann "argue[s] that by employing linguistic features shared by multiple socially and regionally defined language varieties— rather than simply switching among them—Suzanne [the drag queen in his study] is able to effectively perform an identity that frequently blurs gender and racial lines."[7] Some of the linguistic varieties Suzanne switches among are "Southern U.S. English, gay men's English (GME), stereotyped White women's English (WWE), stereotyped masculine language, and African American Vernacular English (AAVE)."[8] Through her negotiation among language varieties, Suzanne plays with assumptions about language and who does and who should speak different varieties of Englishes.

Contestant Manila Luzon draws on cultural and linguistic stereotypes during her time on the show. For example, during the season three episode "QNN News,"[9] Manila acts as a reporter interviewing Kristin Cavallari. She puts on a thick "Asian" accent, telling Kristin, "I have brother. You should hook up with him. You should marry. Immigration. Lots of money." Manila plays up multiple Asian stereotypes here, one of which is linguistic. RuPaul says to her, "When you weren't pronouncing your 'L's and your 'R's, I thought it was a terrible decision. But you know what? You know, that never hurt Barbara Walters." And during judging, guest judge Debbie Matenopoulos says, "It was so wrong that it was so right. And truthfully, if you're going to be groundbreaking, some eggs have got to be broken to make an omelet." Noting that Manila's choice to portray a stereotype was risky, RuPaul asks Manila, "If someone watching tonight were offended by what you did, how would you answer to that?" Manila responds that she was actually trying to bring more representation of Asian people into the culture. She says, "I don't think we have enough Asian people in pop culture. So, I'm here to entertain, I'm here to be farcical and just trying to do my job." And Manila's risk pays off as she wins the challenge, and RuPaul says, "Manila Luzon, this week you broke all the rules, you crossed the line of good taste, and you perpetuated stereotypes. Condragulations, you're the winner of this challenge." Thus, Manila is rewarded for her use of linguistic stereotypes.

While Manila is Filipino in ancestry, however, her speech is not as heavily accented as some of the other contestants, particularly the Latina contestants. Debates about Manila's appropriation of linguistic stereotypes come up among the contestants during the following episode, "The Snatch Game."[10] As Shangela says in the episode, "Oh it was definitely risky. She was making fun of a culture that she *looks* to be a part of but […] she's not. It made me uncomfortable. But the judges seem to enjoy that. So, halle-loo."

Manila's appropriation of these cultural and linguistic stereotypes prompts the questions: What happens when stereotypes become more than caricature-esque send ups of cultures? How do they help or interfere with a contestant's ability to succeed in the competition? Furthermore, what assumptions do the judges and the contestants themselves have about performance based on linguistic ability and linguistic stereotypes? And, taking these linguistic assumptions and potential constraints into consideration, who, really, can be *America's* Next Drag Superstar?

Standard English and Drag

In order to continue discussing assumptions and stereotypes about accented English, it is useful to start with a brief discussion of Standard English. Standard English is a variety of English that is perceived to be free of accent, spoken by educated individuals, and privileged. It is most often thought of as the English spoken in academia and by individuals in power. As Shondel J. Nero notes, Standard English is often assumed, therefore, to be both a "superior" and "fixed" code.[11] As a result, speakers of non-standard Englishes are often seen as uneducated, unintelligent, and unclear communicators.

Often, then, when speakers of other languages come to the U.S. with accented forms of English (or, sometimes, no English at all), assumptions about their intelligence are sometimes made based on their perceived linguistic abilities. These linguistically diverse speakers are also expected to strive to adjust their speech to mimic a Standard English dialect as closely as possible. As Mao says:

> This [Standard English] ideology is further predicated upon the belief that Standard English is simply a better fit for communication" than are the rest of the Englishes and that naturalization or assimilation of ethnic minorities and immigrants into the American melting pot "naturally" calls for these individuals to abandon their native or home languages and to master Standard English.[12]

Thus, the Standard English ideology establishes a hierarchical, problematic, and unwarranted view of language and linguistic ability. This hierarchy can cause problems when individuals who consider themselves to be speakers of Standard English come into contact with speakers of nonstandard Englishes or individuals who are perceived to speak with an accent.

This hierarchy can be seen as a parallel to some of the other hierarchical social constructs that drag queens face. For example, just as nonstandard English speakers are often viewed by Standard English speakers as outside the mainstream or norm, so too are drag queens perceived as outside the norm by those who embrace a heteronormative, mainstream view of gender boundaries. By adding an additional level of "otherness" to an already "othered" group, linguistically diverse, non-standard-English-speaking drag queens push against traditional mainstream conceptualizations of gender and language.

Despite the fact that many of the contestants on *Drag Race* likely consider themselves to be speakers of Standard English since they are from households and communities in which English was spoken as the first, primary, and in most cases, only language, drag queens have a knack for their ability to play with language, creating inside jokes, catchphrases,[13] and neologisms. In fact, translations for different drag terms are often included as captions on the screen during episodes of the show. Through this bending—or dragging—of language, drag queens create their own vocabulary, one that sets them apart from mainstream English language users. This ability for drag queens (and their supporters and fans) to communicate within this particular discourse community and outside perceived language norms is encouraged and celebrated. This celebration is evident during the season five reunion episode[14] as RuPaul encourages both the live audience and the television-viewing audience to shout, "I'm sick and twisted, and I'm not gonna take it anymore!" Through this creation of a shared drag vocabulary, even drag queens who might consider themselves to be Standard English speakers push against mainstream conceptualizations of what the English language is and should be.

Understanding and the "Language Barrier"

Despite the fact that drag queens—such as the example of Suzanne examined by Mann—often bend the barriers and boundaries of the English language, the Standard English ideology is still evident throughout *Drag Race*. The show and its contestants treat linguistic diversity in complex, varied, and nuanced ways. And even though drag queens are often marginalized within mainstream society because of their expressions of sexuality and gender, this does not make them unsusceptible to the underlying belief that Standard English speakers are superior to non–Standard English speakers. It also does not keep them from making assumptions about the abilities and intelligence of linguistically diverse speakers of English who do not speak English as their first or primary language.

Often, contestants and judges seem to have an expectation that linguistically diverse contestants will be difficult to understand because of their accented English. This comes into play during a season three episode, "RuPaul-a-Palooza."[15] During the main challenge, the contestants are given a style of music, and they have to perform RuPaul's song "Superstar" in that style. As the contestants practice their songs, Yara Sofia is shown to grapple with both her seeming lack of musicality and her ability to speak English. Shangela notes, "Maybe tone is lost in translation," and during an interview, Alexis Mateo, laughing, jokes about Yara, "She's not singing in Spanish, she's not singing in English, she's not singing in any language." However, when the contestants receive their recordings of the song, both Yara and Raja express surprise that Yara's recording is not as problematic as expected. Yara responds, "I am so excited to hear my song. I can not believe it! I could understand me. And my English is very well looking darling." And in the workroom, Raja says, "Wow, Yara, I love that I can actually understand you." This exchange shows some of the uphill battles the linguistically diverse contestants face on the show and how they struggle to overcome the perceptions about them that not just the judges and contestants have, but also the ways that they think about themselves. The linguistically diverse contestants worry about being understood in part because other contestants expect to not understand them.

Often, when the language of the international contestants is discussed in a way that suggests this linguistic diversity is detrimental, the phrase "the language barrier" is used. One example of this is during the season four episode "Glamazons vs. Champions."[16] The contestants work in teams to create commercials for two of RuPaul's albums, *Glamazon* and *Champion*. Kenya Michaels,[17] one of two queens from Puerto Rico during this season, wins the mini challenge and becomes the leader of Team *Glamazon*. However, Kenya's ability to lead the team is called into question by Milan. During an interview, Milan says, "I think we all knew that Kenya had a language barrier, so I decided to take control of that situation and help Kenya." Because Kenya's ability to speak English is not as strong as some of her teammates,' Milan believes Kenya needs "help" and she establishes "control" over the situation. Thus, Milan establishes a power hierarchy, placing herself at the top and Kenya at the bottom, despite the fact that Kenya was the one who was chosen to be the team leader. However, when RuPaul comes to the workroom and asks the team who is in charge, Milan responds with a more egalitarian picture, saying, "We decided to share it because of, you know, the language barrier." Milan presents the situation as "sharing" rather than a struggle for dominance. In an interview, Kenya responds to this by saying, "I think Milan talked too much. The English is not my first language. But I'm trying." In this interview, Kenya reacts to the perceptions about her that other contestants have based on her linguistic abilities.

This shift in the power hierarchy—and its ostensible root cause, the "language barrier"—is called into question by some of the other contestants. For example, The Princess says during an interview, "Kenya is supposed to be the team leader, but Milan is stepping in. And I'm sorry, I don't think it's the language barrier." The Princess suggests that Milan uses this perceived "language barrier" as a reason to establish her own authority and gain power over Kenya and their other teammates. The Princess' reaction shows that not all of the contestants necessarily buy in to the problem of the language barrier.

The "language barrier" also comes up in season five on various occasions regarding contestant Lineysha Sparx, who, like Kenya Michaels, is from Puerto Rico. During the episode "Lip Sync Extravaganza Eleganza,"[18] the contestants are challenged to lip sync to scenes from previous seasons' *Untucked*[19] episodes. During an interview, Vivienne Pinay says of Lineysha, "Quite honestly, I think Lineysha is going to struggle the most because of the language barrier." Even though contestants themselves do not have to speak during this challenge, Vivienne still assumes that Lineysha will struggle with pronouncing the words to the lip sync. However, this "language barrier" does not seem to slow down Lineysha, and she ends up winning the challenge.

Lineysha's linguistic abilities also come into question during the season five, episode five "The Snatch Game," when the contestants select a female personality to impersonate. Then, the contestants participate as that persona in a panel game show, similar to television's *The Match Game.* One of the major goals of the game is to be humorous. Often, drag queens will use humor to entertain their audiences, and "The Snatch Game" challenges them to use their wit in order to win. As the contestants prepare in the workroom, Lineysha tells RuPaul that she plans to impersonate Michelle Obama, but RuPaul encourages her to choose someone different. Lineysha opts to impersonate the "Queen of Salsa," Celia Cruz. Lineysha describes her rationale during the judging: "It's very hard to make comedy in other language. It's more comfortable me make uh, somebody Latina." Lineysha acknowledges the difficulty in trying to do humor in a language that is not one's first or primary language. She thought, by impersonating someone with a similar linguistic background, she would potentially find it easier to communicate humorously.

Lineysha's acknowledgment of this potential "language barrier" is evident in her first interaction with the host of "The Snatch Game," RuPaul. RuPaul introduces Lineysha by saying, "It's the Queen of Salsa, Celia Cruz. Hola!" Lineysha responds with "I'm very fine here. My English is not very good looking." It is unclear if Lineysha is making a joke regarding her own learning of the English language. However, it does seem as if, by noting this at the outset, that Lineysha is acknowledging the fact that she is concerned about the perceived "language barrier."

However, during judging, it does not seem as if the judges accepted Lineysha's acknowledgement of her "not very good looking" English. Indeed, it seems as if her accented English is what ultimately led to her elimination. Judge Santino Rice jokes that Lineysha's "'Snatch Game' was lost in translation," and when Lineysha is eliminated after the lip sync, RuPaul says, "Lineysha, your beauty transcends *language.* And there's no *barrier* to how far you will soar" (emphasis added). While the phrase "language barrier" is not used extensively throughout this episode as it is in some others, RuPaul plays on this phrase by using each of the words "language" and "barrier" in different ways as she eliminates Lineysha. While Lineysha's accented English and struggles with English seem to be one of the major reasons she was eliminated, RuPaul ultimately flips this negative association with the "language barrier" by using both of the words in a more positive, encouraging way.

Reunited

This complex nature of the "language barrier" comes up during some of the seasons' reunion episodes, and many of the linguistically diverse contestants are given a chance to express their multilingual identities during these episodes. During the reunions, the seasons' contestants hash out issues from the previous season and look back at their experiences on the show. It seems as if the reunion episodes are intended to give the contestants an opportunity to speak out about misunderstandings from the season, and the reunion episodes usually paint most of the contestants in a positive light.

While, during the seasons, the "language barrier" is sometimes seen as a detriment, the reunion episodes seem to treat linguistic diversity in a more lighthearted manner. Yet at the same time, this lightheartedness can be both celebratory and also somewhat superficial, failing to dig deeply into the complex linguistic identities of the contestants and providing the audience with a less-than-nuanced picture of the contestants. During the reunion for season four,[20] RuPaul introduces Kenya Michaels by saying, "Next up: Little Kenya Michaels. She had the looks, the moves, but what the hell was she talking about?" Then, they show a brief clip where Kenya talks to the other contestants about how it's easier for her to do dancing challenges than speaking challenges because "I don't speak more English." And Sharon Needles responds with "I understood about four words of that." After establishing Kenya's accented English as a discussion point, RuPaul brings Charo on stage as an "interpreter" for Kenya at the reunion. This is done for comedic effect, as Charo, the Spanish-American entertainer, is known for her own accented variety of English and for speaking in a mix of Spanish and English. Kenya and Charo speak in Spanish with each other for a few moments, and Kenya finishes by saying, "Baby, it's not what you say, it's what you do." RuPaul asks Charo to translate, and Charo responds, "RuPaul, I'm very confused. I cannot understand a word that bitch said." This humorous response, along with the bubbly and vivacious personalities of Kenya and Charo, seems intended to show Kenya and her linguistic diversity in a positive way. And RuPaul ends the segment with Kenya by saying, "Kenya, you are a fierce queen in any language." However, even though Kenya and her language are treated with a lightheartedness and humor, the fact still remains that Kenya becomes a bit of a caricature based on her linguistic diversity.

During season five's reunion episode,[21] two more linguistically diverse contestants express themselves with multiple languages—Lineysha Sparx and Serena ChaCha. As RuPaul reunites with Lineysha, the issue of Lineysha's language comes up. As a reference back to Kenya's reunion episode, RuPaul says to Lineysha, "Charo couldn't make it tonight to translate, so why don't you address the audience in Spanish. It might be easier in your native tongue." In Spanish with English subtitles, Lineysha says, "I am very happy and proud to be representing all of my Latinos, so a big kiss for all of you!" Continuing the lighthearted, joking nature of the reunion episode, RuPaul says, "I couldn't have said it better myself. Really. I couldn't have." RuPaul continues to joke with Lineysha as they discuss Lineysha's lack of knowledge about Diana Ross. When RuPaul asks Lineysha if she can name one of Diana Ross' songs, Lineysha fails to answer, so RuPaul jokingly calls for Immigration. While this is done in a joking tone and does not seem to be intended to cause any harm to Lineysha, the fact remains that Lineysha, like Kenya before her, is viewed as a stereotype or caricature of a Latina, someone worried about speaking the language and being deported.

This episode also brings forth the linguistic diversity of Serena ChaCha, another linguistically diverse contestant on season five. Serena ChaCha, the second contestant eliminated during season five, was born in the Republic of Panama. When RuPaul asks Serena which challenge she would have excelled in, had she stayed longer on the show, Serena says she would have done well with the telenovela challenge and then displays her ability to do so by speaking dramatically in Spanish, as is the style of telenovela actresses. RuPaul responds with "Escandolo!"[22] a Spanish word that has become a catchphrase on the show, corresponding to the Latina contestants as well as the telenovela episode nine "Drama Queens" in season five.[23] In contrast to Kenya, Serena's Spanish telenovela speech was captioned, and she was not provided with a "translator."

In the cases of Kenya, Lineysha, and Serena, the show seems to deem necessary the use of either a translator or captions in order for the contestants to communicate clearly with their audiences. This variance in tone throughout the seasons—from discussions about the contestants' "barriers" with language to the lighthearted, joking nature of the reunion episodes to the use of translators and/or captions—demonstrate how the show as well as the contestants negotiate linguistic diversity and deal with the complicated issue of doing drag with an accent. As linguistically diverse contestants push the language boundaries of drag, the show responds in complex and varied ways.

Translingualism: Audience and Identity

An analysis of the linguistically diverse contestants and their treat-ment by judges and fellow contestants shows that linguistic diversity, like many other personal attributes of a contestant, contributes in many mean-ingful ways to that contestant's performance. Viewing the show through a translingual lens helps us to see the complexities inherent in the linguis-tically diverse contestants. The field of composition and rhetoric has a rich body of scholarship[24] addressing the writing and communicative prac-tices of international, linguistically diverse English speakers. Within that field, scholars are beginning to explore and encourage translingualism, an approach to linguistic diversity that emphasizes movement across and through language boundaries. That is, a translingual approach to language examines how individuals use *all* the language resources available to them to write and speak in a variety of communication situations.

A translingual lens also helps us to analyze how linguistically diverse contestants on *Drag Race* push against the Standard English ideology. LuMing Mao argues, "[w]e must study and promote words, concepts, cat-egories, and discourses that can debunk the Standard English ideology and that can reveal relationships of subordination, resistance, and re-presentation."[25] Thus, a translingual approach toward language is a way to "debunk" this monolingual language norm. In this way, while *RuPaul's Drag Race* contestants push against gender norms and boundaries, a translingual approach to language can be used to examine how contestants and judges subvert (or uphold) *linguistic* boundaries and norms. In his introduction to *Literacy as Translingual Practice: Between Communities and Classrooms*, Suresh Canagarajah states, "The best way to understand the term *translingual* is by focusing on the prefix. What does 'trans' do to language? Firstly, the term moves us beyond a consideration of individual or monolithic languages to life between and across languages."[26] A trans-lingual attitude toward language embraces the seemingly "other," even cel-ebrates it, and it does not attempt to homogenize language or language speakers. Just as translingualism celebrates what is outside the norm and pushes us to reconceptualize how norms are defined, so too does drag.

One of the major aspects of translingualism is that it encourages lan-guage users to use the best form(s) of communication available to them in any given circumstance to communicate with any given audience. This can apply to different varieties or dialects of a language as well as differ-ent languages all together. Many contestants on the show proceed with this translingual mindset. For example, during the season three episode

"Totally Leotarded,"[27] Yara Sofia, a contestant from Puerto Rico, introduces her workout in the workout video in a mix of Spanish and English. She begins in Spanish and then concludes, "'Cause you like Latin guy, you have to work your body, darling. If you don't understand me, don't worry, I will include a translation at the end of the video." Yara uses her ability to speak both Spanish and English to play up the campiness for comedic effect, and this approach is apparently successful as it gains a laugh from RuPaul. During judging, RuPaul says to Yara, "You took a potential liability, which is your accent, and you made it work for you," and guest judge Susan Powter agrees, saying, "That whole Latin thing, that sexy swish, you had everyone roaring." Yara has read her audience correctly, and realizes that the inclusion of her cultural and linguistic background would help her in this challenge.

Season four also has some international, linguistically diverse contestants who seem to approach many of the challenges with a translingual mindset. For example, during "Glamazons vs. Champions,"[28] Madame LaQueer and Kenya Michaels both use multiple languages in their commercials to communicate with their audience. However, the response from the judges is different for each of the contestants. In Madame LaQueer's commercial, she says, "I don't speak much English" in English and then she switches over to Spanish. She finishes by asking the audience, "Do you remember your first time?" Madame seems to have chosen to use both English and Spanish because she thought she could communicate more clearly by mixing multiple languages.

Judge Michelle Visage does not respond positively to Madame's use of Spanish, and indicates that she relies on Spanish too heavily. Visage cautions her, "In the video, in the pitch, a little too much Spanish, so remember that." However, guest judge Amber Riley disagrees, saying that Madame was being "true to herself" and her use of Spanish was funny. Yet, she does seem to believe Madame used Spanish as a crutch, saying, "I think that's a place where you're uncomfortable. I would encourage you to push yourself a little bit." This reaction may be based on Madame's statement at the beginning of her commercial when she says, "I don't speak much English." This statement could seem like an admission of inferiority or vulnerability to the judges, which opened up Madame LaQueer for criticism. Yet it remains difficult to determine where the line is drawn between a contestant's appropriate use of their first language and when they use it too much.

Kenya Michaels also switches between English and Spanish in her commercial in the same episode. However, her use of multiple languages seems to come off as more confident and self-assured than Madame LaQueer's, and the judges have a different reaction to her mixing of languages. In her sales pitch, Kenya begins by saying in English, "When you are in a competition that no one speaks Spanish, you think," and then she switches to Spanish. In this instant, Kenya's switch to Spanish is appropriate because it is most likely that she would, indeed, be thinking in Spanish. She then switches back to English, saying, "but in that moment, get your rebel on." The name of the song she promotes in this commercial is RuPaul's "Get Your Rebel On," so she is able to weave in the title of the song while at the same time using the song title as an affirmation of female pride and confidence. By using the term "rebel," Kenya expresses confidence, making her use of multiple languages seem well-planned and self-assured. The judges' reaction to Kenya's commercial is correspondingly more positive than it is to Madame LaQueer's use of multiple languages. During the judging, Santino Rice says, "I really like Kenya. She has less of a handle on the English language, but she was able to just push through it and have fun." So, according to Rice, Kenya's enthusiasm and confidence overshadowed her lack of "a handle on the English language." Interestingly, this is also the same episode in which Kenya supposedly struggled with, and overcame, the perceived "language barrier" that her teammate Milan thought she had when Kenya acted as team captain.

While both Madame and Kenya approach this challenge with a translingual mindset, choosing to use their multiple languages to communicate as clearly as they can with their audience, the audience's (in this case, the judges') reactions are not uniformly positive. Thus, it seems that if contestants want to gain the respect of their audiences and convince them to buy in to the translingual approach, they should not admit any perceived weakness and have confidence in their linguistic approach.

Another translingual moment occurs in the season two episode "Once Upon a Queen"[29] during the "Reading is Fundamental" mini challenge. During the challenge, the contestants "read" each other, or make humorous remarks, similar to a roast. During the challenge, Jujubee, a contestant with Laotian ancestry, reads Jessica Wild and switches between English and Laotian, and she even uses a word of Spanish because Jessica Wild is from Puerto Rico. Jujubee says, "And let me tell you something, *puerca*. You won't understand this anyways," switches to Laotian to say, "You have a dog face, your body is *huge*" (this is subtitled). Then she switches back to English to say, "Get my gist? Do you understand?" Jujubee uses three different languages in this exchange as a way to express herself and make her reading stand out from her competitors.

Earlier in this same episode, while many of the contestants discuss being bulled throughout their lives, Jujubee and Jessica Wild further express themselves via their multiple languages. They both highlight the names they were called when they were teased by telling the other contestants about the non–English words used to tease them. Jessica says that she was often called "*malo.*" And Jujubee says, "You wanna hear it in my language? *Kathoey.*[30] Doesn't that sound dirty?" By calling attention to the "dirty" sound of this word and the negativity that accompanies both of these insults in languages other than English, Jujubee and Jessica show how bullying occurs in all languages. The inclusion of this scene suggests that it does not matter which language(s) the contestants speak because they have *all* been bullied based on their homosexuality and regardless of their language. The language(s) the contestants speak are just one part of their identities. And just as sharing a common drag vocabulary unites these contestants across different language boundaries, they are also united through their experiences with bullying.

Catchphrases

In many ways, linguistic dynamism is woven into the fabric of the show, such as through the use of drag vocabulary. Another way we see this negotiation of language is through the use of catchphrases. Catchphrases are nothing new to RuPaul. Since the drag queen has gained prominence on the national stage since the 1990s, she has come to be known for repeated phrases, often from her music. For example, some phrases from her music such as "You betta work," "I have one thing to say," and "Sashay, shantay" have become part of the common vocabulary on the show. Throughout the show, RuPaul repeats common phrases such as "Gentlemen, start your engines, and may the best woman win" when introducing the contestants to challenges, and "Shantay, you stay" and "Sashay away" are used during eliminations.

Some of the catchphrases that have caught on for single seasons and/or across multiple seasons come from—or are used in reference to—the linguistically diverse contestants on the show. As previously mentioned, one such catchphrase that cuts across seasons is "*escándalo.*" RuPaul often uses this catchphrase to refer to moments that are scandalous (the direct translation of *escándalo* is "scandal") or noteworthy/notorious in some way. One of the earliest examples comes in the season two episode "Here Comes the Bride."[31] Continuing with the theme of scandal that runs through the episode, during judging, RuPaul says to Jessica, "Jessica, *mucho escándalo*. You're safe."

The phrase takes a hiatus during the rest of this season. However, it returns during the season three "Casting Extravaganza."[32] As Yara Sofia is introduced, RuPaul says, "Will Yara's edgy style get her to the finish line? *Escándalo*." It is not exactly clear what is scandalous about this question, but perhaps it has something to do with an "edgy" and/or Latina contestant being crowned. What does seem clear, however, is that the Spanish word is used because Yara is from Puerto Rico. Thus, we see an association between Latina contestants and the Spanish phrase *escándalo*.

Later in the season, during the episode "QNN News,"[33] RuPaul introduces a mini challenge where contestants have to take scandalous red carpet photos. As she prepares the contestants for the challenge, she says, "Ready, set, *escándalo*!" which plays on the "scandalous" nature of the challenge. During the challenge itself, RuPaul invokes the name of another famous Latina performer, Shakira, saying to Yara, "Hey Shakira. Uno, dos, tres! *Escándalo*!" And later in the episode, contestant Shangela picks up on the catchphrase as the teams film their segments for QNN News. Shangela, acting as the team's gossip correspondent, says the pictures from the mini challenge were *escándalo*, and to confirm her analysis of the photos, she says to Yara, "Yara Sofia? *Escándalo*?" and Yara agrees. We see here, that not just RuPaul but some of the contestants pick up on the catchphrases that are borrowed from other languages. After this season, use of the term becomes less prominent.[34] So while the term seems to have gained purchase for a few seasons, it mostly corresponds to Yara's run on the show.

While *escándalo* is most frequently used in relation to Yara, the contestant has another catchphrase for which she is perhaps even more well-known: *echa pa'lante*. Yara first introduces the phrase in "Totally Leotarded."[35] In the workroom, RuPaul asks all of the girls about what they plan to do in the workout challenge, and Yara responds, "It's called *echa pa'lante*." RuPaul responds by requesting, "Oh help me with that." And Yara defines the phrase in the following way: "It means 'move forward.' If you wanna look like this, you have to work it out darling [...] so *echa pa'lante*." The phrase is later repeated as the name of Yara's workout and throughout her exercise in the workout challenge. Thus, Yara makes a point of using the phrase as a way to make herself stand out in the competition.

Echa pa'lante comes up again during episode seven "Face, Face, Face of Cakes."[36] During this episode, the contestants have to decorate a cake that is in the shape of a doll. The decorations are supposed to reflect the personality of each contestant. Yara Sofía opts to decorate her cake with the Puerto Rican flag. During judging, Yara says, "This is mini-me. She is wearing a national costume with the Puerto Rican flag." RuPaul responds to this pronouncement with *"echa pa'lante."* The phrase takes on the virtues of a positive adjective, with RuPaul adopting the phrase to describe Yara's cake. At this point, the phrase seems to start morphing from its literal definition to a catchphrase that is used to describe something fierce or positive associated with Yara.

The strength of the phrase's association with Yara is evident in the episode in which Yara is eliminated.[37] RuPaul tells Yara to "sashay away"; she also says, "Remember this: *echa, echa, echa pa'lante.*" During her exit interview, Yara tells the camera, "This is for Puerto Rico. So I'm gonna *echa pa'lante.*" Interestingly, this phrase seems to be associated with Yara, and Yara alone. Even though the phrase is in Spanish, it is not used in conjunction with the other Puerto Rican contestant during the season, Alexis Mateo.[38] This Spanish catchphrase allows Yara to express her individuality and uniqueness even within the larger category of Latina contestants on the show.

RuPaul also adopts the custom of shouting the names of the countries that international contestants are from as a catchphrase or a shout out, especially when the contestants walk the runway. For example, season one winner BeBe Zahara Benet is from Cameroon, and RuPaul will sometimes shout "Cameroon!" when BeBe is on the runway. RuPaul also refers to Puerto Rican contestant Jessica Wild in a similar way in season two's "The Snatch Game."[39] As Jessica walks the runway, RuPaul says, "Jessica Wild. Puerto Rico. Okay?" This custom is referenced in a tongue-in-cheek way during the season four episode "RuPaul Rewind."[40] At the beginning of the episode, which is a look back at clips from the previous season, judge Michelle Visage stands on the runway, and she is dressed like RuPaul. She opens the show by mimicking RuPaul, saying, "Can I get an amen up in here? Cameroon? Halleloo?" In this brief segment, Michelle echoes three separate catchphrases from the show, one of which is the catchphrase associated with BeBe.

Catchphrases are part of the culture of *RuPaul's Drag Race*, as acknowledged by Michelle Visage. They become a way for the contestants to express their own individuality and to be recognized for their unique culture and linguistic heritages. The use and repetition of these catchphrases throughout the show's run indicate an acceptance of and celebration of the diverse linguistic and cultural backgrounds of the show's international contestants.

Conclusion

Scholars in academic fields, such as composition and rhetoric and linguistics, have been discussing the presence of linguistically diverse students in their classrooms for decades. However, assumptions about the intelligence, abilities, and skills of linguistically diverse individuals are prevalent not just in academia, but most especially in the public sphere. Canagarajah argues,

> The urgency for scholars to address translingual practices in literacy derives from the fact that they are widely practiced in communities and everyday communicative contexts [...]. Social relations and communicative practices in the context of late modernity—featuring migration, transnational economic and production relationships, digital media, and online communication—facilitate a meshing of languages and semiotic resources.[41]

This "meshing of languages" is both evident in and complicated by the contestants and judges of *RuPaul's Drag Race*. While linguistically diverse contestants whose primary language is not English are sometimes challenged by their efforts to communicate in English, they are often also able to draw on their various linguistic backgrounds to participate in the competition in a way that sets them apart from the other contestants.

In many ways, *Drag Race* takes a translingual approach toward language, encouraging contestants to use their linguistic diversity as a way to communicate and compete. LuMing Mao asks us to "begin to view 'speaking with an accent' not as a liability but as an asset, as a contact-zone experience that deserves not censure but celebration."[42] As contestants use their various language resources and accented Englishes throughout the competition, they push the other contestants, the judges, and their viewers to see and hear language diversity differently. While *RuPaul's Drag Race* pushes gender norms and challenges traditional perceptions of sexuality, it also encourages its viewing public to view drag—and dragging with an accent—as something worth celebrating and something worth watching.

Notes

1. Luming Mao, "Why Don't We Speak with an Accent? Practicing Interdependence-in-Difference," in *Cross-Language Relations in Composition*, ed. Bruce Horner, Min-Zhan Lu, and Paul Kei Matsuda (Carbondale: Southern Illinois University Press, 2010), 189.

2. Mao, 189.

3. For the purposes of this discussion, I will focus on seasons two through five, including a few moments from season one. I will not include more evidence from season one because the season is, for the most part, unavailable to view because it has not aired again after its initial broadcast.

4. Throughout this essay, I will use terms like "linguistically diverse" and "international" to describe contestants in the competition who speak English as something other than (or in addition to) their first language(s). Throughout the literature, there are many different terms for such individuals, such as non-native English speaker (NNES/NNS), English as a Second Language speaker (ESL), and multilingual. I chose to vacillate among different terms because I do not perceive one term to be appropriate in all circumstances. Correspondingly, one term cannot encompass the complex and nuanced experiences and abilities of all individuals. For more reading on this, see Michelle Cox, Jay Jordan, Christina Ortmeier-Hooper, and Gwen Gray Schartz's *Reinventing Identities in Second Language Writing*, among others.

5. Rusty Barrett's "Markedness and Styleswitching in Performances by African American Drag Queens," in *Codes and Consequences: Choosing Linguistic Varieties*, ed. Carol Myers-Scotton (New York: Oxford University Press, 1998).

6. Stephen L. Mann, "Drag Queens' Use of Language and the Performance of Blurred Gendered and Racial Identities," *Journal of Homosexuality* 58 (2011): 793.

7. Mann, 794.

8. Mann, 794.

9. *RuPaul's Drag Race*, "QNN News," Logo TV, 14 February 2011.

10. *RuPaul's Drag Race*, "The Snatch Game," Logo TV, 21 February 2011.

11. Shondel J. Nero, "Discourse Tensions, Englishes, and the Composition Classroom," in *Cross-Language Relations in Composition*, ed. Bruce Horner, Min-Zhan Lu, and Paul Kei Matsuda (Carbondale: Southern Illinois University Press, 2010), 144.

12. Mao, 190.

13. Catchphrases will be discussed in a later section.

14. *RuPaul's Drag Race*, "Reunited," Logo TV, 6 May 2013.

15. *RuPaul's Drag Race*, "RuPaul-a-Palooza," Logo TV, 21 March 2011.

16. *RuPaul's Drag Race*, "Glamazons vs. Champions," Logo TV, 12 February 2012.

17. For the most part, I will use female pronouns (she/her) throughout this essay to refer to both the contestants and RuPaul, whether they are in or out of drag. It seems that the contestants, themselves, use female pronouns for one another most of the time, so I try to remain consistent with that pattern.

18. *RuPaul's Drag Race*, "Lip Sync Extravaganza Eleganza," Logo TV, 4 February 2013.

19. *Untucked!* is an online series that offers glimpses of what happens behind the scenes with the contestants as the judges panel discusses who will be eliminated on the show.

20. *RuPaul's Drag Race*, "Reunited," Logo TV, 30 April 2012.

21. *RuPaul's Drag Race*, "Reunited," Logo TV, 6 May 2013.

22. This catchphrase and others will be discussed in a later section.

23. *RuPaul's Drag Race*, "Drama Queens," Logo TV, 1 April 2013.

24. See Bruce Horner, Samantha NeCamp, and Christiane Donahue's "Toward a Multilingual Composition Scholarship: From English Only to a Translingual Norm," in *College Composition and Communication* and Bruce Horner, Min-Zhan Lu, Jacqueline Jones Royster, and John Trimbur's "Opinion: Language Difference in Writing: Toward a Translingual Approach" in *College English*.

25. Mao, 191.

26. A. Suresh Canagarajah, "Introduction," in *Literacy as Translingual Practice: Between Communities and Classrooms*, ed. A. Suresh Canagarajah (New York: Routledge, 2013), 1.

27. *RuPaul's Drag Race*, "Totally Leotarded," Logo TV, 7 February 2011.

28. *RuPaul's Drag Race*, "Glamazons vs. Champions," Logo TV, 12 February 2012.

29. *RuPaul's Drag Race*, "Once Upon a Queen," Logo TV, 22 March 2010.

30. *Kathoey* translates to "lady boy."

31. *RuPaul's Drag Race*, "Here Comes the Bride," Logo TV, 8 March 2010.

32. *RuPaul's Drag Race*, "Casting Extravaganza," Logo TV, 24 January 2011.

33. *RuPaul's Drag Race*, "QNN News," Logo TV, 14 February 2011.

34. The phrase does appear in a few other instances. For example, RuPaul uses it during season five's reunion episode in response to Serena ChaCha's telenovela speech.

35. *RuPaul's Drag Race*, "Totally Leotarded," Logo TV, 7 February 2011.

36. *RuPaul's Drag Race*, "Face, Face, Face of Cakes," Logo TV, 28 February 2011.

37. *RuPaul's Drag Race*, "Make Dat Money," Logo TV, 11 April 2011.

38. Alexis has her own catchphrase throughout the season: "Bam!"

39. *RuPaul's Drag Race*, "The Snatch Game," Logo TV, 22 February 2010.

40. *RuPaul's Drag Race*, "RuPaul Rewind," Logo TV, 16 April 2012.

41. Canagarajah, 2.

42. Mao, 194.

Policing the Proper Queer Subject
RuPaul's Drag Race in the Neoliberal "Post" Moment

KAI KOHLSDORF

"What we're looking for is someone who can really follow in my footsteps: Someone who can be hired by a company to represent their product, someone who can put together a sentence on television and present themselves in the most incredible way."[1]

RuPaul, above, unabashedly claims that her reality television show's quest is to crown none other than a person who can embody what the product needs and show off their exceptional intellect.[2] What does the drive to commodify mean in the context of the wildly popular reality show *RuPaul's Drag Race*? How does it echo racist histories? What happens when we move drag queens from the space of the gay bar to the space of mainstream television? The move to reality television, while loudly celebrated in some LGBTQ communities as a modern triumph of visibility, has a more dangerous undercurrent. Where queen's performances, personas, and charisma exhibit fluidity, outrageousness, or fabulosity[3] in the space of a queer bar, these same performances on screen shift in meaning such that they become tokenizable, purchasable. Instead of expanding and exploding stringent identity categories, what we see as a result of the inescapable political economy of television is an ironic turn towards normalization of the very categories these queens, in other spaces, tend to disrupt.

One might wonder what cultural moment created the market for and sustainability of a show like *RuPaul's Drag Race* beyond the "pink," or LGBTQ focused, economy.[4] In an interview with RuPaul, Tanner Stransky of *Entertainment Weekly* asked what prompted what could be viewed as her "comeback" after several years of decreasing popularity. RuPaul responded, "It wasn't a meltdown or anything. It really had more to do with understanding the temperature socially. Now it's the perfect time to reemerge." Now, according to Tanner Stransky, means "the Barack Obama era." This could be read as code for the increasing popular acceptance and ideology of the "post" race and feminist era. Echoing the legacy of colorblindness, the "post" landscape believes that we no longer need to talk about racism, sexism, or even homophobia, because oppression is over. Very often the election of Barack Obama is given as the proof that the U.S. has reached full equality. Ralina Joseph argues against the validity of arguments that we are in a "post" society in her work on *America's Next Top Model*.[5] As Joseph explains, "Post-race is an ideology that cannot escape racialization, complete with controlling images or racialized stereotypes."[6] The example of Obama's presidency does just that, racializing and utilizing a tokenizing image, and an incomplete one at that, as proof serves to re-center the dominant whiteness and shut down the conversation. I argue *RuPaul's Drag Race* follows a similar post-racial, exoticizing trajectory to most mainstream ideology, and through transphobia connects to a post-feminist landscape. As Joseph argues, here race is again crafted to "echo capitalist rhetoric of individualism and choice, which [...] goes hand-in-hand with the ideology of black transcendence [...] present[ing] race as a lifestyle choice and reconstitute[s] the centrality of whiteness."[7] Those contestants whose identities could be exploited through discussion of exotic "otherness" re-centers the dominant U.S. race as white, much as the reliance on the transformation from men to queens re-centers biological gender and sex norms.

As Ralina Joseph connects post-racial landscapes with post-feminism expectations in her work, I also understand the move from the bar to the screen as an undoing of both race and gender. While race is systematically silenced, despite its consistent and haunting presence, the fluidity of drag queen's experience, which is consistently invoked, is contained and forcibly marketed for mainstream appeal and production approval. Although I talk about both race and gender here as policed behaviors and identities, each category has different specificities of historical oppression and its own relationship to multiplicities and fluidity. What I hope to impart is an intersectional analysis that takes into account how in order to police one identity category, other identities and specificities are made invisible, and hence naturalized. The post-racial era allows for an easy elision of race discussion, while current and ripe transphobia broadly allows gender policing to go unnoticed. Both work together to restrain and limit the freedom with which contestants are able to show the complexity of their lives such that any risks that are too "outside" of the dominant white, heteronormative, binary gendered norm result in either firm moments of containment or contestant's dismissal from the competition.

As we see RuPaul as the "face, face, give me face" of *RuPaul's Drag Race*, RuPaul's character becomes inescapably important to understanding the overarching narrative of the show. RuPaul, as an arguable LGBTQ icon in the community, is often set up as an authority on not only drag, but gender non-conformance more broadly. Therefore, her authority is invoked in the show alongside her clear commodification. RuPaul initially acknowledged the production of her persona as a commodity in her autobiography *Lettin' It All Hang Out*[8]:

> A part of my fame has nothing to do with me. I came along at just the right time [...]. Because I am not the sole and exclusive author of this process, I have been able to watch it one step removed. That's why I often think of myself in the third person, not because I think I am royal—although I am a queen—but because I see RuPaul as a product. The RuPaul experience is rather like a ride in a theme park: You put a quarter in the slot and off I go.[9]

Importantly, RuPaul articulates a distancing of herself from communities that take up her persona, as she is paid to watch from afar. As the show utilizes her as an iconic model of how the drag queen contestants should behave, understanding RuPaul's identity as it relates to the show can also provide us with an understanding of why it might be that the show itself similarly cannot hold the complexity of the contestant's lives. In 2014 the show airs its sixth season, making *RuPaul's Drag Race* the most successful show to date on the LGBTQ network, Logo television. It is also co-broadcast on VH1.[10] In order to maintain wide viewership and marketability, the identities of the contestants are packaged as exotic and policed into dominant understandings of drag queens when they disrupt or challenge binary expectations of race and gender, which has a clear connection to RuPaul's sanitized and safe fame.

Despite the fact that it is called reality television, viewers see only the cuts that production and marketing deem the most worthy of ratings.[11] While the show is based on drag and gender performance, the show ultimately distances "drag" from any and all things "transgender." Surprisingly, this occurs despite the realities that many drag queens identify as transgender at times, or consider their identities and realities as part of the trans* community. To see clear divisions arise in *RuPaul's Drag Race* upholds an ironic understanding that gender and sex, despite what fluidity may be on the screen at any given moment, are in fact easily categorizable and offer no complicated understandings to the viewers at home. Those who are most able to police themselves, by creating a drag image in the best respectable drag just like RuPaul, advance the furthest in the competition. The how-to-win policing dynamic is shown through explicit policies and procedures, spoken and unspoken rules that the queen's understand as their guidelines, and through counter narrative examples. When something happens directly in conflict with these directives, those queens are either policed back into their assigned roles, or are unilaterally eliminated by RuPaul herself—who has ultimate say in who stays and who goes. Ironically, in the act of laying bare the creation of their queen selves, many other identities of the contestants are made invisible and are naturalized alongside a narrative that contains and makes presentable that which would otherwise disrupt.

Commercializing Identities: Creating New Drag Queen Superstars

So what is a drag queen anyway? In the context of *RuPaul's Drag Race,* the answer is RuPaul. However, in the gay men's community, drag is historically thought of as a variety of things, including a social commentary on gender presentation itself.[12] Drag has a long history of performance within bar and ballroom cultures, underground and commercialized, performed for queer audiences and heteronormative ones. However, drag in these underground, bar, and ballroom cultures often exhibits different kinds of expectations than we see in *RuPaul's Drag Race.* There is room in the bar or the ballroom for queens who identify as transgender, who identify with transgender women regardless of personal identification, and who understand their worlds as more gender complicated than simply men who impersonate women (the show's understood definition).[13] These spaces, specifically the ballroom, have rich histories of support for queer and trans* queens of color.[14] By providing a narrow definition and a narrow set of expectations in *RuPaul's Drag Race,* we begin with a different understanding of drag than has historically been connected with LGBTQ communities. RuPaul, and the producers of the show, know that her gender presentation as a queen is what sells her products and her music; a stylized drag performance becomes articulated as talent and a claim to fame. A connection to the historicity of drag in LGBTQ communities is tenuous at best.[15]

A study of *RuPaul's Drag Race*, by proxy of being on an LGBTQ network, would seem to necessitate connection to work on homosexuality within media studies.[16] While *RuPaul's Drag Race* is implicitly linked to homosexuality through the sexual orientation of the queens on the show, gayness is rarely discussed on screen. However, the exclusion of transgender people and the emphasis on the transformation from men into queens is reminiscent of gay television's stereotypical portrayals of homosexuality. Battles and Hilton-Morrow utilize the sitcom *Will and Grace* to show how it creates a safe homosexuality for audiences. They argue it equates gayness with a lack of masculinity wherein homosexuality can only be understood through existing heterosexist categories and language.[17] Similarly, *RuPaul's Drag Race* makes drag safe and confines gender transgressions within heteronormative discourses as well as binary gender codes, even while the queens exhibit gender transgression that could be read as "deviant" or subversive. Although the show is aired on Logo television, ostensibly for a queer and queer-friendly audience, the emphasis on transformation of men into queens marks participants as outside the norm. For instance, even the phrase RuPaul utilizes to get the queens motivated to work on their challenges sets up a reminder of gender binaries, "Gentlemen, start your engines, and may the best *woman* win!" Her emphasis on the word "woman" includes a raised eyebrow and a nod to the performers and those watching that the performances of womanhood they are viewing are not, according to heteronormative discourse, real. What could be read as a nod to queers, and may even be meant as such, comes off as reifying when directed at a mainstream audience.

While RuPaul, in her early career, seemed to appreciate and acknowledge the categories of drag queens and transgender women have a complex relationship, the contemporary RuPaul character is more invested in distancing herself from transgender people, arguably as a necessity to her fame. While I take RuPaul to task for the transphobia exhibited in her show, I also argue that in order for her continued success, she is limited. For instance, in RuPaul's early career she often performed gender fuck drag,[18] but she is careful to note that is not what made her famous. Her androgynous look ended when she was unable to secure a career.[19] When she returned to New York, she shifted to drag that would make her a star—perhaps because reinforcing gender binaries paid the bills. RuPaul may have had a more fluid sense of self than what we currently view. However, in her autobiography, and in her contemporary interviews, she consistently asserts pronouns are formalities, which undercuts and diminishes the experiences of transgender and gender non-conforming people for whom pronouns are especially important. Despite her connection to transgender women and other gender non-conforming people, the famous RuPaul must distance herself from threats to un-marketability.

The linkage between drag queens and transgender women primarily exists in the widespread conflation of any gender transgressive person as either gay or transgender—without regard to the person's chosen identity. Indeed, this is why RuPaul consistently distances herself from transgender women. Transgender women are often policed in similar ways in mainstream culture, as well as by medical professionals, in order to access services and rights. For instance, transgender women face difficult access to medical interventions as a result of gatekeeping by the medical industrial complex through having to present a particular transgender identity, with a proper transgender narrative.[20] The underlying ideology in these examples is that we are who we were assigned at birth, that reality is genitals and upbringing, and that any deviation or alteration from the original body is deceitful. This ideology is transphobic at heart, and is often the same argument used against transgender people to justify violence or prejudice. The push to assign definitional sex identities to those who transgress, establishing "what they really are," is a concern throughout the show, wherein bodies must conform to a particular narrative, echoing the medical history of transgender experiences, in order to prove they are *other than* transgender identified. The transgender narrative is invoked as "born in the wrong body," a limited scope of transgender in and of itself, and any indicators that queens may be transgender are then cause for concern and potential elimination.[21]

RuPaul's gendered roles and, at times, use of transphobic ideology to maintain her position, are important to understanding how the show distances itself from transgender women, as we can see her rhetoric shapes both her identity and the iconic image the queens are meant to mirror. RuPaul's books articulate a distancing from all things gender "freak." Early in her rise to stardom, RuPaul began distancing herself from these stereotypes, "I particularly wanted to do this because, as a drag queen, people generally see me as some kind of thing or freak with a sex fetish. I've never understood why people find it so hard to recognize the real person inside of me."[22] While RuPaul starts out with potential to be critical of these problematic views of drag queens (and also of transgender women) as "unreal" and a "sex fetish," ultimately RuPaul re-enacts the idea that she is "just like everybody else" through seeing the supposedly real RuPaul inside. The means through which the contestants make the products desirable mirrors the ways RuPaul sells her own products, embodying her supermodel identity through sex appeal and double entendres. The double entendres consistently relate to binary expectations of gender, and the sex appeal of the contestants can be read as crossing the line to voyeurism and exoticization. Her reliance on a universal sameness works to enable the post-race and post-feminist landscape the show perpetuates, and also erases all potential conflict from the bodies on screen so viewers may feel safe to purchase the show and its products. It is precisely this sameness that enables gender fluidity to be viewed in the first place, because it is made safe through reliance on a narrative highlighting the transformation—ultimately upholding the status quo.

While we may assume that RuPaul, the persona, invokes this, while RuPaul Charles, the individual behind the persona, may not, it is not her personal experience that I find impactful. It is that her persona, writ large in mainstream popular culture, gives license and authority to the idea of universal sameness, reveling in the post-race, post-feminism age. In RuPaul's rise to fame, she must articulate non-threatening politics, for it is her identity as a queen that people buy. In order to maintain a celebrity status, she is limited in what she is able to express and must continuously make claims to appease readers and viewers that she is "just like them," even if it means erasing race, gender, and sexuality differences.[23]

In *RuPaul's Drag Race* these instances overtly showcase the historical moment and ideology of gender and racial dynamics within the cultural landscape of the "post." The fascination and exoticized marketability of gender and racial "others" is still very high, and occurs in contrast to widespread claims of gender and racial equality. These moves signal the "post" moment, and operate from the expectation that race, ethnicity, and gender can always be played with because we're past oppression. For instance, in the first season's Absolut Vodka challenge, an advertisement for their new flavored series of vodkas—complete with a bolded imprint on each bottle "IMPORTED"—uncritically utilizes sexual exoticization of racial and ethnic minorities, sexual minorities, and gender non-conforming people to sell "exotic" and "tropical" vodkas. During this challenge, the final four contestants are given the task of portraying one "exotic" fruit and must utilize the fruit in their costume creation for the drag ball.[24] While the "fruit" is shockingly unremarked upon, what is most disturbing about this challenge is the dominant discourses of racialized and exotic sexualities are re-enacted by the contestants in an effort to win.

The Absolut Vodka challenge's phrases "exotic" and "tropical" code non-white contestants and gender transgressors as other, and also require white performers to enact cultural appropriative ideology to "win" the challenge. These stereotypical usages are in service to Absolut Vodka's campaign, but are written on and through the contestant's bodies. While RuPaul's universal "we are all the same" argument reinforces that of all contestants are equal and everyone is "post-race" and "post-gender," what we see here instead is a re-inscription of dominant racist ideologies that turn queens of color into stereotypical purchasable commodities, and white queens into tokens for how white people can access "authentic" exotic identities. The sexualized imagery of the ads utilized both on the show and on the show's website further serves to other the queens in homophobic and gender normative ways. The ad "In an Absolut World, True Taste Comes Naturally," depicts a mandarin held softly by wavy lines, at the bottom of which is a phallic-shaped Absolut Vodka bottle—apparently penetrating the dark opening surrounding the mandarin.[25] Clearly, this is a message about penile-vaginal intercourse—and can be contextualized as a moment of containment of the transgressive potential of the show. On air, the Absolut Vodka spokesperson, Jeffrey Moran, stated, "We at Absolut believe that starting with something simple and natural can lead to something really big." Placing these two images together is striking. The coded references to sexuality—"natural," "something really big," and the visual imagery of fruit—can be read together to reinforce the ideology that these queens are born male, targeting the supposed real sex of the contestants to display and highlight the obsession with their transformations.

RuPaul's attitude of sameness, with regard to gender, started a little bit of a stir in January of 2012 when she backed the use of the word "tranny" in an interview with *SiriusXM*, *OutQ*, and *HuffPost Gay Voices*. This is not out of character from RuPaul, as she and other queens frequently use the derogatory slur to refer to themselves and other queens on the show. However, in her interview she takes it a step further by declaring, "If you're offended by someone calling you a 'tranny,' it was only because you believe you are a 'tranny!' [*laughter.*] So then, the solution is: Change your mind about yourself being a 'tranny.'"[26] While some might read this as reclaiming the word, it also smacks of classic victim blaming and shaming language, which she also espouses in her answer to a question about the gulf between transgender activists and drag queens around the issue of representation on the show. She argues that if transgender people want to be represented, "you do it yourself. It starts on a personal level. If you want to change the world, change your mind. *Your* mind. Not anyone else's mind. *Your* mind." Again, RuPaul neglects that widespread oppression exists, and blames those who suffer from oppression for their problems.

While season one set the tone for the series, season three held a particularly fascinating moment of racial stereotyping, and marked the first time the concept of race was discussed by name on the show. Manila Luzon's character highlights her identity as an Asian queen, shown early in the first episode with her choice to wear sushi earrings. In "QNN News" Manila acts as a news reporter for the "Morning After Show." Throughout her news interview with Kirsten Cavallari she exaggerates an Asian accent, does not pronounce Ls or Rs, and is loud and extremely over the top in her presentation. Manila's make-up always has a lighter white base, signaling geisha make-up, and in this interview her facial expressions further the effect through wide eyes as she dramatically keeps her mouth open in a consistent expression of surprise. She alludes to Asian stereotypes as she tells Kirsten, "Oh shoes, I ruv shoes [...]. You don't have boyfend? Oh I have brover, you should meet. Immigration [...] lots of money."[27] While her presentation is indicative of racial stereotyping being taken up without regard to nuances in ethnicity, as Manila is from the Philippines and her drag encompasses many different Asian stereotypes that originate out of Japanese and Chinese cultures, it is the way the judges discuss her presentation that is most informative. Kirsten Cavallari begins by applauding Manila, "It was so wrong, that it was so right. And truthfully if you're going to be groundbreaking, some eggs have got to be broken to make an omelet." RuPaul, in an uncharacteristic show of concern about offending audiences, then asks Manila, "If someone watching tonight were offended by what you did, how would you answer to that." Manila answers, "I don't think we have enough Asian people in pop culture so I'm here to entertain. I'm here to be farcical. I'm just trying to do my job" and shrugs. After the queens leave the stage and the judges confer, Kirsten, who is white, again applauds Manila's performance: "She's an equal opportunity offender. Doesn't mean you're racist you hate everybody, including your own race. Then it's funny." RuPaul agrees, and awards Manila's performance: "This week you broke all the rules. You crossed the line of good taste, and you perpetuated stereotypes. [Pregnant pause, then in a much deeper voice] Condragulations you're the winner of this challenge." Here RuPaul signals the invisible line of camp—what is going too far. However, even as she and the other judges note that Manila went too far, this performance wins the challenge—driving home the message that racism and racist stereotypes do not need to be addressed because they are "funny" in the post-race moment.

Containing the Subversive: Policies and Policing

The first season of *RuPaul's Drag Race* had 4,500 contestants from which nine are chosen, not all of whom begin the race on equal footing.[28] Some queens are chosen to highlight the kind of queen the show is *not* looking for—their presence on the show produces the fallible foil against which the queens who are sufficiently marketable can prove their respectability. The first queen of season one to be asked to "sashay away" was Victoria "Porkchop" Parker.[29] While she asserts sewing skills were the reason for her dismissal, she is also a self-described fat queen. She played on her fat identity in her performances by eating out of her handbag on the runway, for instance, but the judges were not impressed. Victoria was also the first, and, until the retrospective episode, only queen in the first season to reference the real potential for violence in each queen's life. Fat positivity and the reality of transphobia and gender transgressions' effects in queen's lives are policed out of the show in order to create profitable discourses of who a drag queen should be. One could argue that since these moments were allowed on air, the show wishes to engage with them on some level. However, what is most notable of these moments is that they are shown immediately preceding the queen's dismissal from the contest, undercutting the weight of their message. This same pattern is also exhibited in Ongina's dismissal in season one, which comes in the episode following her disclosure of her HIV positive status, and also involved judgment about her refusal to tuck as well as being judged as too masculine at times. I will return to the specific gender policing of Ongina later in this section. The suggestive pattern of who is dismissed tells us something about RuPaul's vision (and indeed, the vision of the companies who purchase portions of the show) of who is a proper drag superstar. Queens like Victoria and Ongina provided the context for *RuPaul's Drag Race* to explicitly demonstrate who aberrant queens are and who can sell a product.

While we understand RuPaul's insistence on personally distancing herself from the word and identity "transgender," we also know the show does not allow for transgender women to compete. No queens have been knowingly cast who identify as transgender, a requirement that is in part manifested through the application process in which the queens must conduct at least half of the personality portion of their video submission out of drag in addition to inclusion of all legal documentation. Although *RuPaul's Drag Race* fan page at one time stated that the "contestants must be born male, be over the age of 21, and not identify as transgender," it has since been removed and the show's site itself has never displayed such information. The unspoken and yet required distancing from transgender identities signals a containment of transgender identities in order to keep a binary gender experience naturalized. The requirement to appear out of drag allows the show to be sure that they can videotape the transformation from men into queens—it is the transformation that makes the fetishization work, which would be undercut if transgender women were on the show. To be clear, the obsession with transformation does not only exist in *RuPaul's Drag Race*, but is a widely accepted trope found in talk shows, reality television, and media broadly. The "before and after" trope is popular due to somatechnic possibilities in the age of technology, and reflects a fascination of how bodies can change to appear different than they were. The reliance on all-powerful experts to judge the "makeover" that arguably takes place in each challenge for these contestants is consistent throughout the makeover canon: "doctors are glorified, powerful, and full discursive agents; patients (a disproportionate number of them women) are passive and yielding, even grateful for their transformations, creating a culture of docile bodies eager for discipline."[30] Brenda Weber argues that the "corrective" function on makeover shows comes from the desire to rewrite gender norms onto women's bodies. She explains that women who have no interest in their appearance are first shamed and policed into proper behavior, and only then can be instructed on how to appear differently.[31] In order to fully praise a woman for her makeover, she must, as Weber states, be shamed through her inability to be a "real" woman. The shaming takes place through the claims of empowerment—cased in language assuming a feminist purpose in which the women being made over are being given esteem boosters to take more pride in their appearance—which ultimately press that women who do not take pride in their appearance are not "real" women before, only after.

Utilizing Weber's work on the makeover genre with specifically drag queens whose success depends on the best impersonation can show us how policing RuPaul's standards appears where you must look real but not too real, cheeky but not too mean, and desirable, but not too feminine. The queens learn early what kind of queen RuPaul is looking for, and they begin to police their own behavior after being shamed into being a better queen—and if they refuse they aren't "really" queens. What we see happening repeatedly in the judgments of RuPaul and the guest judges is the policing of drag queen gender into the right kind of queen—not transgender and not quite woman—mirroring the RuPaul persona enough to also embrace the "post" landscape. The queens must be able to become anyone, across racial identification, gender presentation, and style. The fascination, which is consistently highlighted through confessionals with queens not in make-up, to up close shots as they transform their faces, to after transformation exclamations, is used to uphold the gender binary as safe, present, and available for viewers at home.[32]

During season four RuPaul dismissed a contestant for breaking the rules, and the internet exploded with accusations that centered around the arbitrary and crafted divide between drag queens and transgender women the show created. While RuPaul would not inform the audience why Willam was asked to leave until the show concluded, an online frenzy began immediately in which many posited that Willam must have been taking estrogen. While it later came out that Willam had snuck her boyfriend onto the set, the speculation itself is another example in which the "reality" versus the illusion of drag creates a norm based in biology. Although the queens regularly use breast plates, silicone models of breasts that lay over their chests, and many other technologies to enhance their looks, it would appear hormone usage crosses into the unacceptable terrain of transgender—which is potential grounds for elimination. However, in season three contestant Venus Delite stated that she had had a number of facial enhancement surgeries to look like Madonna.[33] The producers felt this did not cross too far into being coded as transgender and she was allowed to compete. Chad Michaels, on season four, had surgical work done to appear more like Cher, proving this example to not be exclusive.[34] Detox, on season five, confessed to numerous facial and bodily surgeries to appear more womanly, as well.[35] The focus is on transformation, not on an equal playing field—the surgeries and the breast plates, the padding and other techniques used to enhance a queen's look are fine, so long as hormonal treatment that may suggest an interest in living as a woman full-time, and hence less or no access to a before and after look, does not appear. These rules and policing of gender transgression serve to underline the arbitrary definitions of drag queen and transgender that RuPaul's fame necessitated and police queen's behavior from pre-application through the competition itself.

In order for queens to succeed on *RuPaul's Drag Race* it is also very important they display a particular kind of proper feminine behavior while performing, wherein the meshing of gender lines is heavily policed. As potential RuPaul replicas, it is helpful to return again to RuPaul's persona. RuPaul has and continues to perform and identify as both RuPaul Charles and RuPaul, and publicly states that she does not have a pronoun preference. However, the image that sells best is the one that clearly has RuPaul acting as a "man" while appearing as a "man" and acting as a "woman" while appearing as a "woman." In fact, in RuPaul's *Workin' It* she pulls off a quite impressive image of herself dressed and coiffed in the likeness of the Obamas. In a photo called "The Rubamas" RuPaul is shown as both Michelle and Barack Obama, hugging amongst red, white, and blue imagery, with "Barack's" arm around "Michelle."[36] They appear in a stadium, with radiant expressions: Barack's head tilted upwards, mouth open, showing bright teeth and looking into the future; Michelle's head level looking into the camera, mouth open to show not teeth, but a pink tongue—a somewhat suggestive pose. Both appearances are realistic, a quite convincing photograph unless one further inspects the image to realize both persons in the photograph are RuPaul. This crafted look is where RuPaul proves she can "pass" as both the President and the First Lady at the same time.[37] Although one could read this photograph in reference to performances of gender, here RuPaul's interest in "passing" as both persons highlights her interest in the gender binary through proving she can perfectly become either or both of them through incredible transformation.

Gender policing occurs regularly in season one, setting the tone for further seasons by example. On episode one, "Drag on a Dime," three queens are challenged explicitly about their androgynous looks during judging. For example, Ongina was called "just a boy in a dress" for not wearing a wig. RuPaul told her, "When I see you I still see a little boy. I'd love to see more of a little lady."[38] The following episode Ongina admits in a confessional with the camera that she decided to wear a wig after the judges criticized her presentation. Here she tells the audience that she will also tuck, which she does not normally do. Her drag persona was androgynous, but she altered her appearance the second episode—for which she was praised and won the challenge. Nina Flowers, another androgynous queen, was told by RuPaul, "Your image is so strong. I'd love to see a softer side. I'd love to see your flowers."[39] The next episode Nina changed her look, and RuPaul responded with "I have to give her more props for becoming more feminine."[40] The explicit attention to the "creation" of a queen's identity mirrors the mainstream gender ideology that when "men" dress as "women," they are, and always will be, "men."[41]

Nina and Ongina are not the only ones in the first season to be judged on not presenting a "real" enough womanly illusion. Merle Ginsberg judged Rebecca Glasscock's presentation in the first episode explaining that although she presented as a girl in the first challenge, her runway look was "very boy as girl." RuPaul answered with "Looks a little cheap. Looks like you're ready to give a twenty dollar hand-job." However, surprisingly, RuPaul also whispers under her breath, "And that's not a bad thing."[42] This whisper is so hidden that although I had seen the episode several times, it was not until I showed this clip to a lecture hall, with the volume turned all the way up, that I heard the whispered positivity of sex work. Given the high mainstream correlation between sex work and transgender women (particularly trans* women of color), her acknowledgement of sex work as positive is both a nod to transgender women and also a moment that connects trans* experience to the runway. Importantly, the whisper occurred on the very first episode of the very first season— and we never see that kind of positivity from RuPaul again. One could infer that the stakes became higher as the season sought renewal, VH1 picked up the show, and the wider viewership required a more traditional RuPaul to sell it.

However, the "boy as girl" insults rely on the concept of reality in which "boy as girl" is derogatory and ultimately, a failure. The judges consistently police the queens away from any drag that is less than perfectly polished, wherein a complete illusion displays the transformation for which advertisers pay—the process and fascination of someone able to "fool" consumers, but readily able and willing to consistently remind them of the reality of their biological identities. The first season made the explicit point by policing gender transgressions early and rewarding those who conformed such that latter seasons did not require as much—the queens policed themselves into the image of RuPaul.[43]

Indeed, the first time a transgender identity was explicitly broached on the show was after the contest had ended. A contestant on the second season, Sonique, confessed in the "Reunion" episode that after the show's end she realized that she identifies as a transgender woman, and that when she wasn't in drag she was depressed.[44] When RuPaul very somberly prompts her, asking her what she had wanted to share with the audience, Sonique tears up and leaves the stage. RuPaul and another queen follow her off set, to where she is crying, and she dejectedly tells her story of realizing she is transgender. The movement off set and RuPaul's easy pat of her shoulder, followed by RuPaul's quick return to the set to change the subject, are visible cues that transgender identities are not accepted within the show's environment. Indeed, if Sonique had identified as transgender before her participation in the show, she very likely would never have been cast.

The emphasis on the performance aspect of creating the perfect "womanly" image in *RuPaul's Drag Race* is subtly undermined through negation of other performances also at work in each queen's identities. In particular, the racial identities of the queens as they sew their outfits, apply their make-up, and craft their performances are assumed unimportant and/or "obvious" to the audience, and are possibly also considered "taboo." As Judith Butler explains in an essay about the queens' performances in the film *Paris Is Burning*, "realness" is determined by the ability to produce a naturalized effect, resulting from impersonation of norms for which there is not an original.[45] These queens are constantly performing much more than gender, however, the show is unable to focus on more than gender through its erasure of racial identities. As Butler explains here, the standard of "real" as applied to the genders of the contestants requires a naturalizing of stereotypical ideologies of gender and sex. The explicit focus on gender performances obscures other identities, naturalizing them for the purpose of consumption.

For example, the winner of the first season, BeBe Zahara Benet, was constantly asked to invoke her childhood and adolescence in Cameroon, with repeated references and allusions to her dress as "authentic" and/or "animalistic." As the winner of the show, her performance of an "authentic" queen won over the judges. Her authenticity showed up in challenge after challenge as explicitly racially coded to her experience of her ethnicity. In one challenge, BeBe won the best performance, in which she most accurately portrayed Oprah and wore a leopard print "jungle" outfit on the runway. RuPaul remarked that she was "carrying all of Africa on her shoulders" and "you are serving Africa, you are serving the Lion Queen."[46] These problematic moments serve the dual purpose of "othering" BeBe as well as naturalizing the other contestants' identities and marking them as center. Michael Rogin has theorized that ethnicity has become a way of discussing race in a particularly diluted form: "History, not biology, distinguishes ethnicity from race, making the former groups (in the American usage) distinctive but assimilable, walling off the latter, legally, socially, and ideologically, to benefit those within the magic circle and protect the national body from contamination."[47] Rogin describes the push towards highlighting the ethnic identity over and instead of racial identity as a way to contain the racial "threat" and protect the nation. Through the diluted and less taboo subject of ethnicity, *RuPaul's Drag Race* is able to "get away" with these moments, which have the ironic result of attempting to assimilate their bodies and identities but ultimately highlighting the performative nature of race. BeBe's, and others', experiences of their ethnicities on the show proved a post-racial landscape in so far as the queen's acquiesced and performed racial stereotypes, and celebrated their successes without any mention of race.

It is precisely this climate that allows Sharon Needles, a controversial performer who has performed in a swimsuit with a swastika on it while calling members of the audience racial slurs, to win season four.[48] When her fame on the show brought her past performance to light, Needles exclaimed, "I'm an artist and I don't [...] have to answer for my work."[49] Her attitude is strongly reminiscent of racist ideologies that pass through mainstream culture unchallenged due to the claim that the artist is making the person viewing it think about race. However, Needles, a white queen, exhibits a different, racist history when she performs these kinds of acts, and her attitude of pushing boundaries on purpose does have an edge that, for many, is too far. More than that, her response is squarely within the frame that there is no need to discuss matters of race—art, and apparently Sharon Needles—are beyond criticism. However, it is no surprise that her outrageousness won her the season, as RuPaul is a known supporter of Shirley Q. Liquor. Liquor is a white queen who performs in blackface with shockingly specific stereotyped characters imbued with racist ideology.[50] In fact, the language she uses in support of Liquor's act is, again, classic victim blaming language,

> I could tell there was nothing but love there [...]. I realized the people who came out against him were using him as a tool to confirm their role as a victim. They needed figures to reconfirm their own misconception of themselves as a victim. It's going to be interesting with Obama in the White House and how the black community responds to that because you can no longer say, "The world has made it so hard for me and there are people out there trying to keep me from moving forward." So, I think Shirley [...] is brilliant, funny. You can't do those kind of impersonations without a certain amount of love that it takes to really get it right on the nose like that.[51]

With that kind of argument, it's no surprise the show functions as a space fully indoctrinated into the idea of the "post."

Bought and Sold: Commodification of the "Post"

In season five, we see something that shocks viewers and cast members alike. In the second episode, Monica Beverly Hillz discloses her transgender identity to the cast. What ensued has been lauded as praise within the show, and RuPaul's behavior appeared supportive. In an interview published the day following the episode, Monica tells her interviewer that she felt it was time, and that she was supported and respected by the show members and production team after her disclosure.[52] However, what ultimately happens is she finds herself following the same pattern wherein the episode directly following a grand step outside of the bounds of the directives on the show she is asked to "sashay away."[53] The actions of the show do not match the supposedly supportive environment. For instance, Monica also alludes to a fear of an inhospitable environment, stating that she intentionally hid her identity in order to be cast on the show. When asked if she was "freaking out about how the judges might react" Hillz stated, "That was the main reason why I didn't want to say anything. I took a huge chance. That could have been my ticket [off the show]."[54] Hillz's strategic move mirrors the requirement of trans* people to tell a particular story in order to access services, or, in this case, opportunities. For her to exhibit a different narrative in order to be cast on the show, and to have her admission lead directly to her dismissal, despite her initial belief that it would not, upholds the show's reluctance of and policing of transgender bodies throughout the show. It does not, as it may be desirable to believe, indicate a shift in environment of the show. In fact, Monica discusses several of the queens who had competed before her who had come out as transgender after their dismissals from the show as her role models. She had intended to follow the same trajectory, but found that she could not be anyone else for the purposes of the show. Unfortunately for her, this meant that her refusal to follow a script necessitated by policies and expectations of this reality show ultimately led to her dismissal.

What Monica's example, and the policing and use of contestant's bodies shows, is that while we can, on the surface, believe that the fluidity the queens display expands and explodes stringent identity categories, what we see as a result of the inescapable political economy of the show is a turn toward the very opposite. The contestants' racial and gender fluidity is overshadowed by forcible normalization of the very categories they could potentially disrupt. This leaves our audience with a take home message that is not so very far from their initial impulse for watching—a glimpse into a "freaky" world—while the categories of gender, sex, and race, are kept stable to replicate the dominant white, two gender, two sex, heteronormative system from which they are supposedly positioned. *RuPaul's Drag Race* is unable to hold the weight of these queens' multiplicities, given that the show is produced by and for a wider audience than can understand the multiplicities as they manifest. There is an overarching force behind the show driving the queens to act and react in ways that uphold a post-racial and gender normative culture, even if their identities and fluidities seem to contradict the broad messages in brief glimpses. What we are left with in this move from the bar and ballroom to the small screen are winners and viewers who embrace the post-racial, transphobic, post-feminist society.

Notes

1. Kyle Buchanan, "RuPaul on *Drag Race, Hannah Montana*, and 'Those Bitches' Who Stole Annette Bening's Oscar," *Vulture,* http://www.vulture.com/2011/04/rupaul_on_drag_race_hannah_mon.html (accessed November 18, 2013).

2. While I use she pronouns for RuPaul as her presentation in this work is mainly her in drag, she has been famously quoted as saying, "You can call me he, you can call me she, you can call me Regis and Kathie Lee, just so long as you call me." RuPaul, *Lettin It All Hang Out: An Autobiography* (New York: Hyperion, 1995), viii.

3. Martin F. Manalansan IV, "Queering the Chain of Care Paradigm," *The Scholar & Feminist Online* 6, no. 3 (2008), http://www.barnard.edu/sfonline/immigration/manalansan_01.htm (accessed on March 22, 2013).

4. Wendy Peters, "Pink Dollars, White Collars: Queer as Folk, Valuable Viewers, and the Price of Gay TV," *Critical Studies in Media Communication* 28, no. 3 (2011): 193–212.

5. Ralina L. Joseph, "Tyra Banks Is Fat: Reading (Post-)Racism and (Post-)Feminism in the New Millennium," *Critical Studies in Media Communication* 26, no. 3 (2009): 237–54.

6. Joseph, 237–54.

7. Ralina Joseph, "Recursive Racial Transformation: Selling the Exceptional Multiracial," in *America's Next Top Model Transcending Blackness: From the New Millennium Mulatta to the Exceptional Multiracial, 1998–2008* (Durham: Duke University Press, 2012), 188–224.

8. A play on "untucking" that can be read to reify her identity as male.

9. RuPaul, 201.

10. The success created two spin-offs, *Untucked!,* a play on "tucking" (tucking refers to the practice of tucking up ones external genitals to create the appearance of a smooth genital area under clothing), in which queens go off record, and *Drag U.* On *Drag U* RuPaul's drag queens cross over and become "professors" who compete each episode to produce the best transformation of a "real" woman. Vh1 and Logo are owned by the same parent company, Viacom, and the concurrent viewing helped the show produce income and boost sales. Ted Madger, "The End of TV 101: Reality Programs, Formats, and the New Business of Television," in *TV: Remaking Television Culture,* ed. Susan Murray and Laurie Ouellette (New York: New York University Press, 2004), 137–156.

11. John Kraszewski, "Country Hicks and Urban Cliques: Mediating Race, Reality, and Liberalism on MTV's The Real World," in *TV: Remaking Television Culture,* ed. Susan Murray and Laurie Ouellette (New York: New York University Press, 2004), 179–196.

12. Esther Newton, *Mother Camp: Female Impersonators in America* (Englewood Cliffs, N.J.: Prentice-Hall), 1972.

13. Marlon M. Bailey, "Gender/Racial Realness: Theorizing the Gender System in Ballroom Culture," *Feminist Studies* 37, no. 2 (2011): 365–86.

14. Bailey, 365–86.

15. Drag balls are most known to those outside ballroom culture through the

film *Paris Is Burning*, which RuPaul notes. The concept of gender reality arises as contestants compete as "real women" under the title "executive realness" does occur in season 1, episode 6, is here designated as, "not a drag queen." While this is one moment where viewers "in the know" may be able to connect the explicit link to ballroom culture in which gender play, presentation, and transgender identities often circulate meanings, what it shows to a mainstream audience is that those who can "pass" the most win. Indeed, it connects back to the ideology that a significant transformation must take place in order to uphold binary definitions of gender stereotypes.

16. See George Gerbner and Larry Gross, "Living with Television: The Violence Profile," *The Journal of Communication* 26, no. 2 (1976): 173–199; Michelangelo Signorile, *Queer in America: Sex, the Media, and the Closets of Power* (New York: Random House, 1993); Mary Kirk, "Kind of a Drag: Gender, Race, and Ambivalence in The Birdcage and To Wong Foo Thanks for Everything! Julie Newmar," *Journal of Homosexuality* 46 (2004): 169–180; Wendy Peters, "Pink Dollars, White Collars: Queer as Folk, Valuable Viewers, and the Price of Gay TV," *Critical Studies in Media Communication* 28, no. 3 (2011): 193–212; Christopher Pullen, *Documenting Gay Men: Identity and Performance in Reality Television and Documentary Film* (Jefferson, N.C.: McFarland, 2007).

17. Kathleen Battles and Wendy Hilton-Morrow, "Gay Characters in Conventional Spaces: Will and Grace and the Situation Comedy Genre," *Critical Studies in Media Communication* 19, no. 1 (2002): 87–105.

18. "Gender fuck" drag doesn't fully present as the opposite gender from the performer's identity offstage. It is often more androgynous, risqué, and subversive. The drag popularized by RuPaul is "supermodel" drag, in which she seeks to fully read as a woman, with an over the top edge and a consistent wink that she is male.

19. RuPaul, 106.

20. Dean Spade argues that medical discourse infantilizes and boxes transgender identities to the point that one must opt in to a transgender narrative of body dysphoria and sexlessness in order to access resources.

21. Dean Spade, "Resisting Medicine, Re/modeling Gender," *Berkeley Women's Law Journal* 18 (2003): 15–37.

22. RuPaul, vii.

23. Stuart Hall, *Representation: Cultural Representations and Signifying Practices* (London; Thousand Oaks, Calif.: Sage in association with the Open University, 1997).

24. *RuPaul's Drag Race*, season 1, episode 6, Logo TV, 2009.

25. Image can be viewed at http://adfactory.ecrater.com.au/p/3822688/in-an-absolut-world-vodka-magazine-ad

26. Michelangelo Signorile, "RuPaul Sounds Off on New Season of 'RuPaul's Drag Race,' Obama, The Word 'Tranny,' and More," *Huffington Post,* http://www.huffingtonpost.com/2012/01/13/rupaul-on-rupauls-drag-race-obama-tranny_n_1205203.html?ref=gay-voices (accessed on November 2, 2013).

27. *RuPaul's Drag Race*, season 3, episode 5, Logo TV, 2011.

28. *RuPaul's Drag Race*, season 1, episode 1, Logo TV, 2009.

29. *RuPaul's Drag Race*, season 1, episode 1, Logo TV, 2009.

30. Brenda R. Weber, "Makeover as Takeover: Scenes of Affective Domination on Makeover TV," *Configurations* 15, no. 1 (2008): 77–99.

31. Weber, 77–99.

32. I do not intend to suggest that anyone who identifies with the gender binary as fitting for them is at fault or to blame, but that the societal imperative to do so is problematic. It is not my aim to impose a gender hierarchy, but to acknowledge and name the cultural moments in which the policing of queen's identities in *RuPaul's Drag Race* occurs and to theorize upon why those moments occur.

33. *RuPaul's Drag Race*, season 3, episode 1, Logo TV, 2011.

34. *RuPaul's Drag Race*, season 4, episode 1, Logo TV, 2012.

35. *RuPaul's Drag Race*, season 5, episode 6, Logo TV, 2013.

36. RuPaul, *Workin' It! RuPaul's Guide to Life, Liberty, and the Pursuit of Style* (New York: It Books, 2010), 174. Image can be viewed at http://ernestsewell.com/post/20938867312#.Ux434vmwJcQ.

37. "Passing" refers to being read as something other than what you "really" are.

38. *RuPaul's Drag Race*, season 1, episode 1, Logo TV, 2009.

39. *RuPaul's Drag Race*, season 1, episode 1, Logo TV, 2009.

40. *RuPaul's Drag Race*, season 1, episode 2, Logo TV, 2009.

41. Judith Butler, Gender Trouble: Feminism and the Subversion of Identity (New York: Routledge, 1990).

42. *RuPaul's Drag Race*, season 1, episode 1, Logo TV, 2009.

43. While the argument could be made that since the winner of season three, Raja, had a more androgynous appearance the show evolved to consider androgynous characters worthy of winning. However, Raja's androgyny takes a back seat to her couture fashion sense and her emphasis on style. Raja came to the show after working as lead make-up artist on *America's Next Top Model* for 8 seasons, with modeling experience, and began winning challenges on the very first episode (Fitzgerald, "Meet the Queens"). Raja is supermodel size and crafts her appearance and mannerisms to be what RuPaul seeks. Therefore, Raja was able to give supermodel realness so effectively that it overshadowed her punky and at times androgynous style. In fact, her androgyny often serves to reinforce binary representations of gender, as opposed to being read in a subversive way. For instance, while she does begin the season without crafting breasts, and with an androgynous club kid style, she always wears a wig, tucks and emphasizes feminine traits on the runway.

44. *RuPaul's Drag Race*, season 2, episode 12, Logo TV, 2010.

45. Butler, Bodies That Matter: On the Discursive Limits of "Sex" (New York: Routledge, 1993), 129.

46. *RuPaul's Drag Race*, season 1, episode 3, Logo TV, 2009.

47. Michael P. Rogin, *Blackface, White Noise: Jewish Immigrants in the Hollywood Melting Pot* (Berkeley: University of California Press, 1996), 12.

48. Lauren Daley, "Dragged into Debate: Reality-TV Fame Puts Spotlight on Sharon Needles' Controversial Act," *Pittsburgh City Paper,* http://m.pghcitypaper.com/pittsburgh/dragged-into-debate-reality-tv-fame-puts-spotlight-on-sharon-needles-controversial-act/Content?oid=1535799 (accessed on June 20, 2012).

49. Daley.

50. Clay Cane, "BET.com: RuPaul on LL CoolJ, Shirley Q. Liquor and more… ," *Clay Cane Blog*, retrieved from http://claycane.net/2009/01/28/bet-com-rupaul-on-ll-cool-j-shirley-q-liquor-and-more/ (accessed November 18, 2013).

51. Cane.

52. Noah Michelson, "Monica Beverly Hillz, 'RuPaul's Drag Race' Contestant, Discusses Coming Out as Transgender," *The Huffington Post*, http://www.huffington post.com/2013/02/05/monica-beverly-hillz-transgender_n_2617975.html (accessed on November 3, 2013).

53. *RuPaul's Drag Race*, season 5, episode 3, Logo TV, 2013.

54. Michelson.

"For your next drag challenge," You Must Do Something
Playfulness Without Rules

Fernando Gabriel Pagnoni Berns

In *Project Runway* (Bravo-Lifetime), competitors must demonstrate their skills as future great designers making the best dress within a short time and a small budget. In *Master Chef* (Fox), the contestants must demonstrate their culinary skills by outperforming their peers, and in *Survivor* (CBS), participants must … well … survive. In contrast, contestants on *RuPaul's Drag Race* must do a lot of things. In each episode, they must first compete in a mini challenge and proceed to the main challenge, which culminates on the runway. The two queens who have performed the worst in the judges' opinions must then "lip sync for their lives." One may wonder why each episode of *Drag Race* consists of so many challenges per episode when most of the other reality TV show have one or, at most, two per episode? The answer is rich and complex because it reveals both the complexity of the figure of the drag queen and the arbitrariness of reality TV shows. Participants must prove that they are "America's Next Drag Superstar," but which skills do they need to display in order to accomplish this? What exactly do drag queens do? Apparently, they must be "talented performers,"[1] i.e., characters who can make a spectacle of themselves and capture the viewers' attention. However, the show's insistence on prettiness and "realness" in which "the simulacrum actually replaces the model"[2] challenge this definition. Personality is another important feature for any drag queen, but they are criticized if they are not flexible enough in appropriately altering their personas between challenges. To complicate matters further, the catwalk almost never has anything to do with the main challenge; and in the "lip sync for your life" conclusion, participants choose either to do a perfect imitation of the original performance or make a spectacle that grabs the judges' attention, as if they, the contestants themselves, do not know what the ultimate goal of this challenge is.

In this essay I will argue that this lack of definition is interesting to analyze because (a) the indeterminacy of drag is built on the basis of "a failure of definitional distinction"[3] which prevents its labeling in a world where gays and gay culture are increasingly assimilated into society[4]; and (b) the fact that a drag queen must do a bit of everything is countercultural to the modern idea of increasing specializations "that marked the transition of market capitalism to corporate capitalism"[5] and frames our current capitalist culture. Most authors of "step-by-step" business guides stress that a clear purpose is the heart of any successful business,[6] to the point where even to write without a clear purpose is a sin in the business' world.[7] The arbitrariness of the challenges, framed within unfocused goals[8] make *RuPaul's Drag Race* a sort of inversion of many reality shows which are based on professional success. This will be supported by focusing on an analysis of the different challenges that make up the show.

Defining Drag Queens

First, it must be noted that, although the term "drag queen" is commonly believed to be socially well-established, it is, like almost all terms relating to gender issues, actually somewhat complicated. In the popular imagination, for example, the term "drag queen" overlaps with several others relating to gender issues. Rusty Barret seems to explain clearly what a drag queen is: "The basic category of drag queens is men who dressed as women, especially those who perform in gay bars. As a social group, drag queens are often confused with other groups: transsexuals, transvestites, cross-dressers, and female impersonators."[9] He then proceeds to explain each category: transsexuals are individuals who feel that their sex of origin is wrong; transvestites "refer to those who wear the clothing of the opposite sex," but "unlike transsexuals, transvestites (or cross-dressers) categorize themselves as members of the gender corresponding to their assigned sex."[10] It is to be noted that, first, and before explaining what cross-dressers are (anyone who wears the clothing of the opposite sex, regardless of their sexual orientation), the author equates transvestites with cross-dressing.

It is not my intention to criticize extensively Barret's definitions, but rather to note how terms overlap in academic discourses when gender issues are discussed, ultimately revealing the "political tensions between the identities that fall under the transgender umbrella."[11] Within that umbrella terms sometimes overlap, especially in categories such as transsexual, transvestite, cross-dresser, genderqueer, androgyne, and bigender.[12] News media is important in disseminating gender categories or "gender blending" labels, sometimes without a proper explanation. As Daniel Harris points out, in the popular imagination, "drag is often mistakenly conflated with transvestitism. Even in much of the scholarship on the subject, the two phenomena are never sufficiently distinguished but are indiscriminately lumped together."[13] For many people, the media often fail "to cover the immense diversity of (gender) identities and performativities and the social structures inside the drag queen sub-cultures, instead reducing the drag queen to a stereotypical caricature: the entertaining transvestite."[14] Interestingly, Rusty Barret's definitions come from a book on linguistics. Language is very important when defining and categorizing, as reality is nothing more than a construct of a discursive nature. Everything must have a name. If not, then it's considered a risky element. Categorizing is a means to gain control over a thing or subject.

That is why monsters are always uncategorizable beings, since they are liminal. Gays were such monsters years ago. Homosexuals were classified as sodomites who deserved punishment. But in a great many parts of the world today, gays are not monsters anymore. In Western societies, a wave of tolerance now invites everyone to enjoy their private lifestyle, if it implies consumption. In our stage of late capitalism, being part of the consumer class is to be part of society. Gays, lesbians, and transgendered people are a new target market. Homosexuals are now so integrated into society that capitalism has created products especially designed to please this specific group: hotels, food, clothes, TV shows, and even wines are especially created for a non-heterosexual market.[15] Gays and lesbians, the most "easy" labels, have a great quantity of commodities created especially for them. As for new terms such as "bigender," new products will appear if the term endures the passage of time. Integration into society, then, means not only a newly acquired respect, but also being regulated by the classification of capitalism into consumer citizens.

However, at the moment of classification, "drag" is still a blurred category. And if naming is power which imparts control over some thing, then this is not necessarily a bad thing. As Verta Taylor and Leila Rupp state, "up against the assimilationist tendency of gay and lesbian activism, from the homophile movement of the 1950s to the present, drag queens have been an embarrassment."[16] In fact, some decades ago, drag queens were fiercely rejected even by the gay community since it felt that the gay subculture was not appropriately represented by these loud men/women.[17] Then, as embarrassment, as marginal monstrous subjects, drag queens would almost work against the commodification of homosexuality. I choose to say "almost" because, of course, a loose classification does exist.

Now, what exactly does a drag queen perform? Keith McNeal states that a dynamic of "conflict and ambivalence"[18] reigns behind the make-up and the camp of drag. Drag involves parody (of culturally codified feminine traits) and self-parody (of the man performing drag and his subjectivity/identity). In a last gesture of ambivalence, the character behind the costume is not entirely "him," but a blend between him (his life's story) and a created persona with her own identity. Thus, a drag queen's performance is a very complex one.

I have no desire to resolve the conflicting aspects of the definitions because, in fact, I do not want to find a unique, stable classification. It's good that "drag queen" is such an unstable term, which seems to combine comic performer, female impersonator, and cross-dresser without being any of these specifically. Drag favors an unclassifiable and fluid identity against one that is closed and fixed. Thus, this construction of identity in constant motion makes subjects more difficult to subdue and categorize under capitalism, which attempts to find a commercial niche for every citizen. The terms and notions of what a drag queen is are so complicated and so little established that RuPaul and the producers of the show do not seem to know what to ask of the participants, to the point that, rather than having just one challenge per episode, they ask for many challenges to be completed before deciding who is the best. Perhaps this happens because it is not entirely, exactly defined what the qualities of a drag queen are.

In brief, in our time of the commodification of gay identity within a world of classification, drag queens, as an "enormous displacement of context"[19] seem to possess the "charisma, uniqueness, nerve and talent"[20] necessary to defy easy categorization in favor of ambivalence. This ambivalence is illustrated in the nature of the challenges of the show, which combine playfulness with competitiveness. The challenges are so different and have so little logic that they work as anti-establishment performances since they do not have a clear mechanism or regulation beyond RuPaul's judging. The challenges and assessments privilege notions of humor, camp, and confusion that bring a new way of understanding the logic of the competitive world market and counter the rationalism that permeates capitalism. If the challenges are multiple, unrelated to each other, confusing, and difficult to judge, then it appears they are performed for ludic reasons rather than for competition, even if the show has a prize for the winner. Every contestant has the same possibility to win regardless of prior experience, which is contrary to the current notion of accumulating education and job experience on a resume in order to be more prepared to compete in the market through a race to be the best. *RuPaul's Drag Race* denies this, privileging unruly confusion and the basic management of many skills over finely tuned perfection in some specifically specialized task.

Drag and Identities Within the Show

The first episode of season one (2009) includes only nine queens.[21] The first to enter the main stage is Shannel, a performer with several years of work as a drag queen in Las Vegas. And with Shannel, the first ambiguity/discordance/ambivalence enters the show. She makes her triumphant arrival with her butt hanging out of her dress. Interestingly, she considers her persona as "realistic." One, then, can wonder what exactly a "realistic" persona is to her and what the audience can infer from this definition. A well-defined personality? A drag version of womanhood? Again, drag seems to be not that well defined as a term in the cultural imaginary.

Since the other participants (Nina Flowers, Rebecca Glasscock, Ongina, etc.) do not enter displaying their naked bodies, it is possible to infer two things: first, that showing skin is not some kind of concrete characteristic of drag queens but just a personal interpretation of what a drag queen is in the construction of a given persona; and, second, that, to Shannel, "realistic" must refer to presenting an uncanny resemblance to a real woman, which brings her closer to a female impersonator than a drag queen. So drag seems to be open to a broad range of stylistic varieties. This is supported by Rebecca Glasscock's persona. After Shannel and Nina Flowers (who enters the workroom with both an eccentric dress and hairstyle), Rebecca's outfit is basic: a t-shirt and a pair of jeans. This denies Harris' affirmation that the stylistic choice of a drag queen "is screaming vulgarity, the overstated look of the balloon-breasted tramp in the leopard-skin micro-mini skirt who strives to be loud, tawdry, and cheap. The transvestite, in short, tries to tone it down; the drag queen, to tone it up."[22] By this definition, then, Rebecca Glasscock will fit the transvestite's image more than the drag queen definition, but no transvestite would chose to use a name like Rebecca Glasscock.

Hence, if we attempt to define what a drag queen exactly is by taking *RuPaul's Drag Race* as a paradigm, then we will find such a variety of stage personas that such a task is almost impossible in their variety. Here in the first episode of the first season, we see a very rich spectrum of drag: for Shannel, a drag queen seems to be a drag version of a woman; for Nina Flowers, a drag queen is someone who exhibits a loud appearance; and, for Rebecca Glasscock, a drag queen just cross-dresses, indicated more by the use of make-up and a wig than by glamorous or flamboyant clothes.

With so many stylistic variations, it is difficult to arrive at a closed definition of what exactly a drag queen is. The question, then, is how the selection process for the program's participants is accomplished. That this process of selection seems to be rather ambiguous is not necessarily to be chastised: all reality TV shows choose their participants without a clear statement about what they are looking for from them. Clearly a set of skills and professionalism are required, but the selection process is always under suspicion. Spectators and fans always suspect that some of the participants are chosen more for their personalities than their skills. People with aggressive behavior or antisocial conduct are always used as devices to boost ratings. Fans love to see bad behavior in their favorite reality TV show, but they also criticize a show if they feel that some of the competitors are there only for their lack of social skills or an obstreperous personality. But can the competitors in a reality TV show about drag queens be chosen for any reason *other* than their personalities? Drag is, to a certain degree, about bitching about other queens and about the construction of an entertaining persona. Displaying some personality *is* a skill. What in other reality TV shows is something to be criticized here is the core of the project. In *RuPaul's Drag Race* participants are chosen in large part for their (entertaining) personalities. In other shows, this simple fact is hidden so that the show meets certain vague requirements about the "reality" of the competition.

"Give me body, give me face" (and Some Comic Skills Too)

Throughout the seasons, the girls went from performers with finely tuned comedic skills (Pandora Boxx) to queens who rely too heavily on the display of their bodies, for example, Raja and, especially, Carmen Carrera in season three. In fact, Carmen will take all the challenges from the same perspective: displaying her body seems to be enough to go through week after week even when this approach received critical comments from RuPaul and the judges. This must be understood not as a criticism, but as an indication of how malleable the term drag queen really is and how different the approaches that the queens take to face the challenges are that I will analyze.

Let's begin by considering what the challenges of the first episode of the first season were. The show consists of an opening mini challenge and a main challenge. Some mini challenges are repeated from season to season. For instance, the first mini challenge of each season is a photo shoot that includes some kind of special twist. In this episode, the twist was being doused with water while in full drag, posing over a car with the pit crew (two hunks) working as props. Two things must be noted of this mini challenge. First, it is obviously a rehearsal of the main challenge of *America's Next Top Model* (UPN-CW). In both shows, the contestants have to displays skills as a model to win the mini challenge. The best photograph, i.e., the best model, wins. This is similar in *RuPaul's Drag Race*, but here the fact is that the challenge is not a direct consequence of being a drag queen since drag queens do not have to have any modeling skills *per se*. The show asks of the competitors skills that are not part of the job of being a drag queen. The show seems to disregard professionalism understood as a unique set of qualities which are used to perform a simple task. And since professionalism and expertise in some area are highly valuable in global capitalism, the show seems to make fun of these ideas, more so if we take into account that this particular challenge has a concrete gain: a modeling contract. So this transfer to the capitalist marketplace is doubly traversed by drag: first, probably none of the girls is a professional model even if vogueing (striking a pose) is in the drag queens' movements roots.[23] And, second, they get the contract after winning a challenge which has no specific parameters. In other shows, winning a contract of this kind implies that some participant has proven to be the best in that challenge. Here the situation is disrupted because the end result is very subjective. In fact, RuPaul does not even clearly mention to the participants what things that went wrong during the challenge or who did it badly and why. Simply, someone is declared the winner.

Almost all of the queens in this specific mini challenge use a parody of the "sexy cover girl" routine to pass it. It is then possible to infer that comic skills were to be displayed in the challenge, but that is never clearly specified. Humor is the chosen path, and the contestants act as if they were real women striking sexy poses for the cover of a men's magazine. Modeling and sleazy covers are parodied for a humorous, drag effect. Drag is all about artificiality and its presence reveals how fake those postures are and how constructed the sexiness really is. As in other challenges on the series, the contestants have to transform all that they touch into drag. This quality of dragging common objects is what is expected from the queens, more than any other concrete skill. This is not unreasonable, but again, difficult to measure, to qualify as a result, and therefore, to judge.

I take, for example, the main challenge of the first episode of season one. It consists of making a dress created with materials and accessories from thrift shops. This is, of course, a challenge clearly picked out from the reality TV show *Project Runway*. One of its most popular challenges is to make dresses with unconventional materials. It is possible then to call into question the originality of the challenges in *RuPaul's Drag Race*. In addition, it seems like drag queens do not have skills which are entirely their own as a definable category. But their skills are to turn into drag what is given to them. And again, the problem is that if this is the very goal of the challenge, it is not explicitly mentioned. Hence, the results will be very hard to measure to declare a winner. It is impossible to determine the quantity and quality of "drag-iness" of a thing that is transformed by the contestants as part of the challenge.

I will examine other challenges from the show to see how unclear the parameters are. Many mini challenges have as their main goal to work over a common object with the idea of making it ... what? Drag? Funny? Queer? Tasteful? Tacky? The answer seems to be to turn into drag the objects with which they work and the results are always very different in approach. In season two episode five, each queen has to embellish a box, even when the word "embellish" is never mentioned. Rather, the competitors must "work over," or, "werk," the boxes. There are no clear parameters to follow, and this is the same when the objects to work on are shoes, brassieres, or teddy bears in other episodes.

Most challenges and games are based on the principle of equilibrium, meaning, "mutual rationality and mutual consistency."[24] Each participant, then, in order to win, can presuppose what the other participants are likely to do. But even with personalities very well defined, it is almost impossible to know what the other competitors will do precisely because rationality and consistency have no place in *RuPaul Drag Race*. The viewer will know that Sharon Needles from season four will (probably) work a twisted look on the catwalk, or that Carmen Carrera will display her body as her main strategy. But this does not allow one to mathematically (rationality) calculate how Carmen Carrera will decorate a cardboard box or Sharon Needles a shoe. This is not to say that some parameters are not in play in these challenges. Camp taste and imagination can play an important part at the moment RuPaul's chooses the winner, but the problem is that neither taste nor imagination are really particularly measurable. It can be argued that the same thing can be said about the dresses on *Project Runway* or the haircuts on *Shear Genius* (Bravo), but it must be noted that a dress or a haircut (or a cake or a decorated room) are all integrated within the circulation of what is "fashionable" in some concrete society in some concrete space/time. Even more, the global capitalist configuration of our contemporaneity makes the question of taste a transnational matter that increasingly obliterates boundaries between countries.[25] All of these things (purses, dresses, cakes and desserts, decoration, even colors) are measurable in response to some "metanarrative" of what is of some use and what is not: some classical desserts reborn in some specific time are forgotten again, styles of decoration are hot and then pass away, and, in the fashion world, as Heidi Klum says on *Project Runway*, one day you're in, and in the next day, you're out. Global capitalism has universalized taste as a commodity in which subjectivity has little space. Someone else decides what is of use and what is not, even when consumers have the last word at the moment of buying. *RuPaul's Drag Race* puts subjectivity on the main stage because everything depends on the decision of the host, because the challenges are based on entertainment rather than an explicit logic. In this way, the show denies the possibility of a unique way to meet the challenges, favoring instead a multitude of approaches which follow the subjectivities of the competitors rather than a "metanarrative" about taste. It can be argued that camp aesthetic plays an important part, but unlike global taste, camp taste favors polysemy and openness. "Embellishing" (for want of a better word) a cardboard box, a teddy bear, or a doll is not something that is framed within global taste. If we cannot establish with precision what a drag queen is, it is impossible to establish which of the queens has more successfully made a "drag" brassiere.

Games, like the challenges on *RuPaul's Drag Race,* must comply with some basic premises to be reasonable, i.e., to have the capacity of being judged: there have to be well-defined goals[26] which, in turn, lead to a clear evaluation, limited alternative courses of action, and rules that limit the possible behaviors.[27] The mini challenges often have no clear goal to establish how they can be evaluated. This creates suspicions of partiality when RuPaul chooses the winner. But reality TV shows are all about "artifice and fakery,"[28] and drag queens are all about "artifice and fakery." What

RuPaul's Drag Race does is recognize that reality TV works with artifice presented as non-mediated reality and that the decisions of judges are strongly biased towards the participants that are most entertaining. As Tomandlorenzo's blog argues, "The judging on this show is defiantly not transparent and no one ever really bothers justifying the decisions because they all come down to Ru. This makes it easier to accept even when we don't agree (unlike Project Runway where the judging is presented as if it's far less biased than it actually is)."[29] The fact that everything comes down to RuPaul's decisions is not a fact hidden from viewers. At the moment of judgment, RuPaul states, "I have made my decision." This simple sentence explicitly makes clear that the final decision is RuPaul's only, even when there are other judges. Without specific rules and perfectly delimited goals, what is left? First, a judgment far from any idea of impartiality since there are not any clear parameters to judge. Second, as Dinda Gorlée argues, the rationality of rules "must leave out an essential aspect of the nature of games, namely, the element of fun,"[30] turning games into competitiveness, which is key in the current global market. This is what the show carefully avoids, favoring fun more than aggressive expertise in an individualistic race against each other since the true nature of the challenges and their aims are left unclear. Competition in the global marketplace establishes consistent rules that regulate the behaviors of the different competitors/actors in which a business-like attitude is rewarded. It should be clear what can and cannot be done, and how the projects should be addressed. Here rules are lax and the parameters unclear and subjective, unlike the rational parameters that regulate the professional world.

The mini challenges sometimes are not even particularly drag-related. For example, in season three episode nine, the mini challenge was "musical chairs." This classic game has nothing in common with drag except that the competitors must perform it in high heels. What problematizes the true nature of the challenges of the show remains the question of what is expected from the competitors and what set of skills they must have in order to successfully compete in the professional world of drag queens. Clearly, *RuPaul's Drag Race* favors the playful aspects for the pleasure of playing in a game which can not be easily transferred to a conventional workplace.

The Main Challenges

The main challenges require the queens to perform a broad variety of skills. They must sing, dance, perform stand-up comedy routines, or impersonate famous popular culture icons in a parody of *Match Game* called "Snatch Game." All these challenges have the common theme of performance, which is an integral part of what a drag queen is, at least, in all the definitions of this profession. But the main challenge, in fact, is often essentially two different challenges. After the main challenge, the contestants must walk the runway. In some episodes, the catwalk is the main challenge. At other times the runway bears some relation to the main challenge and sometimes it is another challenge entirely. As an example of the first, we can consider episode six from season three. The competitors must create a dress inspired by a cake and present it on the catwalk. As an example of the second category, in season four episode nine, the main challenge has each of the girls presenting a platform as a (drag) candidate for the presidency. Obviously, the goal of the challenge is to perform and show skills in comedy presenting a humorous platform. The catwalk is related to the main challenge since the queens must present a dress which can be used in a drag inaugural ball. As an example of the third category, in season four episode two, the competitors have to perform as drag wrestlers in the main challenge. In the catwalk, they have to perform as "quinceañeras." This episode is an example of the multiple challenges that the queens have to endure in a single episode and how hard it is for the audience to make judgments about who should win, since a queen could do very well in the main challenge, but have a poor performance on the catwalk. In that same episode, the mini challenge asks for the queens to fabricate their own fake asses for RuPaul to judge. It is unclear whether the asses must look fake and funny or realistic and natural. This is the ludic polysemy of drag. Clearly the mini challenges work many times as fun for fun's sake. When the goal of a competition is just to be playful, the games turn "exploratory" of their ludic possibilities and are not "based on existing power relations"[31] since there are not any previous skills which can place one competitor above another one. Since there are no parameters to use as tools to judge, any queen can win. This seems to be unfair, but all reality TV shows are manipulated. The true difference is that *RuPaul's Drag Race* plays with the notion of competition and judgment turning the show into a countercultural version of other reality competition TV shows where the fakery is hidden under the moniker of "true reality."

Comic and performance skills are basic traits of drag queens. It is understandable then that the competitors have to display these abilities in the various challenges of the show. But some challenges ask the contestants to exhibit skills to win the games which are not part of the drag queen's arsenal. For example, in season four episode seven they must work as editor-in-chief of their own "dragazines." The true goal of the challenge is kept, as always, in the dark, to the point that Jiggly Caliente considered for a minute to approach the challenge in a serious way. This specific challenge has no relation to the drag world, nor are the drag queens prepared to perform this particular task. Again, the idea behind the challenge is to turn a magazine into drag. Here it is particularly difficult because to make it drag, participants should perhaps have some previous knowledge of publishing and possibly none of the queens have this. At least in terms of modelling, the queens might have some experience since modelling relates to performance. It is interesting to note that this episode's main challenge prompted some criticism: "usually the show's pretty good about connecting the challenges to the real-life of being a drag performer, and for the life of us, we couldn't see the point to making them all play editor for a day. It just didn't feel like a naturally draggy thing to be doing."[32]

It can be argued that "games can serve as a skeletal analogy of many social situations and contexts. In constructing a game analogy, an attempt is made to dissect from the complexities of real social interactions some fundamental structural aspects that can be employed to facilitate our understanding of the actual situations."[33] This analogy to the real world is what is lost in these types of challenges. It seems that, since the true nature of what a drag queen is is so fluid, the challenges can be about everything and anything. Since the term "drag" is so polysemic, and the variety of styles so broad, it is difficult to establish a definition about the exact status of what the work of a drag queen is. Not a comedian or an actress, not a singer, not an imitator but all that at once without encompassing a single category. They are "performers," but any attempt at a more specific definition is difficult since the variety of styles prevents a closed classification. Such a loose definition denies the centrality of "expertise" so well appreciated in global capitalism, favoring instead the constant flow from one knowledge or ability to another. This way, the show moves away from any articulation with the professional world which demands increasingly expertise to be the best in some area and to beat possible competitors. The analogy with the real world is cut and the game loses its link with the professional market so much regarded in other reality competition TV shows. Creativity and subjectivity win over professionalism understood as expertise and categorization. Since the other reality TV competition shows are presented as an opportunity for employment once the contestants are anointed as "the best" (although few participants actually achieve that entry to the marketplace), this show "drags" the "real" world in a double way: first by mocking the idea of the corporate capitalist who is instrumental to the labor market through the development of knowledge presented as clearly defined areas (X is an expert in global markets, while Y is an expert in local markets). This clear division of tasks means that each worker within the global market replicates the Fordist idea that each worker should have a role and only one to save time and resources and gain in efficiency. The drag queens, however, are more aligned with the non-specialist Renaissance man, as they must know a little of everything: how to sew, sing, design, impersonate, and more. And if you do not know how to do all this, *RuPaul's Drag Race* will force you to improvise. For better or worse, the competitors must comply with the requirements, even when asked to do something that they are unpracticed in or unfamiliar with.

The mockery is double because, moreover, the show also makes fun of the idea of an expert coming out of a reality competition TV show anointed as the best when often they only won because of public preferences or their personalities. *RuPaul's Drag Race* denies the real possibility of finding the best at something through play because the stylistic varieties of drag queens and the skills that they must display are too varied. If creating experts in specific areas is critical to maintaining the power of the hegemonic classes, because this allows a better "acquisition and use of this knowledge,"[34] then the drag queens from *RuPaul's Drag Race* come up as disruptions in the current capitalist climate as they systematically refuse to be classified or fit into a unique frame.

But, before an episode ends, there is still one last challenge for two queens to face: the "lip sync for your life." The two competitors who are judged to have performed the poorest in that week's challenges must compete to outshine each other lip syncing a song by a female pop icon which was previously chosen for that week (enabling preparation by all contestants). This final challenge looks easy enough to understand, but again, it is in fact not that easy to judge. It is not clear if the contestants must perform a perfect, imitative lip sync or make a spectacle of themselves by showing a great display of gymnastics and dance abilities. A good example was during the final lip sync of season four episode ten. Kenya Michaels and Latrice Royale were lip-syncing for their lives and the song was Aretha Franklin's "(You make me feel like) a Natural Woman." The approach with which both competitors face the task is very different. While Latrice performs as the singer would, Kenya develops a very broad set of gymnastic moves with the intention to grab RuPaul's attention. Latrice does not even move from her spot on the main stage as she lip syncs, while Kenya occupies all of it. In the end, it seems that the only form of evaluation is to grab RuPaul's (and by extension, the audience's) attention—which is likely the best way to approach this final challenge, as *RuPaul's Drag Race* is a reality TV show about performers whose job is to grab audience's attention by any means. Since the judging comes down to RuPaul's prerogative in the end, getting her attention is often effective, even if RuPaul and the audience do not always share the same investment in certain participants.

Conclusion

As stated previously, many reality TV shows choose their competitors based solely on personality. Many competitors have in mind not so much to expose their skills as the future great X (designer, chef, model) in order to ensure a lucrative job outside the TV world, but, rather, to create a fashionable persona that they can easily sell on TV. Many contestants of reality TV shows seem to have in mind not so much to get a job but to have their own reality TV show. But this "problem" does not affect this particular reality TV show as much since it is all about personalities. The drag queens must sell themselves because they are their own skills, the only thing that there it is to sell as people capable of doing a little of everything. But the required skills are never fully explained, which has led to criticism about what the show rewards: comic skills? Performative abilities? Realness and prettiness? This means that *RuPaul's Drag Race* works differently from other reality shows. There is not a clear and concrete definition about what drag queens are and what differentiates them from other gender benders. Nor is there a coherent set of skills that drag queens have to possess to succeed in the challenges. Even reality TV itself "lacks definitional coherence as a genre."[35] It is absurd to ask, then, for coherence and impartiality, or, for that matter, "reality" from a televised version of a competition.

But this departure from other reality TV shows is something extremely successful for many reasons. First, reality shows present themselves as unmediated reality in which the relationships of the participants are not scripted and the winner is the one person who demonstrated better skills and willpower. But, in fact, televised reality never can be that unmediated since it does not represent reality itself, but reality mediated by editing. If any reality had truly existed, this was transformed and triturated in the editing room. *RuPaul's Drag Race* has no such problems since it never supports the problematic idea of "unmediated reality." The competition is not, in fact, a standard "reality" competition since rules, methods of evaluation and characteristics of the different challenges resist the naïve idea of a fair game. It is not because the show is fixed, but because RuPaul never denies that the final decision is only for her to make and the tools of judgment and the skills necessary to pass the challenges, as well as the approaches possible to face any challenge, are totally flexible and open to ludic manipulation. Fakery takes center stage since it is a reality show starring drag queens whose main goal is to display enough personality to become "America's Next Drag Superstar." There is nothing serious about the game since the show is based on camp. Meanwhile, the competitors must accomplish a series of challenges more focused on playfulness. The range of challenges is so broad that the competitors come to the show without a clear idea of what is expected of them, especially in the early seasons. Delta Work says in the first episode of the third season (when she is required to make a dress from scratch), that she can sing and act, but that she does not have the abilities to make a dress. This, then, is the only reality TV competition show where the contestants have to perform a broad range of tasks rather than be the best in any one particular skill.

Here lies the second and most important point of *RuPaul's Drag Race*. Every reality TV competition asks for individualism which is articulated within the actual experience of capitalism and its neoliberal ideology.[36] People are pit against each other and only the fittest will survive. The person with more tuned skills wins over other competitors that may not have the same opportunities to achieve education or experience, and may not have a strong will to defeat other competitors week after week. William Hudson astutely sees the proliferation of reality competition shows, in which one competitor comes out on top in some discipline, as the triumph of "radical individualism"[37] where cooperation is dropped in favor of eliminating each other. Every contestant must outsmart the others to prevail. This mirrors the corporate capitalism of today, in which each individual must gain more and more education and skills, accumulate academic careers and titles, and, especially, extend her/his knowledge in some area in order to be the best in it, with the ultimate goal of improving in competitiveness for the actual global market. But since the ludic aspects prevail in *RuPaul's Drag Race*, the entire show disengages itself from current ideas of vicious competition.

Every book about business and management explains that every enterprise must have, first of all, a clear goal towards which to apply all resources. *RuPaul's Drag Race* lacks such a clear focus and its competitions are based more on ludic aspects than on goals to achieve. The challenges are too broad in range. The objectives of some challenges are unclear. The evaluation is opaque to audiences and highly subjective. This lack of coherence is articulated within the hybridity that is represented by drag queens themselves, whose presence is still not fully integrated into society.

In the contemporary world, where the pursuit of competitiveness is a hegemonic discourse,[38] *RuPaul's Drag Race* stimulates creativity over expertise, denies labeling in favor of blurring boundaries, and explicit fakery over some pretense of reality. The drag queens work more as Renaissance men who must demonstrate abilities within multiple areas than with the actual capitalist subjects with a narrowly specialized expertise. So, this show about falsehood works by mocking and parodying reality competition TV shows and their pretense of unmediated reality and articulation within the current stage of global capitalism.

Notes

1. Jessica Hicks, "Can I get an 'amen?'" in *Queer Love in Film and Television: Critical Essays*, ed. Pamela Demory and Christopher Pullen (New York: Palgrave Macmillan, 2013), 157.

2. Roy Grundmann, *Andy Warhol's Blow Job* (Philadelphia: Temple University Press, 2003), 109.

3. Marjorie Garber, *Vested Interests: Cross—Dressing and Cultural Anxiety* (New York: Routledge, 1992), 11.

4. Katherine Sende, *Business, Not Politics: The Making of the Gay Market* (New York: Columbia University Press, 2004), 228.

5. Kathy Ferguson, *The Feminist Case Against Bureaucracy: Women in the Political Economy* (Philadelphia: Temple University Press, 1984), 4.

6. Cheryl Rickman, *The Digital Business Start-Up Workbook: The Ultimate Step-by-Step Guide to Succeeding Online from Star-Up to Exit* (Chichester: Wiley, 2012), 195.

7. *Harvard Business Essentials: Business Communication* (Cambridge: Harvard Business School Publishing Corporation, 2003), 14.

8. There is an overarching goal in the show: be named "America's Next Drag Superstar." Granting a "title" as the ultimate prize (plus a certain amount of money) is at the heart of every televised reality competition. This essay, however, is organized around the various challenges within the show leading to the crowning of a winner.

9. Rusty Barret, "Markedness and Styleswitching in Performances by African American Drag Queens," in *Codes and Consequences*, ed. Carol Myers-Scotton (New York: Oxford University Press, 1999), 139.

10. Barret, 139–140.

11. Heinz Duthel, Kathoey Ladyboy: Thailand's Got Talent (BoD, 2013), 383.

12. Duthel, 384.

13. Daniel Harris, "The Aesthetic of Drag," *Salmagundi* 108 (1995): 62.

14. Carsten Balzer, "The Great Drag Queen Hype: Thoughts on Cultural Globalization and Autochthony," *Paideuma* 51 (2005): 117.

15. Andrew Ross, *No Respect: Intellectuals & Popular Culture* (New York: Routledge, 1989), 204.

16. Verta Taylor and Leila J. Rupp, "When the Girls Are Men: Negotiating Gender and Sexual Dynamics in a Study of Drag Queens," *Signs* 30, no. 4 (2005): 2117–2118.

17. Carsten Balzer, "The Great Drag Queen Hype: Thoughts on Cultural Globalization and Autochthony," *Paideuma* 51 (2005): 113.

18. Keith McNeal, "Behind the Make-Up: Gender Ambivalence and the Double-Bind of Gay Selfhood in Drag Performance," *Ethos* 27, no. 3 (1999): 345.

19. Harris, 64.

20. This phrase, whose acronym is "c.u.n.t." is used repeatedly in the show. They are the qualities that RuPaul looks for in the contestants to be crowned as winners. While this seems to establish some defining parameters about what is expected of the participants, the fact remains that these qualities are very difficult to measure and judge.

21. The number of participants would increase in the following years once the show proved successful.

22. Harris, 63.

23. Balzer, 115.

24. Colin F. Camerer, Teck-Hua Ho and Juin-Kuan Chong, "A Cognitive Hierarchy Model of Games," *The Quarterly Journal of Economics* 119, no. 3 (2004): 861.

25. Miguel Centeno and Joseph Cohen, *Global Capitalism: A Sociological Perspective* (Cambridge: Polity Press, 2010), 116.

26. Anna Wierzbicka, *Semantics: Primes and Universals: Primes and Universals* (New York: Oxford University Press, 2004), 159.

27. Barry Schlenker and Thomas Bonoma, "Fun and Games: The Validity of Games for the Study of Conflict," *The Journal of Conflict Resolution* 22, no. 1 (1978): 11.

28. Hal Niedzviecki, *Hello, I'm Special: How Individuality Became the New Conformity* (San Francisco: City Lights, 2006), 16.

29. TomandLorenzo.com, "Cover Girl Put the Bass in Your Walk," http://tomandlorenzo.com/2012/03/rupauls-drag-race-cover-girl-put-the-bass-in-your-walk/ (accessed February 16, 2014).

30. Dinda Gorlée, *Semiotics and the Problem of Translation: With Special Reference to the Semiotics of Charles S. Peirce* (Atlanta: Rodopi, 1994), 80.

31. Quentin Stevens, *The Ludic City: Exploring the Potential of Public Spaces* (New York: Routledge, 2007), 37.

32. TomandLorenzo.com, "Cover Girl Put the Bass in Your Walk," http://tomandlorenzo.com/2012/03/rupauls-drag-race-cover-girl-put-the-bass-in-your-walk/ (accessed February 16, 2014).

33. Schlenker and Bonoma, 9.

34. Jane Parpat, "Deconstructing the Development 'Expert': Gender, Devel-

opment, and the Vulnerable Groups," in *Feminism/ Postmodernism/ Development*, ed. Marianne Marchand and Jane Parpart (New York: Routledge, 1995), 223.

35. Jason Mittell, *Genre and Television: From Cop Shows to Cartoons in America Culture* (New York: Routledge, 2004), 197.

36. Jen Harvie, *Fair Play: Art, Performance and Neoliberalism* (New York: Palgrave Macmillan, 2013), 79.

37. William Hudson, *American Democracy in Peril: Eight Challenges to America's Future*, 7th ed. (London: Sage, 2013), 133.

38. Gillian Bristow, *Critical Reflections on Regional Competitiveness: Theory, Policy, Practice* (New York: Routledge, 2010), 3.

Cover, Girl
Branding Puerto Rican Drag
in 21st-Century U.S. Popular Culture

R. Gabriel Mayora

No outlet in popular media, and certainly in popular U.S. gay culture, has more consistently represented queer Puerto Rican sexuality than *RuPaul's Drag Race*. Each season, the show features a number of contestants of Puerto Rican descent, something that makes it stand out from most popular texts featuring gay characters. Yet, I must confess that as a gay Latino male *and*, perhaps more importantly, an avid fan of *RuPaul's Drag Race*, I have waited season after season to see a Puerto Rican queen take the crown. It seems like just about every season a Puerto Rican queen makes it far into the race, and, each season, she loses to a queen the judges generally consider more "cutting edge," more "sophisticated," or more "polished." More significantly, the show—intentionally and unintentionally—positions the Puerto Rican queens' struggles throughout their journey in specific relation to their race and ethnicity in more explicit ways than it does to the other queens of color. While my initial reaction is to attribute my indignation at the losses of splendid contestants like Nina Flowers and Alexis Mateo to my personal investment in the show, there is something else lurking behind my disappointment, something that remains well after the queens are done untucking in the (in)famous Interior Illusions lounge.

Focusing on the journey of the Puerto Rican queens from seasons one to three, this essay argues that *RuPaul's Drag Race* functions as a mirror of the relationship between the gay mainstream and queer Puerto Rican identity in the United States. In my reading, the popularity of the show both complicates and cements the notion of homonormativity and gay cosmopolitanism. To unquestionably celebrate the show's status as the ultimate pinnacle of success for gay and/or trans individuals would not only be misguided, but it would flatten the intricacies inherent in the show. At the same time, to dismiss the show as "problematic" would equally miss the valuable opportunities to explore issues of gender, race, class, and sexuality that the show offers every season. Following this idea, I argue that the presence and the season arcs of the Puerto Rican queens in the show function in two major ways: (1) through the contestants, the judges, and the producers' constant "othering" of the Puerto Rican queens, the show displays how queer Puerto Rican identity is commodified and packaged for the consumption of dominant gay culture; and (2) this position, somewhat counterintuitively, presents opportunities for the Puerto Rican queens to disidentify with the gender, sexual, and racial categories they are asked to inhabit, thus creating a potential for challenging typical representations of queer Puerto Rican performativity in the context of 21st-century U.S. gay politics. In this way, the show becomes a particularly valuable tool to explore the space of queer Latino men in today's political atmosphere.

"America lets me be Latina": Contemporary Gay Rights and Puerto Rican Queens

My argument is connected to two major trends in academic queer theory. On one hand, many established queer scholars—such as Michael Warner and Kenji Yoshino—have identified the apparent drive toward normativity plaguing the contemporary queer movement. For example, Michael Warner's canonical indictment of turn-of-the-century gay politics, *The Trouble with Normal*, famously argued that "repudiating its best histories of insight and activism, [the gay movement] has turned into an instrument for normalizing gay men and lesbians."[1] On the other hand, Latina/o queer theorists—like the late José Esteban Muñoz, Lawrence LaFountain-Stokes, Hiram Perez, and Frances Negrón-Muntaner—have criticized the ways in which queer Anglo-American culture (including white academic queer theory), mirroring dominant discourses about Latino/a identity, has figured itself away from needs or concerns related to queer Latino/a subjects. As Hiram Perez writes,

> If queer is to remain an effective troubling of the normative and its attendant regimes, it must painstakingly excavate its own entrenchments in normativity.

Establishmentarian queer theory houses itself not only in the academy but also within the identificatory boundaries of U.S. nationalism. The shaming of brown bodies is fundamental to dominant U.S. cultures, among them now a dominant queer culture.[2]

Thus, through their criticism, queer Latina/o scholars implicate white queer theory in the call for normativity the latter form of scholarship so deeply criticizes.

The topic of a "now dominant queer culture" is of particular significance to an analysis of *RuPaul's Drag Race*, given the show's popularity within and outside gay circles. In this way, the show has reached a type of mainstream status that sets it apart from more niche popular gay texts.[3] Of course, the word "mainstream" has to be used with caution here. Indeed, referring to a show about drag queens—some of the most controversial figures in U.S. queer culture—that airs on the self-identified gay network LogoTV seems to reject most understandings of what the mainstream is.[4] However, the show's popularity corresponds to the emerging national acceptance of gay men in both popular culture and dominant politics, an acceptance that matches the emergence of a gay culture which has closely figured itself along the politics associated with heteronormativity. In the past few years, a slew of TV shows featuring gay characters, like ABC's gigantic hit *Modern Family* and NBC's less successful copycat *The New Normal*, have premiered. In addition, gay marriage is one of the current hot topics in the United States following the Supreme Court's decision in June 2013 to declare the controversial Defense of Marriage Act unconstitutional. *RuPaul's Drag Race* is very much a part of this trend: recaps of the show can be found along recaps for other reality TV programs on websites not targeted toward a gay audience like EW.com (Entertainment Weekly) or TVLine.com, clips of the show are constantly featured on E! Network's *The Soup*, and many straight and gay celebrities have appeared as judges. Hence, the question of whether gay culture has made its way into the mainstream representation is not really a question anymore; the question now pertains to the types of representation allowed to be part of this process, as well as the costs associated with this relationship with the mainstream.

Queer lawyer and scholar Kenji Yoshino and Puerto Rican queer scholar Hiram Perez provide useful ways of critically engaging with this particular socioeconomic context. Rather than celebrating this newfound visibility, Yoshino points to the ways in which such visibility has created a new problem for queer people in the U.S, a problem he deems "the demand to cover." According to Yoshino's understanding, this demand to cover refers to how "gays are increasingly permitted to be gay and out so long as we do not 'flaunt' our identities."[5] Though such a claim might not at first be so easily applied to a show that asks its gay male and transgender contestants to constantly "flaunt" their drag queen identity, a closer look at the implications of Yoshino's work and the show's treatment of Latino/a identity highlights the value of "covering" to an analysis of the series. Anticipating his critics, Yoshino writes,

> Some might question whether anyone is imposing a cultural covering demand on gays. Far from forcing gays to mute gay culture, America seems increasingly to ask us to flaunt it [...]. The selective uptake of gay culture—gay fashion, yes; gay affection, no—shows that *acceptance is driven by the desires of the straight cultural consumer rather than the dignity of the gay person* [emphasis mine].[6]

To this conceptualization of covering, I would add that the differences between the desires of the straight cultural consumer and the gay one are becoming less and less defined. Hiram Perez uses the term "gay cosmopolitanism" to describe contemporary dominant gay male culture in the United States, a culture which has adopted a set of values rooted in "white, urban, leisure-class" masculinity. What is so valuable about Perez' use of gay cosmopolitanism is that he always conceptualizes it in terms of its origins in "urban whiteness," while clearly stating that gay men of color are a part of it even if they "do not emerge unscathed." Particularly important to my discussion of the show is Perez' argument that participants of gay cosmopolitanism

> can occupy an ambivalent position as both exoticizing/exotic and subject/object in relation to a cosmopolitan gay male desire. His experience of this subjectification can be simultaneously resistant and ecstatic.[7]

Following both Yoshino's and Perez' ideas, I frame drag queen culture as something that has been associated with the demands of dominant audiences, especially when it concerns drag queens as performers/entertainers.[8] Furthermore, as Yoshino and Perez note, dignity often takes second place to such demands precisely because those demands tend to require the minoritarian subject to give up her/his dignity. *RuPaul's Drag Race*, like most reality TV, is certainly a show not concerned with the dignity of its contestants even as it celebrates their stories and depicts drag as a genuine art form. This is obvious from the first episode of each season, which immediately presents the queens with a photo shoot challenge that consists of engaging in some sort of difficult and often embarrassing physical act in drag. In season two, the contestants had to pose with a wind machine blowing air at them at the highest speed; in season three, they had to find a sexy pose while jumping on a trampoline. What exactly these challenges test is unclear, since it is hard to think of a time when a drag queen performer will ever have to pose under those conditions; clearly, their point is to elicit laughs from the audience as the challenge often results in key accessories (like wigs, fake eyelashes, and fake breasts) falling off, revealing the contestants as "fakes."[9] As I will show later, the Puerto Rican queens, in particular, are not given many opportunities to keep their dignity as they struggle with the language or suffer some of the most scathing criticism from the judges.

Covering then becomes a highly significant term when it comes to exploring the relationship between the show, the mainstream, and the queer Puerto Rican contestants. It is in this process of covering through which the most complex tensions surrounding race in the show emerge. I argue that for most of the queens, covering is about adapting themselves to a version of drag identity relatable to a larger audience. For some of them, like Chad Michaels, it means they are good impersonators; for others, like Raja, it means they are classy models worthy of the runway. Even the edgier queens of the later seasons, Sharon Needles and Jinkx Monsoon, position themselves as actors, as artistic counterparts to their predecessors. What the show offers is the illusion that each queen has the chance to present herself in whatever way without forcing the audience to acknowledge the class position that allows Raja to look as stunning as she does, or the familiarity with American gay icons necessary to make a living as a celebrity impersonator, or the language skills necessary to master acting as skillfully as Sharon Needles and Jinkx Monsoon. The queens in the show who identify themselves as Puerto Rican may want to cover, but they are rarely able to. When they do, they do it in a way that forces them to overplay their raced identity. At other times, through their failed attempts at covering, they stress how their socioeconomic position informs and reinforces their inability to cover.

This essay focuses on the first three seasons of *RuPaul's Drag Race* for both purposes of scope and because these seasons represent the show's formative years, years that went on to define the show's DNA. I focus on the Puerto Rican queens since the show did not feature Latina queens from other countries who self-identified as such during these seasons. Furthermore, because of its status as an American territory, queer Puerto Rican identity in the U.S. is filled with a rich tension informed by the history of colonialism with the United States—this history runs through the Puerto Rican contestants' dynamics with the other contestants, the judges, RuPaul, and the audience. The main queens I discuss here are those who had a difficult time covering, either because of their accent, their skin color, or other features that marked them as Latinas: from season one, Jade; from season two, Jessica Wild; and from season three, Alexis Mateo and Yara Sofia.[10]

"I can see her rice and beans"

Queer scholar Hiram Perez frames his essay "You Can Have My Brown Body and Eat It Too!" as a demystification of "the primitive, exotic, or 'brown' body commodified by dominant gay male culture."[11] This commodification of queer brown bodies has historically been an indelible part of North American gay culture, especially in terms of North American gay culture's relationship with the drag community. Queer artists Andy Warhol and Ronald Tavel have been criticized for their use of Puerto Rican drag queen Mario Montez in their 1965 film *Screen Test #2*,[12] a film where they embarrass and humiliate an unknowing Montez under the auspices of a film audition. Queer Latino/a scholars have also noted the commodification of Stonewall-era Puerto Rican and Nuyorican drag queens, like Sylvia Rivera and Holly Woodlawn, across different sections of U.S. queer culture (academics, historiography, film, etc.).[13] Based on these critiques, I interrogate those moments in the series that recall this oppressive history.

Examining the series then becomes a reminder of how hard it is to let go of a history of oppression, since, as José Esteban Muñoz writes, "understanding that the past has a performative nature [...] rather than being static and fixed, the past does things."[14] Understanding the show in relationship to this history complicates progressive narratives so prevalent in the gay rights movement today. The somewhat recent well-intentioned but politically naive "It Gets Better" slogan only vocalizes the main philosophy of the mainstream gay rights movement: time will take care of everything. Through this philosophy, gayness aligns itself closer to heteronormativity than it does to queerness; buying into the narrative of the American Dream, progress narratives for the U.S. gay community only serve to ignore the intersection between race, gender, class, and sexuality that might keep certain individuals from succeeding more than others. Placing the problem away from institutionalized social inequality and into each individual, the gay rights movement has failed to question for whom exactly are things more likely to "get better."

From the first episode, *RuPaul's Drag Race* places itself in the context of the American Dream. The episode starts with a quick bio of RuPaul narrated by the mother queen herself; as we see an image of a young, working class black boy on the screen juxtaposed with images of RuPaul's modeling photos, RuPaul's voiceover narration talks about going from being a poor black boy to becoming a star. Immediately, the show frames its contestants as equal pursuers of the American Dream, all able to achieve it with the right amount of what RuPaul refers to as a perfect combination of "charisma, uniqueness, nerve, and talent." Examining RuPaul's use of this catchphrase, Ein-Anne Edgar writes, "While on stage, the Queens need to make sure that their C.U.N.T.s are present for the judges to rate."[15] This notion haunts all the Puerto Rican contestants, who are then figured as immigrants in search of the American Dream, their narratives of success only conceived in terms of their confirmation of American notions of progress and individuality.[16] Yet, what becomes apparent watching the show is that there are specific challenges that complicate the Puerto Rican queens' ability to keep their C.U.N.T.s in check, challenges which are tied to their role as ethnic others within the context of the show; thus, their performance in the show suggests that hegemony, something larger than the individual, is at work in the journey of these contestants. For example, when Shannel proudly claims that she brought $20,000 worth of costumes and wigs to compete in the show, I find it difficult to ignore the social forces—like white privilege or class status—that allow Shannel to spend that much money on costumes and wigs.[17] Meanwhile, Santino Rice criticizes Jessica Wild for being "very quinceañera," adding, "her style is pretty bad"[18]; when I hear this criticism my immediate thought is that perhaps if Jessica had $20,000 just for costumes and wigs like Shannel does, she might look more couture. This is just an example of how the fight for the crown is not as equal of a playing field as it might seem at first.

A close look at the challenges in *RuPaul's Drag Race* supports the idea that the show is designed for the queens to prove their ability to build a drag persona around the desires, expectations, and experiences of gay cosmopolitan culture. Therefore, the Puerto Rican queens I discuss here are often unable to get as far as the other queens for reasons that are simply more than individual or private. The area where I see this inequality most pronounced is in the show's focus on the Puerto Rican queens' struggles with the language. Throughout all three seasons I examine in this essay, there is a large emphasis on the Puerto Rican queens' difficulties to handle the language during speech-related challenges. Season two contestant Jessica Wild's initial comments in the season opener establish that the one aspect she is most worried about is the language. In an early episode of that season, when the queens must shoot a scene for a mock sci-fi movie, Mystique—the leader of the group—assigns Jessica Wild what she believes is a small role, telling Jessica, "You can't speak English."[19] Jessica's storyline in the episode is all about her struggle to learn the lines and recite them well, with RuPaul expressing concerns when he checks up on the queens as a mentor. Though Jessica does well in the challenge, she eventually is eliminated later in the season for a very speaking-heavy challenge consisting of promoting an autobiography and a vodka brand. Before she is eliminated, the judges make fun of the way she pronounces the title of her book (*Dreams of a Golden Child*) because her accent has the unintentional effect of sounding like she is saying "golden shower" instead of "golden child," something the judges find even more hilarious when Jessica confesses she does not know what a "golden shower" is.[20] More than anything, I think highlighting their accent serves to both exoticize and diminish the talent of the queens. It frames them as less capable of displaying their abilities as comedians, actresses, and artists, insinuating that their purpose is to look beautiful and be made fun of by their English-speaking counterparts. Curiously enough, as of now, the only queens cast in the show who have thick accents or struggle with the language are Latina queens, which reinforces the association between gay cosmopolitanism and queer brown bodies.

Still, the show's producers, including RuPaul, who is a host, mentor, and judge as well, work hard to make the Puerto Rican queens palatable to normative audiences. They mainly do this through cultural signifiers recognizable to North American audiences. Around fifteen minutes into the first episode, Puerto Rican queen Jade is being photographed during the first challenge, which consists of posing with the Pit Crew against a car while being hosed down. As soon as Jade starts, photographer Mike Ruiz instructs her, "give me every bit of sex that you have" before RuPaul yells at her, "give me J.Lo, honey!"[21] Sure, all the queens are asked to perform according to their looks—at different points in the series, Tyra Sanchez is compared to Beyoncé, Raja to Tyra Banks, and Shannel to Barbra Streisand. These contestants sought those comparisons though, whereas Jade only needed to be Puerto Rican to receive a command to act like J.Lo. The call to cover is implicit in the employment of Jennifer Lopez as both a model for the Puerto Rican queens to follow and a measuring stick for them to determine their level of acceptance by dominant culture. Jennifer Lopez, a performer whose career has been characterized by the right combination of commodified exoticism and universal likability, serves to remind the queens of how far they can go if they allow their bodies to become part of dominant culture. Hence, the show aligns itself with homo-normative values by attempting to package the queens as a product that is recognizable and successful under terms defined by white, normative, middle class audiences.

This type of scene is characteristic of the show's treatment of Puerto Rican identity; over and over, the queens are asked to perform not just gender but their racial identity as well. Yet, what I found most striking about the constant call for the Puerto Rican queens to perform their Latina/o identity is that drag consists of making public that which is private or even foreign to the gay male body. Drag performance, at its most pragmatic, is about adopting an identity that society sees as different from the individual. Moreover, Judith Butler points to the political value of drag by conceiving drag as

> a site of a certain ambivalence, one which reflects the more general situation of being implicated in the regimes of power by which one is constituted and, hence, of being implicated in the regimes of power that one opposes.[22]

RuPaul's Drag Race divests the Puerto Rican queens from realizing this potential since, when it comes to race, the show does not provide room for the queens to occupy whiteness; instead, they must model themselves after Latina/o cultural markers.

This represents a missed opportunity to encourage the Puerto Rican queens to use drag as a way to call attention to the performativity of "whiteness," much like drag has the potential to highlight the concept of gender as a social construct. Indeed, one of the ways in which drag has been read as politically subversive has been through its ability to call attention to the performativity of whiteness; for example, Ragan Rhyne argues that "camp, as a mode of class performance, is often deployed [...] by white drag queens and in fact often subverts naturalized whiteness and renders it marked and visible."[23]

While white drag queens have the opportunity to "subvert naturalized whiteness" by embodying white femininity, the Puerto Ricans are not given the space to interrogate the category of "whiteness" through their drag performance. Of course, the power dynamics implicated in perform-ing "whiteness" are very different from the power dynamics involved in men doing drag. For one, when they impersonate women, men are moving from a position of privilege to a position of social inferiority. Moving down the social ladder, when the possibility of returning to the original dominant role is always available, belongs to a larger tradition. Historically speaking, men have portrayed females for the purpose of entertainment for centuries, and the popularity of the show proves that 21st-century audience members are still entertained by this idea.

Less acceptable today, though still following a tradition, are performances from either white entertainers as members of another race (i.e., minstrel shows, classic Hollywood movies) or from performers of color embodying a different race—except for whiteness.[24] Thus, the show inadvertently creates a barrier around the type of drag the queens of color can represent. Of course, it is important not to ignore the problematics involved in the Puerto Rican contestants' brown bodies being reconfigured in terms of whiteness, and I do not argue that the show should ask the contestants to embody white drag. Rather, I evaluate the show's persistence on racing the brown, Puerto Rican contestants in such a way that they do not typically have the opportunity to disidentify with whiteness.

Going back to Jade, the order to perform Jennifer Lopez also places her within the larger history of Puerto Ricans as objects to be looked at and consumed by the United States. That it happens to Jade foreshadows her ultimate moment of shame later in the season, a moment deeply rooted in this history of objectification. As Frances Negrón-Muntaner argues, dominant culture has commodified visible mainstream Puerto Rican celebrities like Ricky Martin and Jennifer Lopez through a focus on a specific part of their body—hips in the case of Martin, the butt in the case of Lopez; the author sees this discussion as a way to "highlight how the shame of Puerto Rican identity can lodge itself in specific body parts, even when the bodies displaying it are greatly appreciated cultural commodities showing off pride."[25] In the context of a show celebrating gay pride, Jade suffers great shame due to a racialized reading of a specific part of her body—her penis.

In the show's first season, Jade's penis becomes a major subject of discussion. The topic of Jade's penis comes to focus in episode three, when, after her runway walk, RuPaul casually says, "Interesting to see such a beautiful woman with such a big dick."[26] I turn to Eir-Anne Edgar's description of this incident to capture the visual and spoken rhetoric the show employs to address Jade's penis:

> Suddenly, a playback of Jade walking the runway fills the entire television screen with a close-up of her blue panties. While laughter filters through the room, Jade's voiceover explains the embarrassment she is feeling at that moment [...]. The other judges laugh and affirm that they too are able to detect Jade's penis. In the reunion episode, RuPaul returns to a discussion of Jade's penis. She asks her how big it really is [...]. Noticing Jade's discomfort, RuPaul asks why it bothers her that she would point out her penis-tucking failure after her per-

formance. Jade responds by stating, "Obviously, when you're dressed as a woman, you don't want to be asked about your penis. It's very embarrassing."[27]

The close-up of Jade's crotch filling the entire television screen captures the way *RuPaul's Drag Race* is designed for the dominant viewer who will find pleasure in mocking Jade, judging Jade, and desiring Jade. Jade figures her embarrassment in terms of drag failure, as does Edgar's analysis of this particular moment. Indeed, the show's shaming of Jade largely relies on portraying her penis as an obstacle impossible to overcome; as such, her seemingly huge penis (by now imagined not simply as large, but as freakishly large), is figured as an indelible part of her identity that will never allow her to cover. If covering is about maintaining order by not flaunting one's identity for the world to see, Jade's penis is unruly and threatening; as such, it must be laughed away, humiliated, and divested from any power.

Following my argument that the show mirrors the actual dynamics between dominant subjects and queer Latino/as, the shaming of Jade eerily resembles an incident that took place at the 2003 Gay Shame conference held at the University of Michigan. At this conference, Ellis Hanson presented on Plato's *Symposium*, while in the background, he displayed publicity images of an Afro-Latino model called Kiko from the porn film *Learning Latin* as he was presenting. According to Hiram Perez' account, the images of Kiko's penis elicited a series of comments from the very established queer scholars in the room; these comments fetishized Kiko's penis as an extremely "big, purple dick." Unfortunately, even though this all transpired at a conference titled Gay Shame attended by the biggest name in the field of queer theory (queer of color scholars were in attendance though inexplicably no panel at the conference was dedicated to race), there was "no substantive discussion about the representation of Kiko, about fantasy, about racialized desire [...]. Kiko's dick assumed its historical place as the focal point of white fantasy." Perez concludes that brownness then exists as a way to validate the desires of gay cosmopolitan culture without ever having to worry about the power dynamics at the center of this fantasy.[28] When Jade is singled out for her big penis, she is being divested of her power as a drag queen, which places her in a position of shame due to her inability to properly tuck; simultaneously, she is also divested of the power of her masculinity (a sphere where, in the context of U.S. society, large penises symbolize power) by objectifying her penis in such a way that it becomes a fantasy for the viewer, the gazed object rather than the gaze itself. Jade, like Kiko, is relegated to a position of shame that only protects the agency and desires of dominant audiences.

"When I'm in drag, I'm a star"

Rewatching the first three seasons, it seems like Alexis Mateo was the Puerto Rican queen who was able to navigate the show's trappings the best. Alexis' arc in the show points to the tensions that emerge when the minority subject interrogates and critically engages with the mainstream's demands. When Alexis walks into the workroom for the first time, she is aware she will be marked as Latina. Right away, Manila Luzon says, "We got two big girls, and two Puerto Ricans"; her comment prompts an Alexis confessional in which she responds, "What I hate the most is that people label you the Latin queen. I'm not just the Latin queen; when I'm in drag, I'm a star."[29] Manila, an ethnic queen herself, soon (either consciously or subconsciously) sets herself apart from the marginalized girls in the group—the Puerto Rican girls and the big girls. Manila's instant othering of these queens reveals that part of the covering process for minoritarian subjects means embracing hegemonic discourse. Therefore, Manila's own privilege throughout the season comes at the expense of the oppressed groups, something that becomes even more obvious through the challenges in which she personifies a series of negative Asian stereotypes, much to the critique of the othered contestants like Shangela and Alexis. Alexis' response to Manila's comment depicts a level of awareness about her subordinate role within U.S. gay culture that is not as apparent in the performance of the other Puerto Rican contestants. She never denies her race and ethnicity, but she tries to develop a sense of identity around stardom and drag, taking her race into account without always allowing hegemonic desire to disrupt her agency.

The forms of success Alexis finds on the show, though, rely on how she is able to package her own Latina identity for the judges to consume. Just like Jade was going to be compared to Jennifer Lopez before she even stepped in front of the camera, Alexis was bound to be the Latina queen before she started the competition. However, by the time "Totally Leotarded" (the fourth episode of season three) arrives, Alexis has seemingly given up her disdain for being thought of as "just the Latin queen." In this episode, the main challenge calls for the queens to act in their own workout video. Alexis decides to play up her Puerto Rican identity by exaggerating her accent and wearing a tacky getup; she also acts like the stereotype of the American dumb girl. Yara Sofia chooses a similar approach for her workout video. She comes up with the catchphrase "*echa pa'lante*" (a colloquialism that could be translated as "keep moving forward" or "keep going"), wears a short black dress with a flower on her hair, and uses salsa as her background music. While Delta complains that working with Yara feels like she is making a workout video with Charo, the judges praise Alexis for embodying a Puerto Rican Chrissy Snow in her video. Charo is, of course, one of those figures whose shadow looms so large over Latin performers that she seems almost mythical; certainly, the type of loud, dancing, hypersexual Latin femininity she cements is a myth. Chrissy Snow, the famed character from the American sitcom *Three's Company* (1976–1984), represents a signifier for the naïve, hypersexual American blonde so ubiquitous in U.S. sitcoms; the judges favor Alexis' adaptation of this stereotype over Yara Sofia's "Charo performance." Here we see how Alexis subverts the judges' expectations, and even insistence, that the Puerto Rican queens personify Latina/o cultural markers; rather, Alexis chooses to package herself as someone who can perform both Puerto Rican and North American ideas of femininity.

To understand the subversive value of Alexis' victory in this challenge, I turn to José Esteban Muñoz' theory of disidentification. When I refer to disidentifications, I'm specifically invoking the term as developed by the late Latino queer theorist Muñoz in his book *Disidentifications*. Muñoz enlists the concept of disidentification to describe survival strategies employed by minoritarian subjects in order to exercise agency within a hegemonic sphere.[30] Informed by Michel Pêcheux, the author describes the three different ways in which minorities relate to hegemony. Identification refers to uncritically adopting a hegemonic set of social codes and counteridentification refers to those who attempt to completely reject dominant norms; Muñoz sees the latter strategy as equally unsuccessful as the former since he argues that a complete rejection of dominant norms only "validates the dominant ideology by reinforcing its dominance through the controller symmetry of 'counterdetermination.'" Finally, he establishes disidentification as the most valuable and politically subversive form of engaging with oppressive systems. He conceives of disidentification as a mode that "neither opts to assimilate within such a structure nor strictly opposes it; rather, disidentification is a strategy that works on and against dominant ideology."[31] By playing with both Puerto Rican and white myths of femininity, Alexis Mateo's performance in the workout video disidentifies with both hegemonic understandings of race and femininity as a way to get ahead in the race, finally emerging as a victor. On the other hand, Yara, who arguably identifies with the stereotype of Charo, is read by Delta and, more importantly, ultimately loses the challenge. Thus, the results of the challenge highlight the role of disidentification as a form of survival.

I find Muñoz' concept of great value to address the role of queer Latino/as in the United States because it captures the nuances of those subjects' search for agency. Disidentification is not a permanent state of being; it is not imagined as a utopian sense of identity.[32] Muñoz writes, "Disidentification is *not always* an adequate strategy of resistance or survival for all minority subjects [... at times,] queers of color and other minority subjects need to follow a conformist path if they hope to survive a hostile public sphere."[33] Conceiving of disidentification as a tool for survival that is not always available to minoritarian subjects moves us away from picturing Alexis' journey as a Puerto Rican queen solely in terms of a success story. The point I seek to emphasize here is that just because Alexis found a way to disidentify with multiple versions of femininity in the fourth episode, it does not mean she "figured it out" for the rest of the show. A moment where this becomes painfully obvious is in the standup comedy challenge from the episode "Ru Ha Ha." As part of the challenge, the queens have to work with comedian Rita Rudner to develop a standup routine. Alexis' first instinct is to talk about coming to the United States, so Rudner's suggestion is that Alexis opens with a joke about coming here on a raft. Alexis seems uncomfortable with the joke, and tells Rudner that the word "raft" is difficult for her to pronounce, cuing a displeased reaction from the comedian. At the end, Alexis makes the joke in her standup routine, which bombs. Rudner's joke fails on multiple levels. Apart from the fact it is simply not a funny joke, it imagines Alexis as Cuban, since Cubans are generally the immigrants who travel here by boat; for Puerto Ricans, migrating to the mainland is not a question of legality. The show forces Alexis to fully identify with a stereotype that is not even part of her identity; the result is embarrassing for everyone involved.

Moments like these are what make the subversive moments in the show both surprising and exciting, especially when they are so close together. By far, the most complex episode concerning queer Puerto Rican identity in the show's first three seasons is the episode right after the just-discussed "Ru Ha Ha," titled "Life, Liberty, and the Pursuit of Style." The main challenge of the episode finds the queens making a PSA to honor American troops abroad. Given the complicated history between Puerto Rico and American troops, this episode represents one of the very few cultural artifacts in the history of American television that finds queer Puerto Rican drag queens directly engaging with the notions of American nationalism, American loyalty, and Puerto Rican identity.

Unexpectedly, Alexis Mateo and Yara Sofia are a central focus of this episode. Yara Sofia's issues throughout the episode are highly connected to her identity as a Puerto Rican queen; running her main idea by Alexis, she says: "Right now, I'm wearing no clothes because I don't want any brand, any stereotype to cover who I am. I don't want any brand to cover my identify, identity [*sic*]."[34] Later on, RuPaul asks her if she is going to do any of "that sensual Puerto Rican." The contrast between Yara's original plan to not represent any stereotype and RuPaul's question/suggestion about performing Puerto Rican sensuality encapsulates the show's back and forth between Puerto Rican desires and the expectations from gay cosmopolitan culture. For her PSA, Yara decides to play up her Puerto Rican camp identity, which works against her favor; her dress looks tacky, and she has a difficult time delivering her lines during the taping. Meanwhile, Alexis wears a stunning jump suit with a print full of United States flags all over; she has officially packaged herself as a patriotic American, but she still speaks Spanish in her PSA and seems to have a lot of fun while doing it. Yara does not even pretend to embrace typical conceptions of American symbols in her runway look; instead, she wears a *bomba*, a traditional Puerto Rican dress, which she then removes to reveal a bathing suit made to look like the Puerto Rican flag. Unlike the workout video challenge, Yara Sofia seems to have more agency in her performance during the runway walk and the PSA challenge. She not only refuses to reject her national identity as a Puerto Rican, she embraces it in a way that is undeniable and even abrasive, far from the neatly packaged performances some of the queens are asked to provide at times. In another instance of disidentification proving to be an effective survival strategy, Alexis wins the challenge and Yara Sofia ends up in the bottom two with Carmen Carrera, the other remaining Puerto Rican queen of the season.

Carmen Carrera's own Puerto Rican identity comes into focus during this episode, another example of how the show provides a surprising space to discuss the notion of queer Puerto Rican performativity. As I said earlier, this essay zeroes in on those queens whose journeys on the show are defined by their race. Carmen Carrera's ethnicity is never directly addressed until this episode when Carmen, Shangela, Yara Sofia, and Alexis are talking about the challenge while getting ready for the runway. Carmen says she doesn't speak Spanish and proudly claims her mom is very "Americanized." This moment cues a confessional from Yara, where she says she would love to see Carmen embrace her Puerto Rican identity; in her confessional, Carmen says she loves Puerto Rican culture and that it has been a part of her life since she was little, but that Alexis and Yara do not consider her Latina enough. The underlying tension has to do with Carmen Carrera's ability to pass as white because of her lack of a Puerto Rican accent, her skin color, and the way she presents herself. Again, it is difficult to think of another show that explores the nuances that define the relationship between the queens based on race performativity, color, and queerness the way this episode manages to do.

Conclusion: Responsitranity

Analyzing the issue of minority representation in dominant forms of popular media, queer film scholar Richard Dyer writes,

> How social groups are treated in cultural representation is part and parcel of how they are treated in life [...]. How a group is represented, presented over again in cultural forms, how an image of a member of a group is taken as representative of that group, how that group is represented in the sense of spoken for and on behalf of (whether they represent, speak for themselves or not), these all have to do with how members of groups see themselves and others like themselves, how they see their place in society, their right to the rights a society claims to ensure its citizens. Equally re-presentation, representativeness, representing have to do also with how others see members of a group and their place and rights, others who have the power to affect that place and those rights.[35]

Dyer's take on cultural representation assigns responsibility to dominant avenues for their depiction of minority subjects. Based on the ideas he presents, I argue that *RuPaul's Drag Race* is a highly important and valuable site to discuss the commodification, oppression, eroticization, and shaming of queer Puerto Rican subjects. Aligning itself with the politics characteristic of hegemonic conceptions of queerness and Puerto Rican identity, the show is implicated in the losses of its Puerto Rican contestants. And yet, those conditions produce a series of moments that allow for sites of resistance, subversion, and survival, suggesting that the nexus between queer Puerto Rican identity and gay cosmopolitanism is filled with potentiality, a potentiality that must not go untapped. Just like RuPaul reminds his audience of their "responsitranity," she, her producers, and her girls should be aware of their own "responsitranity" to those whose voices, while as loud as the rest, have yet to be fully given an honorable place within the show.

Notes

1. Michael Warner, *The Trouble with Normal: Sex, Politics and the Ethics of Queer Life* (Cambridge: Harvard University Press, 1999), 25.

2. Hiram Perez, "You Can Have My Brown Body and Eat It Too!" *Social Text* 23, no. 3–4 (2005): 175.

3. I'm thinking here of movies like *Priscilla, Queen of the Dessert* (1994) and *To Wong Foo Thanks for Everything! Julie Newmar* (1995).

4. In her essay "Queer Television Studies: Currents, Flows, and (Main)streams," Lynne Joyrich provides an insightful analysis of the tensions between the mainstream and queerness, particularly in terms of conceiving queer television as mainstream.

5. Kenji Yoshino, *Covering: The Hidden Assault on Our Civil Rights* (New York: Random House, 2006), 19.

6. Yoshino, 85.

7. Perez, 176.

8. For example, it is common for gay bars to have a straight night that features a drag show as the main point of attraction. In Gainesville, Florida, where I currently reside, this is a common practice at the only gay club in town, the University Club. The club's connection to *RuPaul's Drag Race* goes beyond drag in general; in fact, this was the club where season five contestant Jade Jolie performed before she was cast in the show. On an even more personal note, I recently attended a drag dinner show in Ft. Lauderdale, Florida—an area known for gay tourism—as part of a bachelorette party and was shocked by the fact I was the only gay man who attended as a customer; the rest of the tables were occupied by seemingly heterosexual women, most of them as part of bachelorette celebrations.

9. When I say reveal them as "fakes," I mean within the context of the show.

10. This is why I mostly exclude Carmen Carrera, who is of Puerto Rican descent, from this study. Unlike the other Puerto Rican queens, Carmen could cover her ethnicity and often did so. Her ability to cover allowed her to be part of the "Heathers"—a group mainly built around queens whose identity performance almost only relied on gay cosmopolitanism. The other Puerto Rican queens were childishly deemed the "boogers."

11. Perez, 171.

12. See Perez, 171–192; Lawrence LaFountain-Stokes, "Gay Shame, Latina- and Latino-Style: A Critique of White Queer Performativity," in *Gay Latino Studies: A Critical Reader*, ed. Michael Hames-García, and Ernesto Javier Martínez (Durham: Duke University Press, 2011), 55–80.

13. See Frances Negrón-Muntaner in *Boricua Pop* (see note 25); Jessi Gan in "Still at the Back of the Bus: Sylvia Rivera's Struggle," *Centro Journal* 19, no. 1 (2007), 124–239.

14. José Esteban Muñoz, *Cruising Utopia: The Then and There of Queer Futurity* (New York: New York University Press, 2009), 28.

15. Eir-Anne Edgar, "Xtravaganza: Drag Representation and Articulation in *RuPaul's Drag Race*," *Studies in Popular Culture* 34, no.1 (2011): 133, 142–143, http://www.pcasacas.org/SiPC (accessed January 15, 2014).

16. While a discussion of their performance in the show is not within the scope of this essay, I would also argue that the contestants who do not neatly fit into the American Dream, like season 1 winner Bebe Zahara and breakout star Shangela are also haunted by this notion.

17. *RuPaul's Drag Race*, "Drag on a Dime," Logo TV, 2 February 2009.

18. *RuPaul's Drag Race*, "Here Comes the Bride," Logo TV, 8 March 2010.

19. *RuPaul's Drag Race*, "Country Queens," Logo TV, 15 February 2010.

20. *RuPaul's Drag Race*, "Once Upon a Queen," Logo TV, 22 March 2010.

21. See note 17.

22. Judity Butler, *Bodies That Matter: On the Discourse and Limits of "Sex"* (New York: Routledge, 1993), 125.

23. Ragan Rhyne, "Racializing White Drag," *Journal of Homosexuality* 46, no. 3–4 (2004): 181–194, http://www.tandfonline.com (accessed February 13, 2014).

24. For example, Russian actor Yul Brynner won an Oscar for his portrayal of the King of Siam in *The King & I* (1956); African American actress Juanita Hall played a Polynesian woman in *South Pacific* (1958).

25. Frances Negrón-Muntaner, *Boricua Pop: Puerto Rico and the Latinization of American Culture* (New York: New York University Press, 2004), xvii.

26. *RuPaul's Drag Race*, "The Queen Who Mopped Xmas," Logo TV, 24 January 2011.

27. Edgar, 133, 142–143.

28. Perez, 183–186.

29. *RuPaul's Drag Race*, "The Queen Who Mopped Xmas," Logo TV, 24 January 2011.

30. Muñoz, *Disidentifications: Queers of Color and the Performance of Politics* (Minneapolis: University of Minnesota Press, 199), 4.

31. Muñoz, 11.

32. In this way, Muñoz works against teleological conceptions of identity and success, an idea he further complicates in *Cruising Utopia: The Then and There of Queer Futurity*, see note 14.

33. Muñoz, 5.

34. *RuPaul's Drag Race*, "Life, Liberty, and the Pursuit of Style," Logo TV, 14 March 2011.

35. Richard Dyer, *The Matter of Images: Essays on Representation* (New York: Routledge, 2002), 1.

"Draguating" to Normal
Camp and Homonormative Politics

JOSH MORRISON

RuPaul's Drag Race (2009–) and its spin-off shows, *RuPaul's Drag Race: Untucked!* (2010–) and *RuPaul's Drag U* (2010–2012), have exploded into American media and become mainstream hits. They are often hailed as beacons of hope, progress, positive representation, and as ambassadors for the inclusion for members of the LGBTQ community. According to Mac McClelland's recent profile on RuPaul's career in *Rolling Stone* magazine,

> The world's pre-eminent drag queen might not consider drag his greatest passion, but he's still a big believer in its power [...]. "You have to go into this complete artifice to figure out who you really are.... There's a certain genre of drag," Ru says, "that is sanctioned and its OK because they are saying to the audience, 'Oh, and by the way, I'm making fun of this,' but then there is the drag that I do, and my girls do, which is really taking the piss out of all identity."[1]

In much of the laudatory discourse around *Drag Race*, however, there is a way that the show is assumed to represent progress for all constituents of the queer community; an assumption I take issue with in this essay. When criticisms are leveled at the show about its treatment of transwomen, people of color, queens with heavy accents, older queens, or larger queens (to name a few), common responses are to point to the show's campy humor as excusing transphobia, racism, misogyny, fatphobia, and ageism on the show. After all, drag is just "taking the piss out of all identity." In the *Drag Race* pantheon, camp becomes an excuse for severely narrowing which queer subjects the show includes in its politics of progress, rather than a humorous social agitant.

In this essay I examine how *Drag Race* and *Drag U* portray women's bodies and bodies of color as objects of a sadistic camp promoting normative gender roles and homonormative political causes. In her essay "Deaths of Camp," Caryl Flinn names this variety of camp, practiced mostly by gay men, as loving assassination. It entails drag and camp performances that intend to subvert norms or create emotional catharsis on the bodies of women, fat people, the elderly, bodies of color, and other minoritized groups through an often loving, well-intentioned impersonation of them, that, in sending up these bodies, unintentionally does them discursive violence.[2] A loving assassination involves gay male camp being brought to bear solely on a particular body or object that, through its camping, is often left ravaged, attacked, and/or represented as dead, morbid, and empty of agency or even subjectivity. Accordingly, Flinn asserts that "'loving assassination' suggests [...] less the unintended nature of camp humor than the sheer morbidity of its aggressiveness."[3] Loving assassination involves an aggressive camping of another object that becomes intentionally malicious, making camp performances that are far more likely to reaffirm the power and privilege of the performer. As camp practices, and drag in particular, have become increasingly prevalent in mainstream culture, RuPaul's shows have increasingly committed loving assassinations against female and racialized bodies.[4] I argue that in *Drag Race* and *Drag U* campy loving assassination is used to capitalize on homonormative political goals, transforming drag into a mainstream cultural commodity whose consumption incorporates (predominantly white) gay men into normative regimes of power. Heterosexuals watching are assured that gays share their values, taking away the threat and destabilizing force of drag and camp through the assimilationist causes featured on the Drag Race shows including marriage equality and the inclusion of GLBTQ in post–9/11 rhetorics of American patriotism.

"Sashay away": Camp Policing Bodies

"Deep in the Lake Titicaca valley, a school was formed by drag queens to help biological women unleash their inner diva and let the world have it! We here at Drag U are in the business of putting drag queen heads on women's shoulders. Welcome to RuPaul's Drag U!" intones RuPaul's voiceover for the credits of *Drag U*. In each episode, three women with a traumatic or painful story and a hardship to overcome enroll at Drag U. Here their drag professors, competitors from previous Drag Race seasons, President RuPaul, Dean of Drag Lady Bunny, and rotating Deans of Dance (including trans choreographer and dancer Candis Cayne) make over female contestants. They become caricatures of the caricature of drag so that they can compete in a lip-sync performance to "draguate," hopefully with top honors, and win a small prize. Each of the women has a short one to two minute interview with RuPaul in his office, where he provides quick and facile life advice about the "trauma" that brought them to Drag U. Almost always, the women cry or open up about their issues to RuPaul, realizing that their painful problems needed only a moment of sound-bite advice to be surmounted. We are told that they confront their issues through the "miracle of drag," and, by the end of the show, have generally reached some kind of closure or resolution of their issue. The show chooses its women based on weekly themes, which are typical reality TV fare rife with stereotypical brands of sexism: "real heroes," including veterans and emergency services women who need to re-feminize; virgins looking for sexiness; fat women with low self-esteem; women who can't get dates but want them; moms who feel unsexy; wives who want to re-invigorate their sex lives; nerds who have "no life"; and moms and daughters looking to bring their families back together. There is even a special episode where RuPaul's three sisters compete to see who can become (almost) as fabulous as their brother. In season two, an ad-break bumper section called "Drag Tips" was introduced where queens from previous *Drag Race* seasons give advice about how drag queens use everyday objects to transform their look, extending the show's helping hand to the audience. Though some tips are useful for everyday life, many of them are drag specific, such as using glue sticks to mat down one's eyebrows before covering them with stage makeup, suggesting that the actual audience and subject of address is more likely to be other queens than the women that the show purports to address. Season two also saw the inclusion of "Lady Lessons," when Lady Bunny, a famous drag queen and friend of RuPaul's, arrives to teach the contestants a lady skill, like how to correctly use spanks or paint on seductive lips. Lady Bunny is assisted by (often male) experts pitching beauty products, bringing a complicity with the fashion industry and its body-shaming norms uncomfortably close to the surface of this "empowering" show. In the bizarre *Victor Victoria* meets *Dr. Phil* universe of *Drag U*, men who act like women tell women how to act like men who act like women to become better women through embracing "the miracle of drag," all the while chastising women for not embodying "proper" femininity.

Much of the show's appeal to its viewers is the inclusion of the drag professors, beloved former *Drag Race* competitors including Pandora Boxx, Jujubee, Raven, Ongina, and Shannel. A side effect of their inclusion is the increasing displacement of the contestants and their agency over their drag persona's creation and execution as the series progressed. In season one, the contestants were left alone at the end of the first day of their ordeal, with homework assignments including sewing their costumes and rehearsing choreography. Though the dragulator had already created a drag persona for them to draw inspiration from, in the first season it was more of a suggestion, and the onus was put on the contestants to make that image come to life through their own sewing skills or choose a different look to execute. As the show continued, this agency is taken away: by season three the costume from the dragulator image was provided, no mention was made of creating anything, and increasingly the three women's looks and drag names became similar in color, cut, theme, and sound. As the contestants' agency over their transformation shrank, the drag professors were featured more, often manifesting in artificial catfights over who had the most wins (Pandora Boxx increasingly mentions this, likely in response to her lack of challenge wins on season two of *Drag Race*), stealing wigs or heels from each other (most often Raven and Jujubee, who are close friends), or reading the other contestants and their professors for being less fabulous than their own duo.

There is more at stake in *Drag U*, however, when discussing the show in relation to queer history and politics. To elucidate my point, I focus specifically on the third episode of season two, "Lesbians Gone Wild," where three butch lesbians are brought to the show to get help "finding" their inner woman, and from the start of the episode it is clear that their butchness is not an acceptable form of gender presentation for these "biological women."[5] For example, in the opening scene of the episode, as RuPaul introduces the contestants to the competition, butch is included in a list of bad words that lesbians are called alongside "lesbo" and "Sir Lick-a-lot," but he still names the contestants as each "one of his girls" despite being butch. In the hallowed halls of Drag U, female masculinities are not an acceptable self-presentation.[6] The winner of this episode, AJ, receives the most attention and screen time, and the entirety of her story arc revolves around her large breasts, which she has spent years concealing. The focus of the show is slyly previewed by the title of the episode, which is a riff on the popular porn series *Girls Gone Wild*, which seeks to get young, "hot" women to show their breasts to a camera for inclusion in a montage of nudity for the objectifying gaze of the straight male audience it presumes and targets. RuPaul and Raven, AJ's professor, focus intently on convincing AJ to show her cleavage at Draguation in a low-cut, feminine dress. This episode even stages a reunion with AJ's estranged mother that centers entirely on her breasts and previous lack of femininity without providing any additional context or reason for their estrangement. When AJ speaks with her mother from the runway, she says, "You've been waiting for me to be a girl," to which her mom replies, "I love you and I've been waiting thirty years to see you in a dress." After AJ wins, there is a cut scene where her mother is shown tearfully saying, "She's a beautiful person inside now, and she showed it."[7] AJ's entire personality and butch history are erased, and her personality, family, and self-esteem are literally tied to her breasts and the makeover which reveals them, implying that she can only be beautiful inside once her breasts are revealed to the outside world as a marker of proper femininity.

Most of the humor in *Drag U* and *Drag Race* is conceived of as being campy: camp is, after all, regularly considered the purview of drag queens and fay gays. Generally speaking, camp is a mode of (mostly) queer humor that uses parody, star worship, overacting, and melodramatic emotion to send up, or to borrow from RuPaul, take the piss out of the object being camped. This object is usually a celebrity, gender norm, and/or political situation that affects queer lives and communities.[8] Though the object being camped is not normally read as being mocked more than played with and ribbed, tongue firmly in cheek, all too often the privilege, agendas, and politics of the performer can seep into the camping, and tip it into the realm of mockery and ridicule. In "Deaths of Camp," Flinn examines gay male camp which is acted out through the visual send-up of the female form, known as body camp. It is the camp genre that *Drag U* engages in most extensively, and which *Drag Race* also regularly deploys in its challenges. One example is the season four mini challenge requiring the queens to don an exaggerated breast plate and participate in a wet t-shirt contest for a crowd of hooting men, once again camping the objectification of women often associated with collegiate life and invoking the *Girls Gone Wild* series.[9] According to Flinn, the moment when the camped object becomes the butt of a cruel joke rather than a harmlessly satirized object is a loving assassination, a term she draws from Leo Bersani's discussion (and condemnation) of effeminate gay male camp.[10] *Drag U* engages in serial loving assassination by partaking in this particular form of body camp: it is not just women who are targeted, but their bodies are made to stand in for a material representation of their inner struggles and conflicts that the show tries to "fix" by bringing out their "inner divas" through "the miracle of drag." I do believe that there is a real desire on the part of the professors to help the women who come on *Drag U*, which is why I have chosen not to remove "loving" from the term, but that does not mean that the resulting television show is kind to the contestants. For Flinn, loving assassination often goes hand in hand with body camp, which "focuses attention on the ways in which this particular body, with its 'certain type of femininity,' can be articulated and 'assassinated' at the same time."[11] In turning the contestants into caricatures of a caricature and a copy without an original, attention is spectacularly cathected onto every nuance of the woman's body, simultaneously bringing it into definition and destroying it through the bizarre copy of their professors that they are turned into. For example, in being turned into a faux drag queen, the body camp of RuPaul and the professors is discursively forced onto AJ and her breasts, overplaying them until they are the only part of her which matters. Rather than the piss being taken out of feminine ideals of beauty, *Drag U's* camp takes the life out of AJ in the name of promoting RuPaul's media empire through a reinscription and grotesque inflation of societal beauty standards.

There are many other examples in *Drag U* of bodies being spectacularly emphasized and defined as a problem, which must be fixed through horribly offensive products or transformations that force women's bodies to conform to normative beauty standards. In the episode "Dangerous Curves," large women are shamed for not being happy about their size, but then are put in loose-fitting, body-obscuring, caftan-like garments that hide their curves even as they are supposedly being held up as beautiful.[12] In the series' final episode, "Time to Grow Up," women who still "dress like girls" are told to grow up and act like proper women, including a lady lesson where the contestants have their bodies re-envisioned as "properly" shaped by a plastic surgeon who designed body pads for breasts, hips, and butts based on what women look for from his surgical practice.[13] In bringing in a plastic surgeon as a guest "expert," the show closes its run only one metaphorical step from surgery based shows like *The Swan*, which literally (rather than discursively) takes a knife to women's bodies, this closeness upping the stakes of cutting camp "humor" significantly. Body camp exaggerates the body-object it targets to the point of gross exaggeration to generate its discursive messages, and at the end of each episode the contestants are left a carnivalesque grotesquerie, no matter how playful and joyous the show makes itself out to be.[14]

Body camp is much more than just parody which sends up norms or conventions. For Flinn,

> it seeks out "deadly" obvious conventions, ones that have become so clichéd and shelfworn as to become visible, if not risible [...]. Camp adores cliché, surface, image. With its emphasis on textures, appearances, materials, and bodies,

camp poses a challenge to depth models [...] of identity (repudiating the belief that external signs of one's appearance "express" inner truths, a stable, "real" self).[15]

The aggressive action of putting the worst clichés of drag onto the female contestants already represented as embodying misogynist clichés of femininity guarantees that by the end of each episode, nothing remains of the depth of character that their individual story is meant to convey. The makeovers follow a formula which inevitably brings all the contestants to a place of resolution, where the woman who best embodies this assassinatory transformation is rewarded by being judged the top "draguate."[16] In erasing the women's individual subjectivities, the body camp of *Drag U* becomes less about the women themselves, and more about the drag queens making them over, and, ultimately, RuPaul's media empire.

Camp's loving assassination takes over the camped person's representation and embodiment while leaving her feeling like she is being loved. This allows for a reading of *Drag U* and *Drag Race* which does not discount the happiness that the contestants seem to feel about their makeover at the end of the show while also critiquing its politics and interventions in queer history. When you are smirked at, if you don't get the joke behind the smirk, it can simultaneously be interpreted as acceptance even though you're the butt of the joke.[17] Furthermore, Flinn reminds us that just because the camper may assert a "willed, smirking control over the object being camped," this sense of power is not often reflected in the camper's actual socio-political status: many queers do not enjoy a lot of social power, though of course some have access to the privilege that comes with whiteness and economic wealth.[18] The point is to elucidate how having the contingent and momentary power to ridicule someone with less privilege than you allows for a "displacing of the social, psychic, and historical anxiety of its subject's disempowerment onto the objects and icons othered."[19] The drag queens smirking at the women of *Drag U* themselves occupy a place of compromised power, which manifests in *Drag U* and *Drag Race* through an attention to contemporary political causes such as the inability of LGBTQ people to marry, serve in the military, or legally and legislatively access these and other civil rights.[20] In assassinating the contestant's bodies in the name of "charity," however, RuPaul and the drag professors displace their own sociopolitical disempowerment onto their "pupils" by leaving them the caricature of femininity that has historically been read onto gay male bodies and ignoring the misogyny of this transference. According to queer scholar Jasbir Puar, who has, following Lisa

Duggan, contributed to discussions of homonormativity I engage with in the second half of this essay, "Violence, especially of the liberal varieties, is often most easily perpetrated in the spaces and places where its possibility is unequivocally denounced."[21] The loving assassinations that *Drag Race* and *Drag U* commit are so regularly couched in notions of charity, selfless help, the safety of queer communities and family structures, and progressive liberal causes that they protect themselves from criticism as they are committed. The queens are presented as humble personal and social crusaders of equality and love, which sets up the assumption that they obviously could not be committing any kind of cruelty against others in the same way that assimilationist gay activists protect themselves against accusations of racism, transphobia, misogyny, and classism.

The politics of ignoring women's embodied and lived experiences on *Drag Race* also encompass transwomen's bodies, both on the show and in its political engagement with trans politics outside of the show. In the season six episode "Shade: The Rusical," the mini-challenge involved the contestants seeing a close up photo of a female celebrity or former Drag Race competitor and holding up a sign to guess if the photo is of a "female" or a "she-male" and guessing if they are looking at a "biological woman" (said in the same tone of voice as used in the *Drag U* credits) or "psychological woman," an indirect reference to a runway quip by Raven in season two (which also references problematic biological determinist notions of trans identity). The segment was widely criticized as being transphobic, adding to a long history of RuPaul's problematic opinions about trans identities.[22] Several weeks after the show aired and the internet was alive with open criticism of the segment's transphobia, increased critiques of the weekly "she-mail" segment of the show, and RuPaul's complicated history with transpeople, the producers issues a non-apology, stating that "we delight in celebrating every color in the LGBT rainbow [...]. When it comes to the movement of our trans sisters and trans brothers, we are newly sensitized and more committed than ever to help spread love, acceptance and understanding."[23] The show has also not yet committed to any substantive changes, such as pulling the "she-mail" segment or removing the offensive mini-challenge from future iterations of the episode.

Former transwomen *Drag Race* contestants Carmen Carrera and Monica Beverly Hillz both spoke out regarding the transphobia of the segment, acknowledging the important role RuPaul has played in their lives, but condemning the use of words like "she-male," "tranny," and "ladyboy."[24] It is worth noting that RuPaul has songs titled "Ladyboy" and "Tranny Chaser" (in which the chasers in question are seeking to hook up with drag queens, not transwomen, further muddling the offensive connotations of the term). Combined with RuPaul's publicly stated distaste for gay celebrities like Lance Bass who apologized for using the term "tranny" and other instances of insensitivity to transpeople's experiences, Hillz's and Carrera's statements are quite generous. According to Hillz, "After my experience on the show, I would say that, to me, the use of the words 'she-male,' 'ladyboy' and 'tranny' are not cute at all [...]. Maybe some things need to be changed about the show, because it's not just a drag show anymore. We have beautiful transgender cast mates paving the way for all transgender showgirls."[25] This most recent instance of egregious transphobia and misogyny on the show demonstrate how the cultural juggernaut that is *Drag Race* continues to carry out its assassinations in the name of "campy" drag humor, and that it has reached a point where RuPaul can openly avoid apologizing or taking responsibility for the hurt his show causes regardless of his personal opinions or politics. Just as Carmen Carrera ended her Facebook post condemning the show with "#shehasspoken," so Queen Ru has decreed her position will likely not change any time soon.

In *Drag U*, the camp performer's attachment to junking women's bodies and the often misogynist conceptions of femininity that are read onto them makes Drag U a site of extremely sadistic camp. The attachment here is one of reproducing stereotypes of femininity through constantly reproducing and (re)appropriating them, which also serve as gateways to playing with stereotypes of race, class, age, obesity, large breasts, surgical procedures, and decaying and sick bodies (among others). Flinn reminds us that the exaggeration and grotesqueification of female bodies happens just as much in mainstream culture as it does in camp performances, which "illuminates the mutual interdependency and heterogeneity of these cultural areas."[26]

Drag U's loving assassination is carried out through the abjectification of women's bodies by making them pale copies of the show's drag queens' stereotyping of women's bodies and femininity. There is one key difference between the loving assassination of most drag performances and those of *Drag Race* and *Drag U* though: these moments occur on television shows that have seen an increasingly large audience of all sexual orientations over the past five years. There is a larger message behind RuPaul's camp destruction: the *Drag Race* empire's loving assassination demonstrates that gay men are ready to take their place in mass society through gender policing, an act of patriarchal oppression which reduces the cultural threat of gay subjectivity.

"If you can't love America...": Race, Nation and Homonormativity

Drag Race and its spinoffs have an interesting engagement with contemporary LGBTQ politics in how they simultaneously promote "universal" values of acceptance and tolerance to mass market television audiences while addressing hot-button LGBTQ rights issues that, given their presence in popular culture, still aren't likely to surprise viewers. RuPaul often states that *Drag Race* and its spinoffs are working to "bring families together," which plays out regularly on *Drag U*, as many episodes feature at least one contestant who has been estranged from her loved ones. On *Drag Race* and *Untucked!*, the queens are often reunited with estranged parents or siblings through video messages, such as the one Alyssa Edwards received from her father asserting that he loves her and is sorry to have abandoned her as a child. The specter of the family and its queer surrogates also appear during the make-over episode of season four, when Phi Phi O'Hara finds a positive father figure in the straight dad she has to drag out who discusses how he would be fine with his kids turning out queer, unlike Phi Phi's biological father. Gay marriage appears frequently, with the most touching example being Jujubee's partner proposing to her through a video message during an episode of *All Stars Drag Race: Untucked!*. *Drag Race* has also offered RuPaul several chances to tearfully assert how queer people get to choose our own families, and that when one drag queen is in pain, they all suffer and support together. Two high profile examples occurred when Ongina revealed her HIV positive status in season one and when Roxxxy Andrews discussed being abandoned by her mother as a child in season five.[27] *Drag Race* regularly engages with contemporary political campaigns taken on by mainstream gay rights groups such as the Human Rights Campaign (HRC), Egale Canada, and the Gay and Lesbian Alliance Against Defamation (GLAAD), giving the show an air of social relevancy without presenting any issues that would appear overtly radical. Examples of this include: the season one episode where the queens shoot promotions for the Mac Viva-Glam campaign, which donates all its proceeds to HIV/AIDS research; a second season episode requiring the queens to create a wedding dress which facilitated backstage discussions about gay marriage; the season three episode where contestants filmed public service announcements for American troops overseas, telling them how much they appreciate the freedom to be gay that the military provides; the season four episode "Frock the Vote," featuring gay sex columnist and marriage advocate Dan Savage as a guest judge, which required the queens to create false political platforms and participate in a political debate meant to encourage LGBTQ people to become politically active voters; and, season five's make-over challenge where the final five queens helped gay veterans become drag queens and express themselves the way they couldn't under the recently repealed "don't ask don't tell" policy.[28]

In its own current-yet-conservative engagement with politics, *Drag Race* is able to espouse a supposedly universal politically correct liberal progress narrative for all queer people, while also pandering to post–9/11 over-zealous American patriotism. These shows use their violent camp to operate as part of the increasing move towards homonormative gay politics which promote "universal" gay equalities at the expense of the concerns of women, many queers of color, bisexuals, transpeople, and working class queers. The term "homonormativity" comes from Lisa Duggan's examination of queer politics under neoliberal capital in *The Twilight of Equality?* She describes homonormativity as "a politics that does not contest dominant heteronormative assumptions and institutions, but upholds and sustains them, while promising the possibility of a demobilized gay constituency and a privatized, depoliticized gay culture anchored in domesticity and consumption." It is produced through "a double-voiced address to an imagined gay public, on the one hand, and to the national mainstream constructed by neoliberalism on the other" and "works to bring the desired public into political salience as a perceived mainstream, primarily through a rhetorical remapping of public/private boundaries designed to shrink gay public spheres, and redefine gay equality [...] as access to the institutions of domestic privacy, the 'free' market, and patriotism."[29] Through its "edgy" yet liberal mainstream politics, *Drag Race* promotes the false universals of patriotism, free market economics, and the idea that gays and lesbians are "just like everyone else" in wanting a domestic, state-sanctioned, neoliberal life.[30] Through this politics, advanced by the loving assassination of the show's sadistic camp, *Drag Race* simultaneously assures queer people that they can take part in the American Dream regardless of their actual material ability to do so (if RuPaul, a black drag queen from humble beginnings can in a dress and heels, so can you!) and assures straight viewers that even drag queens are people who want the same things as them, rather than being a radical threat.

An example of this sanitization comes in season three's "Life, Liberty & the Pursuit of Style," where the queens film messages to overseas troops thanking them for giving the queens the freedom to be themselves in a typical narrative of American patriotism. Alexis Mateo, a Puerto Rican queen who has emigrated to Florida, wins the challenge based on a hilariously campy message asking the troops to come home safely and creating a runway gown out of the uniform jacket of a former lover of hers who is now deployed overseas. Yara Sofia, who at the time sill lived in Puerto Rico, is critiqued for her thick accent and traditional Puerto Rican dress on the runway, and must lip sync for her life to a song in Spanish, chosen to show off America's diversity. In the nature of homonormative patriotism, neither Yara nor her opponent, Carmen Carrera, are sent home: in RuPaul's words, "for the first time in Drag Race history, no one is going home tonight. This is the land of opportunity, and I've decided you both deserve to stay and fight another day. Now remember, if you can't love America, how in the hell are you gonna love somebody else?"[31] The last part of this quote is a paraphrase of RuPaul's usual episode ender, "If you can't love yourself, how in the hell are you gonna love somebody else?" This episode expands the liberal individualist emphasis of reality TV competition and the narcissistic self-love it promotes to also require a love of the nation. For Puar, the love of nation by queer subjects, so regularly not returned by the nation, is an important part of homonationalist politics and rhetoric. Accordingly, "unrequited [national] love keeps multicultural (and also homonormative) subjects in the folds of nationalism, while xenophobic and homophobic ideologies and policies fester."[32] In positioning the queens, queer subjects, and Puerto Ricans as subjects who love the American state which gave a poor black kid from California the chance to be Supermodel of the World, this episode washes away America's racist and neo-colonialist policies and attitudes towards Puerto Rico, as well as more general concerns about the show's racism. One must love the nation to love others, making this homonormative stance a pre-requisite stance for the right to love who you please, neatly tying the show's individualistic appeals for marriage equality and other rights-based queer discourses to post–9/11 patriotic discourses, assuring the watching public that queers are just as attached to the unquestioned social discourse of American patriotism as everyone else.

In this episode, queer (self) love is based on a love of America and its neoliberal, colonialist capitalism, and an assurance to the straight watcher at home that gays, and even Puerto Rican gays, love American just as much as they do. This is most obviously demonstrated through rewarding the Puerto Rican queen who has chosen to emigrate to the continent with a challenge win while punishing the Puerto Rican nationalist in her traditional garb. Alexis' story was presented in such a way as to embody RuPaul's modified statement about loving the nation as loving oneself. Alexis' inspiration for her PSA was a former relationship with an American soldier which ended when he was deployed overseas. Alexis implores American soldiers to come home safely in her PSA, turning her own plea for her love's safe return into a call for all soldiers to return to the nation they share her love for. Alexis turned her lover's uniform jacket, one of his last gifts to her, into a runway gown, praised by the judges for its patriotic glamour. Through loving a soldier and emigrating to the mainland, Alexis has also come to love America, allowing her to find peace with her former relationship and love herself more through it, the final conclusion of her emotional arc in this episode. Yara, meanwhile, is punished for performing the "wacky Latina" routine which she had previously been lauded for, and the judges were lukewarm, at best, about her choice to walk the runways in a traditional Puerto Rican dancing costume, suggesting that Yara's Puerto Rican patriotism was incompatible with Alexis' assimilated Americana. In other challenges, it was apparently acceptable to laugh at Yara for her overplayed otherness, but when the political stakes become tying the show to homonationalist patriotism, she must be punished for not fitting in with RuPaul's progress narrative; a narrative based on her own position as an exceptional black subject "making it" in America, just like other famous people of color who provide the exception to the rule of systemic poverty, racism, and classism which rules the lives of far too many people of color in the U.S.[33] During the lip sync to Toni Basil's "Hey Mickey" in Spanish, the editing focuses almost exclusively on Carmen Carrera as she slinks around the stage, and approaches the judges' bench to kiss guest judge Johnny Weir. This suggests that Yara is losing the lip sync as she dances on stage in a Puerto Rican flag jumpsuit hidden under her dress and waving a Puerto Rican flag. RuPaul ends up saving them both, but these editorial choices reframe the double-safe as a paternalistic gesture of multicultural acceptance and patriotic grace which does little to undercut the ugly, neo-colonialist, and xenophobic discourses perpetrated in the name of the pursuit of life, liberty, and assimilation.

Part of the larger project of homonormative politics is rewriting the history of queer activism to fit a civil rights narrative of "things were bad, then we resisted, we were misunderstood, but now we've nearly reached the systemic equality we deserve." This narrative strips queer histories of their radical politics, intersections with struggles for racial equality, and suggests that moments of radicalism are now past, which allows certain queer subjects access to nominal capital and political privilege through embracing the free market and a politics of domesticity and privacy. This political narrative is evident from the inception of the show: in a review of the debut of the first season of *Drag Race*, journalist Alessandra Stanley invokes the history of gay liberation in explaining the import of the show. She writes that,

> "Drag Race" has a message (besides "You better work"). One contestant, Victoria ["Porkchop" Parker], is a middle-aged, plus-size performer [...] who looks like Dame Edna and was most likely chosen more for diversity than looks and as a reminder to complacent viewers about prejudices past. At one point Victoria reminisces about his early days in the 1980s when he was mocked and worse. "I've been shot at," he says sunnily.[34]

I agree that Victoria, season one's only larger and older queen and the first queen ever to sashay away, seems to have been chosen for the show mostly to invoke this progress narrative: in her single appearance she discusses how much better things are for drag queens now, and that because of RuPaul drag queens are seen as more accepted than ever before.[35] RuPaul herself has invoked the history of the Stonewall riots as a way to place drag queens specifically within the progress narrative of gay acceptance, noting in an interview with ETonline:

> The basic fact is we still are a niche audience—even in the gay community there are still people who think drag is the bastard child of the gay movement. When the truth is, it was a queen who threw the first motherf*cking brick—and people forget that sh*t because it's convenient for them to forget sometimes.[36]

On the one hand, RuPaul's narrative actually participates in the redefinition of the Stonewall riots that some queer scholars have undertaken to give credit for the riots to the drag queens and transwomen who fought the police faster, harder, and longer than anyone else. Yet, in the context of the show and its paratexts, RuPaul's comment also places *Drag Race*, its queens, and himself firmly within the narrative of progressive gay inclusion that the show promotes and goes against the radical act of defiance of the queens of Stonewall. Drag isn't a freak show: it's a legitimate part of a movement and can claim an important, even originating, part of that history.

The clearest staking of this historical terrain is made in season two's makeover challenge, "Golden Gals." The top five queens are paired up with older gay men identified by RuPaul as members of early gay liberation struggles, and the queens must make the men over into their drag mothers. One of the older men even discusses his memories of Stonewall and the death of Judy Garland, which is often credited with contributing to the attitude of defiance present in the bar the first night of the riots. The episode is won by Raven and her drag mother, Ms. Golda Lamé, after Raven

literally carries her mother off stage at the end of their lip sync performance when Raven realized that Golda had grown too tired and was worried
she wouldn't make it through the performance.[37] This episode takes the
radical resistance of Stonewall and recodes it as a relic of the past, ready
to be passed on to the politics of *Drag Race* and its queens, now positioned
as (literally) carrying the burden of past activism. Queer history is remade
to service the contemporary political and economic concerns of this mainstream media show as it turns the drag that fought off the police into a
commodity to be consumed by the mainstream which oppresses it.
"Golden Gals" demonstrates how homonormativity requires a revisionist
gay history to be deployed to legitimate itself as the heir to gay liberation
and the next step in a manufactured teleological narrative of progress.

Shantay, Who Stays? Drag Race and Contemporary LGBT Politics

It is important to remember that discussing homonormative politics
in relation to media requires coupling political analysis with the mecha-
nisms of identity and politics that promote these revisionist histories that
we increasingly see in contemporary "gay" media such as *Modern Family*,
Hunting Season, *Looking*, *Glee*, and other shows that focus centrally on
gay issues or feature prominent gay characters. This brings me back to
"Lesbians Gone Wild" and its plethora of examples of gay male misogyny
and its disciplining of butchness and "non-normative" gender and sexuality presentations. RuPaul often describes the contestants of *Drag U* and
Drag Race as being "her girls," a paternalistic stance that authorizes his
media empire's particular sadistic camp and homonormative politics
which require all subjects, queer and straight, to be tamed into "acceptable," and even "normal" identity presentations. On *Drag U* it is imperative
not only to practice cultural misogyny every week, but also to erase queer
histories that do not conform to the teleological progress narrative which
normative LGBT politics desperately seeks to inhabit. In "Lesbians Gone
Wild," butch lesbian histories, aesthetics, community norms, and subjectivities are erased in the race to "draguate" to normalcy for gay male subjects.[38] *Drag U* reproduces societal misogyny through its loving assassination
of straight and queer women for RuPaul's profit. The show projects a new,
cookie-cutter personality onto its contestants predicated on queer subjects
conforming to traditional gender norms that require the disciplining of
transgressive bodies like AJ's, conventional ideals of citizenship such as

becoming an "empowered" individual who eschews community in the name of consumption, and only questioning the forms of power that prohibit gay civil rights. Social misogyny, racism, classism, sizeism, and ageism go unchecked in the LGBT communities *Drag Race* helps build, since addressing them would distract from the myopic politics of gay civil rights. For example, season three of *Drag Race* regularly saw the judges reward queens purveying racial stereotypes in their performances and costumes, allowing them to claim a place of normalcy by engaging in common media practices of being racist and saying it's all in good fun. These instances include: Manila Luzon winning a challenge through a deeply stereotypical impersonation of Asian-American newscaster Connie Chung; Alexis Mateo, Yara Sofia, and Shangela playing racial stereotypes for laughs in stand-up comedy routines, earning Shangela a challenge win; and, Raja's "editorial," critically acclaimed racist runway including her use of a Native American headdress as a patriotic American outfit and her infamous "tribal" look impersonating the worst stereotypes of African indigenous peoples.[39]

These examples position *Drag Race* within the "color blind" politics of HRC and other assimilationist groups by excluding intersections of race and queerness from "legitimate" queer activism.[40] The HRC is an extremely well known pro-gay marriage group which puts monetary and political pressure on governments largely through funding court cases challenging anti-gay laws. Most recently, it was a major player in bringing the challenge against the Defense of Marriage Act (DOMA) before the U.S. Supreme Court, where it was struck down. During the case, the HRC's activism became ubiquitous largely through the circulation of its re-colored logo, a dark red equal sign against a lighter red square backdrop on social media sites such as Facebook. The HRC, however, has a long history of being critiqued as a racist and transphobic organization. For example, in 2007, the HRC supported congress changing the Employee Non-Discrimination Act (ENDA) to remove protections for people being discriminated against because of gender identity.[41] During the fight against DOMA, the HRC was accused of racism and transphobia during its protests in Washington, D.C., which were reported widely within the mainstream media and queer blogosphere. Among the most egregious incidents reported included HRC volunteers and organizers asking trans activists to remove a trans pride flag from its place within view of the podium, which was taken as a suggestion that gay marriage was not a trans issue. The HRC had also asked Jerssay Arredondo of the Queer Undocumented Immigrant Project (QUIP) to speak against DOMA, then asked him to remove any reference to his undocumented status from his speech so as not to "distract" from the implicitly "more important" issue of gay marriage.[42] The HRC was reported to have apologized for the incident in mainstream media outlets, but many queer news sites and blogs suggested that the "apology" was forced, false, and dodged the issues at hand by pinning the blame on the United for Marriage Coalition and saying that they merely wanted only American flags at the event to show their patriotism, and that any wrongdoing was the fault of individual volunteers and not the HRC organizers.[43]

On a larger scale, one of the most telling examples of the rise of racist homonormative politics was the passing of California's Proposition 8 in November 2008. Prop 8 banned gay marriage in the state, although it was struck down as unconstitutional in 2010. In the wake of Prop 8 passing, a narrative became prevalent which blamed black Christian voters for the ballot initiative passing, leading to waves of blatant racism by largely white gay activists, reporters, and bloggers across the United States. The claim that black voters turned out en masse and voted along racial lines to commit an act of extreme homophobia was easily proven false by many mainstream and blog media outlets, such as on the public opinion website Daily Kos, which produces public opinion pieces held to a journalistic standard of research that puts most mainstream press to shame.[44] As queers of all stripes took to the streets to protest Prop 8, more and more reports of white gay activists indiscriminately targeting black people, straight and queer, and even those protesting with them, with language indicative of hate crimes trickled out, including even mainstream media outlets such as the *Huffington Post*.[45] These horrific examples of the virulent nature of the myopic hatred produced through homonormative political investments demonstrate the high stakes queer media faces in choosing what representations it purveys, and brings into sharp relief the responsibility queer scholars and activists have to question the naturalized histories and goals of the mainstream gay rights movement. Without a more critical engagement with the ways different identities are socially enacted by and through hetero- and homonormativities, *Drag Race* and shows like it will be borrowing and slightly modify Duggan's words for a new political slogan: "Welcome to the New [Gay] World Order! Coming soon to a mainstream near you."[46]

Conclusion

It is telling that in season one of *Drag U*, when the judging panel actually gave the women letter grades for each aspect of their performance, these grades were on the backside of a hand-held mirror: the women are subjected to an arbitrary and uncritical valuation of their (lack of) proper femininity that leaves gender norms unquestioned while the judges keep the reflective surface of the show pointed firmly at themselves, marking them as the true subjects of *Drag U*'s murderous camp. In the erasure of the individual contestant's histories and collective queer histories, *Drag U* and *Drag Race* reproduce narratives of heteronormative history through sending its contestants back into the world "empowered" with the goal of getting dates, going back to work, or taking part in any number of the ways that normative history reproduces itself after experiencing the (normalizing) "miracle of drag." The shows' erasure of history is also productive for RuPaul and participating drag queens as they profit monetarily from acting on the show, with many queens experiencing major mainstream success including Willam Belli, Sharon Needles, Shangela, Pandora Boxx, and Latrice Royale. On *Drag U*, the queens are positioned as being entertainers who use their abnormal gender presentation to induct more people into the norm, containing the threat that their drag might entail (and, perhaps, making their own transgression into a grotesquerie for straight consumption by erasing drag's own history of political transgression in favor of boring, normative politics). The mass commodification of drag in RuPaul's TV empire promotes the history of the homophile movements and their call to assimilate rather than agitate as the only queer history worth bringing back through camp practices. In doing so, camp's history of destabilization is reversed, even as RuPaul cites her shows as being part of a trajectory of inclusion that started at Stonewall. *Drag Race* and *Drag U* actively rewrite the past encouraging the "draguation" of queer communities in the present to normalcy, rather than to a different and better future (increasing RuPaul's profit margin all the while).

Notes

1. Mac McClelland, "RuPaul: The King of Queens: How RuPaul became America's sweetheart," *Rolling Stone*, October 4, 2013, http://www.rollingstone.com/movies/news/rupaul-the-king-of-queens-20131004 (accessed January 28, 2014).

2. Caryl Flinn, "The Deaths of Camp," in *Camp: Queer Aesthetics and the Performing Subject: A Reader*, ed. Fabio Cleto (Ann Arbor: University of Michigan Press, 2002), 431–57.

3. Flinn, 439.

4. I would like to assert that despite my critiques in this essay, I am a huge *Drag Race* fan, though I am not a fan of *Drag U*. I find many of the *Drag Race* queens

inspirational, and will assert time and time again that Tammie Brown is the most talented queen to ever walk the runway, that Yara Sofia is an avant-garde goddess, that Ongina is a superhero, that Latrice Royale is a personal role model, that Courtney Act presented the show's first moment of queer theory in her first *Untucked!*, and that Shannel was unfairly edited to look terrible while Chad Michaels was made to look like the natural winner in *All Stars*. All this is to say that my critiques of the *Drag Race* universe come from a borderline obsessive knowledge, a place of love, and the hope for the show to improve and continue doing the thing that it does so well despite its politics: inspire queer and straight folk alike to be better, more fabulous people.

5. I highly encourage my readers to watch the credit sequence of *Drag U* to better understand why I am returning to the phrase "biological women" and putting it in quotation marks. Though I am sure the tone is meant to be funny or ironic, the way RuPaul says these words in the credits and throughout the show comes across as sneering and condescending, demonstrating who the subject of this television show *really* is and putting the contestants in their naturally-less-fabulous place.

6. Though this episode is one of the most egregious examples of gay male misogyny in the *Drag Race* pantheon, it also presents one moment where a contestant troubles the narrative of acceptable femininity that it portrays. Skylar describes herself at the beginning of the show as a "gender terrorist" who is often mistaken for a man due to her pronounced musculature and butch presentation. She has come to Drag U to get in touch with her feminine side and "earn the right to be called a lady," but doesn't seem to completely embody the usual narrative of self-improvement that *Drag U* trades in. Skylar never seems to have low self-esteem and articulates an interest in using the show for informed gender experimentation rather than jettisoning her butch appearance and life as detrimental to her happiness. However, as commonly happens on *Drag Race*, *Drag U*, and other reality TV shows, when a participant doesn't present in the narrative the show is constructing, she receives less treatment on the show than the others: Skylar receives the least screen time and neither Ru nor the judges seems all that impressed by her, her story, or her transformation. *RuPaul's Drag U*, "Lesbians Gone Wild," Logo TV, July 11, 2011.

7. "Lesbians Gone Wild."

8. For more definitions of camp, see Susan Sontag, "Notes on 'Camp,'" 53–65; Jack Babuscio, "The Cinema of Camp (AKA Camp and the Gay Sensibility)," 117–35; and Andrew Ross, "Uses of Camp," 308–29; in *Camp: Queer Aesthetics and the Performing Subject: A Reader*, ed. Fabio Cleto (Ann Arbor: University of Michigan Press, 2002). Also see Eve Kosofsky Sedgwick, "Some Binarisms (II)," in *Epistemology of the Closet* (Berkeley: University of California Press, 2008), 131–81.

9. *RuPaul's Drag Race*, "Float Your Boat," Logo TV, March 5, 2012.

10. For more, see Leo Bersani's influential and deeply problematic argument, see "Is the Rectum a Grave?," *October* 43 (Winter 1987): 187–222.

11. Flinn, 453.

12. *RuPaul's Drag U*, "Dangerous Curves," Logo TV, July 30, 2012.

13. *RuPaul's Drag U*, "Time to Grow Up," Logo TV, August 6, 2012.

14. Flinn uses the terms grotesque and carnivalesque as outlined by Mikhail

Bakhtin, primarily in relation to camp's loving assassination of women's fat and/or aged bodies, which are two types of female bodies that the themed episodes of *Drag U* have engaged with among many others. Thus I see the terms and Flinn's argument as being more broadly applicable to this show, and to reality TV makeover shows in general.

15. Flinn, 440.

16. There have, of course, been a few sporadic examples of women who don't seem happy with their makeover, or whose troubles have not been resolved, or who defy the normative scripts of the show as much as its heavy editing and doctoring will allow. These women, however, never win the competition and often receive the least amount of screen time, a disciplinary post-production practice which serves to at least partially contain their individuality and transgression.

17. It is also important to mention why I specifically avoid making value judgments of the actual contestants: I choose to believe that many do actually find a measure of happiness and value in their *Drag U* experience and make-over. The great analytical utility of loving assassination is that while it points to the sly motives and representations created by the camper, the inclusion of love also allows for the camp to be free of these negative associations. In analyzing these TV shows, I discuss the way the contestants are portrayed through editing, discursive framing, etc. without ascribing this representation to the lived experience of the women being portrayed. It is important to remember that camp often walks a fine line between its love and assassination, and that an analysis of it points firmly to the camper and his choices, not the person he camps.

18. Flinn, 442.

19. Flinn, 442.

20. *Drag Race* has had episodes dedicated specifically to themes such as the repeal of Don't Ask Don't Tell and gay political involvement, and regularly engages in discourses about teen bullying, suicide, marriage rights, etc. through discussions between contestants who have personal connections to these issues.

21. Jasbir Puar, *Terrorist Assemblages: Homonationalism in Queer Times* (Durham: Duke University Press, 2007), 24.

22. *RuPaul's Drag Race*, "Shade: The Rusical," Logo TV, March 17, 2014. For more on RuPaul's problematic comments and history with transpeople, see Parker Marie Molloy, "Logo, *RuPaul's Drag Race* Respond to Antitrans Slurs," Advocatewww, March 29, 2014, http://www.advocate.com/politics/transgender/2014/03/29/logo-rupauls-drag-race-respond-antitrans-slurs (accessed April 6, 2014).

23. Molloy.

24. James Nichols, "Carmen Carrera and Monica Beverly Hillz Address 'Drag Race' Transphobia Allegations," Huffingtonpostwww, April 1, 2014, http://www.huffingtonpost.com/2014/04/01/drag-race-transphobia_n_5072399.html (accessed April 6, 2014).

25. Nichols.

26. Flinn, 448.

27. *RuPaul's Drag Race: Untucked!*, "Can I Get an Amen?" Logo TV, March 4, 2013; *RuPaul's Drag Race*, "Dads I'd Like to Frock," Logo TV, April 2, 2012; *All Stars RuPaul's Drag Race: Untucked!*, "All Star Girl Groups," Logo TV, November 12, 2012;

RuPaul's Drag Race "Mac Viva-Glam Challenge," Logo TV, February 23, 2009; *RuPaul's Drag Race,* "RuPaul Roast," Logo TV, March 11, 2013. Another form of drag kinship regularly explored by the show is the relationships queens have to their drag mothers, older drag queens who mentor and train younger ones, and drag performance communities that they are part of, such as Alaska and Sharon Needles' participation in the Haus of Haunt in Pittsburgh.

28. *RuPaul's Drag Race,* "Mac Viva-Glam Challenge" and "Here Comes the Bride," Logo TV, March 8, 2010; *RuPaul's Drag Race,* "Life, Liberty & the Pursuit of Style," Logo TV, March 14, 2011; *RuPaul's Drag Race,* "Frock the Vote!" Logo TV, March 26, 2012; *RuPaul's Drag Race,* "Super Troopers," Logo TV, Apr. 8, 2013.

29. Lisa Duggan, *The Twilight of Equality? Neoliberalism, Cultural Politics, and the Attack on Democracy* (Boston: Beacon Press, 2003), 50–1.

30. I do wish to note that homonormative politics are often posited as disproportionately benefitting white gay men, and sometimes white lesbians, usually of the middle or upper class. Obviously *Drag Race* and RuPaul present a complication of this, as Ru herself is African American and has built much of his career around presenting himself in public as a woman. It is only with the advent of *Drag Race* that he has begun appearing as a man regularly in public forums, reminding us that for all her supermodel glamour, Ru is still a man, and thus far more normal than she presented in her younger, more radical pre–"Supermodel" days. Ru is also an African American drag queen, simultaneously marking her as minoritized socially, but part of a racial group with a long tradition of drag. Ru draws on this history to gain legitimacy on the show through the invocation of drag queen lingo that is largely drawn from black drag communities or black culture more broadly. She takes a position of authority in the drag world through this invocation, yet deracializes and normativizes these expressions by simultaneously spreading awareness of black drag cultures, yet invites contestants and viewers to appropriate them through hashtags, social media posts, and idol worship. Like neoliberal politics generally, institutions that generally privilege whiteness, male privilege, and capital accumulation are sometimes accessed by queers, people of color, and women, though more often then not these people are exceptions to the rule that are then held up as examples of why there is no systemic problem for non-white, poor, etc. activists to complain about. RuPaul, Oprah Winfrey, Beyoncé, Colin Powell, Condoleezza Rice, Sonia Sotomayor, and Barack Obama are all excellent examples of this phenomenon. *Drag Race,* however, has its own internal racial politics that I don't have the space to exhaustively explore in this essay, where African American and white queens do very well, whereas the queens from Puerto Rico are regularly discussed in relation to their island home (whether they have moved to the mainland U.S. or not), and regularly face disciplining around their thicker accents and stereotypes such as being the "fiery" Latina/o. Season three's Yara Sofia and Alexis Mateo are excellent examples of the show's racial politics. Alexis, who advanced to the final three, is a naturalized Puerto Rican living in the continental U.S., regularly received praise for her fluent English, and won several challenges, whereas Yara only did well when embracing and overperforming a wild, barely intelligible Latina stereotype. Yara only won one fashion-based challenge in season three, whereas Alexis clocked several wins, largely in performance-based challenges. The show has also seen a decrease in

queens of color, and especially Puerto Ricans as it has continued, with seasons five and six only featuring one Puerto Rican queen each. season five's Lineysha Sparx was called one of the queens to beat early in the season due to her fashion and beauty, but went home early in the season when her lack of pop culture knowledge and thick accent led to her demise in the popular Snatch Game challenge. In the end, homonormative politics often promote white, heterocentric, misogynistic, class-based politics and policies while allowing some queers and people of color to access their privilege primarily to "prove" that these politics are not everything they are in the first place. *RuPaul's Drag Race*, "The Snatch Game," Logo TV, February 25, 2013.

31. "Life, Liberty & the Pursuit of Style." Another layer of meaning in this episode that is important is the way that Yara, who had been consistently praised for playing the "wacky" Latina character, was then criticized for it in this episode. It is telling that in the challenge about American patriotism and militarism, the queens from a colonial territory won the challenge and were in the bottom two: Alexis for embracing American patriotism and being constructed as the exception-to-the-rule of racialized subjects who embrace the American dream, vs. Yara who was disciplined for her Puerto Rican traditional costume and performing a subject she was previously encouraged to embrace.

32. Puar, 26.

33. We see this exceptionalism, a subject Puar discusses at length in *Terrorist Assemblages* in relation to sexuality, become a narrative the show has its contestants take up. Examples of this include: season one winner Bebe Zahara Benet and her ability to move to America from Cameroon and become the first next drag superstar; Shangela, who is regularly praised for her explicit southern roots and the racially inflected humour it influences that wins a comedy challenge, and; Latrice Royale, who went to prison, then rebuilt her life upon gaining freedom to become the soul-singing motherly drag queen we've all come to love. All these queens are presented as turning their socially racialized characteristics into winning traits, following in Ru's "everyone is celebrated in America" narrative as "one of her girls."

34. Alessandra Stanley, "They Float Like the Clouds on Air Do, They Enjoy," *New York Times*, February 2, 2009.

35. *RuPaul's Drag Race*, "Drag on a Dime," Logo TV, Feb. 2, 2009.

36. Jarett Wieselman, "RuPaul Talks 'Drag Race' Hits—and Misses," *ETonline*, September 23, 2013, http://www.etonline.com/tv/138718_RuPaul_Lost_Drag_Race_Season_One_Interview/ (accessed January 28, 2014).

37. *RuPaul's Drag Race*, "Golden Gals," Logo TV, March 29, 2010.

38. LGBT politics are often framed as asking for "normally" feminine lesbians to also be accepted into society's fold as well, but "Lesbians Gone Wild" shows that *Drag U* doesn't even manage to make this case, so I use the term "gay male" here rather than "gay and lesbian" and certainly not "queer."

39. *RuPaul's Drag Race*, "QNN News," Logo TV, Feb. 14, 2011; *RuPaul's Drag Race*, "Ru Ha Ha," Logo TV, March 7, 2011; *RuPaul's Drag Race*, "Life, Liberty & the Pursuit of Style," Logo TV, March 14, 2011; *RuPaul's Drag Race*, "The Snatch Game," Logo TV, Feb. 21, 2011.

40. Even the progression of winners on the shows points to an attention to homonormative progress narratives and the need for gay people to be accepted by

straights based on presenting the queer community as calmingly normal. Though the first two winners, Bebe Zahara Benet and Tyra Sanchez, are African American, and they both embody a pageant-style, glamourous drag that recreates normative feminine beauty standards. Tellingly, the more androgynous, genderqueer style of Nina Flowers was unable to earn the crown in season one, as it might have set a completely different tone for the show's gender politics moving forward into its future seasons. Season three's Raja regularly embraced cultural appropriation and racism in the name of being "editorial," linking her to problematic and beloved supermodels like Tyra Banks (who Raja discussed working with several times and impersonated in the Snatch Game challenge), and using racist fashion to reach mainstream fame. Sharon Needles, season four's victor, was touted as an avant-garde hero-freak, but was only able to win once the show had established itself and by Sharon appealing to narratives like that of the "It Gets Better" campaign which popularized discussions of how bullied kids need to be reached out to in ways that would prevent queer teen suicide. (Importantly, Sharon also won the crucial final-four challenge which was based entirely on glamour and serving life-like drag looks, demonstrating that for all her edge, Sharon was capable of being a glamourous queen too.) After the show aired, it came to light that Sharon Needles has faced criticism over her use of racial slurs and anti–Semitic imagery in her performances and in interactions with fans that has also complicated her status as victor. Interestingly, in "Frock the Vote," sponsor Absolut Vodka's image czar and guest judge, Jeffrey Moran, expressed doubts about Sharon's ability to be a public spokesperson for his brand (and Ru's), then this season became the first to include audience feedback on which of the final three should win. Fans responded in droves cheering for Sharon, and she was crowned, though her win was quickly followed by *RuPaul's Drag Race: All Stars* where season four's perceived runner up and glamourous, "perfect," Cher-impersonator Chad Michaels easily waltzed to the crown, allowing for two reigning queens for most of the year leading up to season five of *Drag Race*. Finally, in season five, Jinkx Monsoon became the first campy queen crowned, but also plied a story about being bullied to elicit sympathy and become so beloved by audiences as to gain wide-ranging fame since the show, including Off-Broadway shows and a high profile performance at the GLAAD Awards for positive representations in the media. All the winners of the show have been presented as palatable in the mainstream in various ways, ensuring that Ru's champions are good ambassadors of homonormative politics. Even the show's top three has seen a whitening as the series has progressed, both in queens who self-identity as a person of color or mixed race, and (especially) in seeing less of the queens branded by the show as "Puerto Rican," "Asian," "ghetto," or somehow foreign (like Bebe, who was regularly greeted on the show by Ru shouting "Camarooooooooooon!"). Season one had three queens of colour in the top (though Rebecca was branded as a fishy queen rather than mixed-race), season two saw two queens of colour, season three back to three (though none African American), then two consecutive years of white queens or queens whose histories as mixed or people of colour was not foregrounded. Even *All Stars* had three white queens and the Laotian JuJubee in the final episode, demonstrating just how white is has become in which queens it lauds the most. GLAAD, "Video: Jinkx Monsoon Performs Sondheim at the #glaadawards," glaad.org, last modified May

14, 2013, http://www.glaad.org/blog/video-jinkx-monsoon-performs-sondheim-glaadawards (accessed January 28, 2014).

41. Karlee Johnson, "Equality for Some: A Critique of the Human Rights Campaign," *Daily Sundial*, October 10, 2011, http://sundial.csun.edu/2011/10/equality-for-some-a-critique-of-the-human-rights-campaign/ (Accessed February 22, 2014).

42. Maribel Hermosillo, "Human Rights Campaign Fails to Advocate For Minorities," *PolicyMic*, March 29, 2013, http://www.policymic.com/articles/31563/human-rights-campaign-fails-to-advocate-for-minorities/424007 (accessed February 22, 2014).

43. Meredith Bennett-Smith, "Human Rights Campaign Apologizes for Censoring Undocumented, Trans Activists at Marriage Protests," *Huffington Post*, April 2, 2013, http://www.huffingtonpost.com/2013/04/02/human-rights-campaign-apologizes_n_2994939.html (accessed February 22, 2014). David Badash, "United for Marriage Coalition Apologizes for Mistreatment of Trans and Undocumented Activists—HRC Signs On, Then Denies," *The New Civil Rights Movement*, March 29, 2013, http://thenewcivilrightsmovement.com/united-for-marriage-coalition-apologizes-for-mistreatment-of-trans-and-undocumented-activists-hrc-signs-on-then-denies/politics/2013/03/29/63826#.Uwja816N-4c (accessed February 22, 2014).

44. shanikka, "Facts Belie the Scapegoating of Black People for Proposition 8," *Daily Kos*, November 7, 2008, http://www.dailykos.com/story/2008/11/07/656272/-Facts-Belie-the-Scapegoating-of-Black-People-for-Proposition-8# (accessed February 22, 2014).

45. Pam Spaulding, "The N-Bomb Is Dropped on Black Passersby at Prop 8 Protests," *The Huffington Post*, November 10, 2008, http://www.huffingtonpost.com/pam-spaulding/the-n-bomb-is-dropped-on_b_142363.html (accessed February 22, 2014).

46. Duggan, 66.

Of Women and Queens
Gendered Realities and Re-Education in RuPaul's Drag Empire[1]

CAROLYN CHERNOFF

Drag queens are a girl's best friend.[2] It's another day on the Internet: another blog gets picked up by the *Huffington Post*, another video goes viral, another pop princess gets anointed queen. In this case, it's 6-year-old Joselyn Molina, host of Spanish-language media giant Univision's children's TV show, *Sabado Gigante Kids*. In response to a *MamaPop* blog post arguing drag queens make better role models for girls than Disney princesses,[3] the then-newly-launched digital network Fusion TV brought *RuPaul's Drag Race* Season three runner-up Manila Luzon and Joselyn[4] together for a playdate: coloring on the beach, practicing their catwalks on playground equipment, then shopping, dinner, and a joint performance onstage at a club.

While the video and article both argue that drag queens can be good role models for cisgender girls, but not necessarily the *only* role models, some of the ways in which both article and video circulated reinforce an age-old catfight: cis[5] women vs. drag queens. The link between cis women and drag queens is an extension of the longstanding concept of fag hags, or of cis women's emotional attraction to gay men (especially femmes or queens). Gamson traces mainstream America's public embrace of gay queens to the late 1990s, and further explores the tropes of "consumption gurus and gay best friends" as available reality TV options for gay men as sidekicks, depicted as accessories or otherwise subordinate to cis women.[6] But drag queens are not exactly gay men. And queens in the media are rarely subordinate to anyone. As queens, they quite literally rule.[7] They dominate a portion of the mainstream imagination, and many become household names. Or, as Martin-Malone writes, in the voice of her daughter, "My favorite princess is Ariel, and yours is Cinderella, and Mommy's favorite princess is Sharon Needles."[8]

A queen can be one of many types of princesses. Martin-Malone's argument is not that drag queens are better women than cis women, but that the hyper-feminized vision of global capital known as the Disney princesses are just another misogynistic aspect of contemporary "girl-hood" that promotes dangerous gender stereotypes and norms.[9] Drag queens have become as visible, although perhaps somewhat less sanitized, as America's favorite cartoon royalty.[10] And RuPaul has been the very public face of American drag since the 1990s, a watershed decade in mainstream drag representation and exploitation.[11] America's revered and reviled royalty includes (drag) queens and (Disney) princesses.

These princesses, like Barbie before them, are not "women," but drag queens can be. Regardless of their gender identity, drag queens reveal the labor of gender, or the work in WERK. *RuPaul's Drag Race* shows some of the complexity of gender among queens and cis women, as well as highlighting the camaraderie and relationships that can emerge from pushing back against assumed roles. There are multiple meanings of girl, woman, princess, and queen at play. Some reinforce a gender binary, a sense of competition, and notions of a "natural" gender or body, while others disrupt these fictions. The Fusion TV video mentioned above, the "Drag School of Charm" episode of *RuPaul's Drag Race*,[12] and Lenae's transformation into "the queen she already is," in the words of her son, on the first season of the spin-off show *Drag U*,[13] all play with these competing discourses to reveal the complexity of gender performance.

That is not to suggest that drag necessarily promotes solidarity across gender identities, or that RuPaul's drag empire presents a trans-inclusive intersectional feminist perspective to the mainstream viewing public. Indeed, *Drag Race* is another showing of the longstanding mass media tradition of the freak show.[14] In highlighting seemingly deviant or atypical gender identities from drag queens to girl fighters to celibate mothers and other women at more than arm's length from heteronormative sexual activity, notions of what is typical or "normal" are always present. But I argue that there is at least one unexpected outcome of RuPaul's various media productions, and that it is queering the body more generally for cis women. In asking what it is that queens and girls have in common, we find a sense of gender expectations, inversions, and experiences not readily represented on big and small screens. These are not necessarily positive, of course. Certainly there is no shortage of evidence of discrimination and misogyny within drag and mainstream American culture. Although RuPaul and *Drag Race* have been criticized for their stance on trans representation, *Drag Race* itself does highlight interesting moments of rupture around the stale stereotype that drag queens are a girl's best friend—or rather, boss. The theme song highlights the centrality of competition: "*RuPaul's Drag Race*/May the Best Woman Win." This is a reality show; the genre demands a winner, and many losers. As more than one contestant snarks, and a season five episode takes as its title, the show is not RuPaul's best friend race. This show makes explicit some of the reality TV codes of competition, subterfuge, manipulation—basically, cattiness or the mean girl writ large. At the same time, *Drag Race* sometimes manages to puncture these illusions. The team approach seen in Manila and Joselyn's playdate, the "Drag School of Charm," and the students and faculty at *Drag U* enable a glimpse into some of the ways that girls and queens can collaborate, in camaraderie, not competition.

Overview: Gendered Realities

From their very first seasons, *RuPaul's Drag Race* and its spinoff, *Drag U*, represent gender collaboration across social identity, and notions of learning in a surprisingly nuanced way for a pop culture production, much less the mass-market camp that is RuPaul's stock in trade. The mentorship frame of Manila and Joselyn's "playdate," the "Drag School of Charm" of *Drag Race*'s season one, and the university frame of *Drag U* offer different ways of looking at gendered realities, expectations, and (re)education for cis women, drag queens, and others across the gender spectrum.

In "Drag School of Charm," the queens make over cis women athletes (female professional fighters). This premise of queens teaching women to be girls is taken up and elaborated in the subsequent three seasons of the *Drag Race* spin-off *Drag U*. In a surprising move for "reality" TV, these makeover shows move beyond the gender binary to reveal gender performance as a conscious cultural strategy.[15] The Pygmalion formula enables a closer look at the challenges and successes implicit in performing femininities, and further destabilizes static notions of gender while complicating the assumed relationships among women and queens.

In "Dateless Divas," *Drag U* contestant Lenae receives a sexy makeover after 20 years of single-parent celibacy. Commenting on his mother's transformation, Lenae's adult son says that he wants her to externalize and make legible for others "the queen she already is." Drawing on the registers of African American femininity, the transformed housewife (or "queen for a day"), and drag performance identities, the multiple meanings of "woman" and "queen" in this context point to the many different, yet possibly concurrent ways one can experience both "womanhood" and "queendom."

Drag Race and Drag U problematize gender and femininity for queens and cis women alike. While most queens choose a "mini-me" approach to the makeover challenge, presenting the fighters in each queen's own signature image, Ongina continues to play with gender, taking a more "masculine" role to enhance Jarrett's "femininity." The "mini-me" approach emphasizes the Pygmalion story of transformation, and adds a sense of lineage and connection between the queens and fighters. The gender-play emphasized by Ongina costs her a place on *Drag Race*, but reveals the conscious effort of performance and the fluidity of gender. Even as Ongina is eliminated, RuPaul muses that Ongina "could have won it all," at least in part *because* of her gender bricolage.

The sense of collaboration implicit in makeovers emphasizes a sense of partnership that punctures the stale notions that cis women latch on to drag queens as exotic others, or choose to play sidekick in yet another showing of female abasement or subservience. Makeover challenges both reinforce and trouble the notion that queens are more "authentic" women than cis women, divorcing "femininity" from gender and revealing the labor involved in gender presentation of all sorts. Collaboration around drag and gender reveal a more nuanced take on the performance of genders than the categories of "drag queen" or "cis women" generally signify. This essay interrogates the categories of "women" and "queens," and of multi-gendered collaboration and performance. I argue that an alliance between queens and cis women resonates not only with the experience of social construction of gender, but of the pleasure and pain in performance.

Drag School of Charm: "It's hard to be a girl"

In a video challenge to the first-season competitors, RuPaul announces in a video "She-Mail"[16] that "drag is part of a sisterhood," and that sisters, in the words of the song, will be doing it for themselves. BeBe Zahara Benet chokes, "Oh, oh no!" as she sees five cis women follow RuPaul into the workroom. They are, presumably, part of the new sisterhood. BeBe falls to the floor in horror as RuPaul announces the challenge. Nina Flowers describes the moment afterwards, referring to the cis women as "fierce girls." She goes on to explain that they are "not fierce like drag fierce—fierce like they looked threatening." From the start, notions of "sister" and "fierce" are recontextualized, or taken out of the drag context. But the gendered context of the "Drag School of Charm" is not entirely "natural," even if such a thing were to exist. Close-ups of the women RuPaul introduces as "girl fighters" zoom in on unsmiling faces, tattoos, muscles, and clenched jaws. Drag queens BeBe, Nina, Rebecca Glasscock, Shannel, and Ongina are introduced to the willowy, blonde, white Krav Maga instructor Jarrett; Swee'Pea, a short African American cage fighter with a shaved head, bulky muscles, and many visible tattoos; capoerista and karate instructor Michelle, with long black hair in a ponytail, bronze skin, and a solid frame in layered leotards; tall, white, muscular Mia with a blonde ponytail, who announces "I am boxer" in a heavy Russian accent; and Tempele, another boxer, a petite African American woman with black and navy micro-braids in a ponytail and multiple visible black ink tattoos. The girls are clearly depicted in a way that emphasizes strength, toughness, and a minimized femininity.

The first part of the episode is a contest: queen vs. queen, presided over by the girls. RuPaul announces that drag queens need to keep in shape, so "these girl fighters" will give the queens a "full-force workout." They are girls, and therefore subordinate—but they will oversee a full-force workout and dominate the queens. The power dynamics are fluid. Girl fighters are at the service of the queens as personal trainers, even as they are diminished as "girls," while the queens are positioned as vulnerable, lacking the physical prowess the girl fighters so readily embody. The queens play with representations of physical strength and weakness. Ongina flexes her biceps with resignation, then a tongue-out grin. The girls demonstrate fighting techniques as the queens giggle, blanch in horror, and tentatively throw punches. The physical awkwardness or uncertainty of the queens in fighting poses along with their reluctance or resistance to the challenge emphasizes the athletic discipline the girls bring to their workout. RuPaul tells the queens that this challenge is about being "the last man standing" as Shannel opts out, saying, "I'm nauseous." She lies down on the couch, only to get up and reenter the competition. After all, she says, "I have a lot of integrity, and I am a fighter. Not physically, but mentally." The queens' strength is mental; the girls' strength is physical; and both groups embody atypical demonstrations of what it means to be a fighter. The "last man standing" will be a queen, trained by girls. Throughout this episode we see overlap and distance between the strength, integrity, and discipline that the queens and fighters each need to succeed in their chosen field. We also see contestations and inversions of gendered terms (boy, man, girl, woman, butch, femme, queen, lady) for both queens and girls.

After the physical challenge, Rebecca is the last queen standing, with Shannel in second place. RuPaul tells the queens that the next part of the challenge will be to make each girl fighter "into a real-life female version of yourself, of your drag persona." This is a chance to "reveal the secrets of drag, something every real woman should know." Again, it is unclear what or who a "real woman" is: is it the queens, with their chosen gender performances? The girls, with their (assumed) biology and anatomy? The cross-gender aspect of the contest is clear as the queens whoop and cheer at the makeover challenge, while the girls are shown with stoic faces and crossed arms. The queens are charged with re-imagining the girls as queens, and the next section of the show focuses on each queen's approach to "teaching" their "secrets" to an atypical novice.

The first season cast represents a wide array of drag, moving back and forth between a more "passing" or "real" approach to a more consciously artificial or genderqueer approach: fishy Rebecca, elegant BeBe, and fabulous Vegas diva Shannel might be read as more "real," whereas edgy club kids Ongina and Nina sometimes literally reveal their bag of tricks. Nina often goes without a wig, and Ongina almost exclusively uses headbands or hats in place of hair. Nina's confrontational presentation brings up shades of her namesake, Nina Hagen, as well as Divine, John Water's drag muse. In particular, Ongina almost never uses breast forms, nor does she tuck (hide her penis and testicles from sight). This is a marked contrast from the flawless femme drag RuPaul serves up.

Across the board, the queens' various gender performances play out in their approach to their girls. Rebecca, clearly not there to make friends, yells at Tempele, weary of her complaining about the pain of high heels. Ongina and Jarrett get off to a slow start, disagreeing about Jarrett's hair along with everything else. BeBe seeks to relate to Michelle as a collaborator. "I can represent Africa," says BeBe, "and you should represent the Middle East." This is a particular cultural strategy, part third-world exoticism, Orientalism,[17] and the cultural Other,[18] but also BeBe's claim to fame. Still, Michelle laughs, a short bark of—embarrassment? Unwillingness? In another show of team spirit, Nina and Mia seem to be delighting in their partnership, with Nina at the sewing machine, whipping up battle gear. After all, "none of my clothes is gonna fit on her." At well over 6 feet out of heels, Mia is the tallest contestant on the show. She towers over Nina and the other queens.

Boys, girls, tomboys, and queens—gender and bodies are understood to mix and match in the experiences of both groups of contestants. As the runway competition nears, we learn that this will be the first time Swee'Pea will wear a bra. She says, "I was always a little tomboy" who was "running around with the boys, jumping fence." She distances herself from conventional gender roles, and RuPaul responds in kind, commenting, "you should have been hanging out with boys who wore bras." Swee'Pea discusses her strategy for the competition, drawing off of RuPaul's comments about hanging out with "boys who wear bras," or trying to fit in with the codes of her peer group. Swee'Pea says that she plans to be "as feminine as I can be," which is both about the effort she is presumably willing to expend as well as her own gender limitations. Again, who is the "boy" in the bra, Swee'Pea or Shannel? Swee'Pea also focuses on her plan to "become Shannel," and "to represent what Shannel stands for." Being "feminine" and being "Shannel" are linked, but not exactly the same thing, which seems to be a helpful strategy for "masculine" "tomboy" Swee'Pea. She doesn't have to be a girl or a woman. She can be a queen. Early in the challenge, Shannel and Swee'Pea are filmed practicing postures in the mirror. Shannel elaborates, saying that what they are doing is all about strength, but also "elegance and beauty," as Swee'Pea nods. In a boxer's crouch, hands up guarding her face, Swee'Pea laughs as she acknowledges this is the first time she has ever worn makeup. Shannel describes Swee'Pea matter-of-factly as "the most masculine of the entire group." But none of the girls read "feminine" or "queen" to the queens. Similarities seem hard to find. Addressing visual appearances of masculinity, conventional or otherwise, is a key element not only of drag in general, but this episode of *Drag Race* in particular. In this episode, masculinity and femininity are divorced from male and female bodies, but norms about appropriate gender (or appropriate gender-bending, or gender inversion) still guide the competition.

Nina foregrounds the aspect of transformation, and perhaps the disconnect between gender and drag, saying that the queens "are really transforming them into what we are. These girls, they never wear dresses, they never wear makeup." Distance between girl and queen in some ways is measured in makeup. Michelle asks BeBe if she's really good with makeup, to which BeBe rolls her eyes and says, "Oh girl…." "This is really not my territory," admits Michelle, nervous that BeBe will "pile a lot on." (She will.) This is training for me in a different way, says Michelle, revealing the frame of the competition for the girls: another fight, another physical challenge. But the challenge is not simply physical. It's symbolic, and the symbolic aspect points to other ways the girls and queens react differently to being read as female. For BeBe, the runway walk is about "seducing." She tries to help Michelle connect to the audience as "the hottest thing" and a delighted and knowing object of the male gaze. BeBe asks, "When you walk with your friends, when you're looking cute, how do you walk?" Embarrassed, Michelle laughs, "I—I just be myself." When BeBe asks to see Michelle as herself, of course, it turns out that Michelle's "self" is lacking. We see that some coaching is empathetic, while some is mostly dismissive or negative. The queens are aware they will be judged by the girls' performances, and struggle with the idea of translating their own signature look into another form.

Meanwhile, the girls are learning with various levels of success and comfort. Asked what she has learned from BeBe, Michelle talks about gestures (the half-smile, the chest grab) and a general embodiment of sexiness. She says of her attempts to be more like BeBe, "It looks fake to me. I don't know how to do this." Throughout the competition, Michelle remains at a distance. Not the mysterious, flirtatious distance BeBe uses to charm onlookers, but a remove that signals discomfort. On the other hand, Mia offers to demonstrate in response to RuPaul's question about what she learned from Nina. In her boxing shorts and boots, Mia draws herself upright, gestures from her eyes using her fingers, demonstrating eye contact, as Nina and RuPaul say, "Yes, yes." Then she slowly walks as if in a pool of water, pivoting at the end, and turning back to RuPaul and Nina at the worktable for approval. Mia is portrayed as enjoying the competition, the transformation, and the hard-won knowledge of how to walk in heels. During judging, Mia is asked whether she was scared of the challenge. She replies, "No, because there's some part of me that likes to be girly." For Mia, the artificial "girlyness" of the *Drag Race* mainstage is more accessible than it is to Michelle.

The girls and queens are more and less accessible to one another as well. During one of RuPaul's team visits, Ongina whispers, "She scares me" to RuPaul while she drapes a black and white satin dress on Jarrett. Ongina continues to voice her "fear" of Jarrett, commenting that "when she first walked in, I was like Holy Jesus Mother Christ. She will beat an ass and it might be mine." For all her conscious gender-blending on the show, Ongina's disapproval of Jarrett in some ways reads as connected to Jarrett's girl fighter physique and stance, or Jarrett's own nuanced blend of gender and sex. In the second episode of the season, Ongina was told by the judges that she looked like a boy in a dress, and she comments, "I wanted to elevate that this week. Not so much boy in a dress but drag queen in a dress." But when Jarrett, tentative in heels, asks whether she looks foolish, Ongina assesses, "Manly, but I'll fix it." Here "drag queen" is an ideal type, whereas "boy" and "man" are negative across the gender spectrum, an interesting inversion of gendered value in the contemporary world.

The queens remark on the butchness or manliness of the girls throughout the competition, sometimes with seeming empathy, sometimes with disgust. BeBe coaches Michelle, "You have to take your mind away from being the butch woman." Gender is a state of mind. Some queens see gender or drag as simply a matter of experience. Nina shakes her head and proclaims, "These girls, they never wear heels, so they don't know how to walk in heels." The scenes of the girls in heels are played for laughs, as what is assumed to be "natural" for "girls" is revealed as a drag. It's another physical challenge for the fighters. Here Ongina gently walks hand-in-hand with Jarrett, almost tenderly, whereas Rebecca barks at Tempele, "Don't walk like a man."

The work of gender is salient throughout the competition. "I didn't know it was that hard being a girl," says Tempele, in an interview segment. Onstage, practicing with Rebecca, Tempele sighs, "I feel like such a wuss!" Strength and weakness are highly contextual. Rebecca, as drill sergeant, points to the runway and says, "Do it by yourself, up and down. Do it, just back and forth." Tempele cries, "Oh no!" In these moments, the audience can fear a lack of connection and a sense of mistrust among participants, and yet we do see a "sisterhood," one formed through challenge. We see shots of the duos cuddling, arms around one another, as RuPaul explains the next wrinkle in the competition—the girls learning to lip sync Beyoncé's "Freakum Dress." Michelle says, "I thought it was enough work to just put on a dress, put on frickin' high heels, and walk," much less perform another embodied aspect of femininity. Even the song is gendered, along with the lip sync performance. Ongina comments on the difficulty of the song, and admits that she can't perform that song, "let alone these butch girls, who have probably never even heard of the song before." Ongina heightens the social distance between the queens and the girls. They simply don't *know,* in her estimation, how to do the things drag queens and women somehow know—but more to the point, they won't *learn.*

Differences are embodied, yes, but also social, attitudinal, and cultural, in the sense of an orientation towards the physical world. Rebecca refers to Tempele as "my fighting bull-dog," but fears that "she won't come through, she'll suck," even as the other queens claim Rebecca chose the most "feminine" girl for her partner. Nina says of Mia, seen with earphones listening to Beyoncé, "She really wants to do it. She's so into it. She's excited. And that makes it good to work with her." Swee'Pea says, "I'm an outgoing person, I love to put myself to the test, but this is—I didn't know what I was walking into." Being a queen, like being a girl, is harder than it looks.

Shannel speaks of herself in the third person to Swee'Pea, observing that "Shannel is about representing *eyes* and *glamour* and *diva* and *body* and *strength*, so if you're going out there as my sister, I want you to embody that." Swee'Pea is the "toughest" or "butchest" of the girls, but Shannel appeals to Swee'Pea as a sister, as a fighter, and as a competitor. There's sweetness in their partnership, and in Nina's and Mia's. The other pairs are shown more in direct competition or exasperation. They can't speak the same language. Rebecca doesn't seem to try, preferring to be the drill sergeant, but while BeBe's charge, Michelle, seems reluctant to engage, Ongina seems uncertain about her girl throughout.

Ongina's failure to connect with Jarrett, to empathize with her, is a surprise to the judges and the viewers. People expect that kind of attitude from Rebecca, but in this episode, Rebecca's "Mommie Dearest" approach to Tempele seems to work, resulting in a win for Rebecca, and elimination for Ongina. For Ongina, the previous week's challenge winner, the elimination rests on her lack of connection to Jarrett as well as an aspect of mis-gendering the task at hand. Commenting on the black and white satin pantsuit and floor-length dress of the duo, RuPaul says, "You look like a prom date." Ongina justifies her costuming as part of a "masculine/feminine challenge," where she herself would be "the more masculine one." But it was never a masculine/feminine competition. RuPaul reminds Ongina that the challenge is about transformation, and turning an "ultimate fighter" into her drag persona. After the contestants retreat to the Interior Illusions Lounge, the judges dissect Ongina. They comment on her boyishness, with cis woman judge Merle Ginsberg saying that "Ongina looked more boyish than usual." This was accentuated by the costuming, or as judge Santino Rice comments, "A woman in a pants suit is really great. A drag queen in a pantsuit not tucking is a man." And this is where the contest is lost. If Ongina's flamboyant club kid/genderqueer interpretation of drag was celebrated in earlier episodes (and prompted RuPaul to write the song "Ladyboy" about her) her jarring appearance as a bald, flat-chested queen with a semi-visible penis onstage in satin pants next to the cis woman Jarrett signaled Ongina's limitations to the judges. She goes from *boy in a dress* to *man*. And men are not queens. At the very least, it signals the drag preferred on the show.

In lip syncing for their lives, Ongina and BeBe both address the artificiality of drag, but BeBe brings vulnerability as well. Ongina and BeBe face off to Britney Spears' "Stronger," embodying the episode-wide themes of effort, struggle, and challenge. While Ongina continues to bring her usual level of performance to the elimination stage, BeBe approaches this as a battle. She says if she is eliminated, at least she will go out fighting. BeBe makes her struggle visible. She also removes her wig mid-lip-sync as she sinks to the floor in a posture of defiance in submission. RuPaul plays up the fierceness of the lip sync. Commenting on the "fire" and "hunger" BeBe brought to her lip sync, RuPaul proclaims that BeBe did the impossible in out-shining Ongina. Ongina looks down at the stage as RuPaul intones, "Shantay, you stay." She continues, "Ongina, the first time I saw you, I thought you could walk away with this competition. You know why? Because you're a winner, baby. And I know you'll take that with you wherever you go. Though this breaks my heart to say, Sashay, walk away." And Ongina does.

Drag U: *From Girls to Queens*

In *Drag Race* and its spin-off makeover show, *Drag U*, a playful, destabilized take on gender prevails. But a drag vision of gender as malleable does not mean everyone has equal access to gender flexibility or equal success with their creations, as we see in the "Drag School of Charm." While Rebecca's bitchiness as a partner is in keeping with her fishy queen persona, Ongina's uncharacteristic pessimism and coldness in her relationship with Jarrett threatens her strength as a queen: her gender play and sense of humor. Some of the girls and some of the queens seem to engage in conscious collaboration and negotiation not only of the official challenge, but around understanding their own multiple gender outlaw identities. But even an atypical and fluid gender also intersects with sex, sexuality, race, and class, among other things. Sexuality, race, and class are constant absent presences onscreen.

Unlike *Drag Race*, *Drag U* is specifically focused on helping cis women learn to more successfully negotiate gender under the expert tutelage of a drag queen. RuPaul gives the origin story, recounting how a school was founded "deep in the Lake Titicaca Valley," a school where drag queens would help cis women "unleash their inner diva." In each episode of the online show, three cis women are given drag makeovers, taught to access their "inner divas," and ultimately evaluated on their Drag

Point Average (DPA), which is made up of the strength of their drag trans-formation, performance, and attitude adjustment. Their mentors are past *Drag Race* contestants, but on this show, the queens have the additional authority of education and credentials in their new title of "professor." "Realness" meets real, in a sense, where the campy theatrics are height-ened, but the overall sense of makeover or improvement is assumed to connect to the cis women contestants' everyday lives. *Drag U*'s "Dateless Divas" episode addresses "real women who've stopped believing in mir-acles." Contestants Pegah, Lenae, and Debbie learn that "*Drag U*, like the real world, is a competition." This episode's featured "professors" are sea-son one's "Miss Congeniality," Nina Flowers; season two runner-up Raven; and season two's 8th place contestant Morgan McMichaels. The queens are already celebrities, known to the contestants and audience of *Drag U* from their tenure on *Drag Race*.

Once the women have matriculated and entered the Drag Lab, the contest begins. Like in the "Drag School of Charm," the tension around gender norms and gender-bending for contestants and professors makes this show more than just another way to show typical cis women ways they have failed. On this episode, in particular, racialized tropes are con-sistently deployed without the same sense of awareness and inversion that the queens bring to gender. Just like on *Drag Race*, RuPaul appeals to a certain sense of solidarity across the gender spectrum, saying, "I know it may seem odd for a group of single straight women to come to a drag university to find love, but you've come to the right place. It's just us girls." Unlike *Drag Race*, however, RuPaul appears in his male guise, with a mous-tache and in men's suits. So again, who or what makes a girl? How much of gender is inherent, regardless of body, and how much is illusion?

The students are matched with their professors, and they suss out similarities and sex appeal. Raven announces in a mock stern voice, "I'm going to work you out, girl," to which Lenae responds with a giggle and a squeal, "I know you is!" Blackness and working-class womanhood are frequently parodied in drag culture, particularly by white queens and those with class privilege. Lenae's embodied black womanhood is unlike Raven's racial and gender experience, but Lenae seems willing to connect. She seeks similarities between herself and her professor, linking them as similar even in their (very different) bodies. Lenae comments that Raven "was tall like me. She had the diva lashes and the lips. This could not be more perfect for me!" When Nina and Pegah are matched, Nina comments, "She has all the elements to be a very sexy woman." Morgan and Debbie exchange sweet-voiced hellos, and Morgan muses that Debbie is "like a sponge," and should be able to absorb her professor's teachings. Unlike at the "Drag School of Charm," the queens are invested in finding similarities with their pupils, or at least sizing them up as promising raw material.

In the interview segment, the professors assess some of the things that are keeping their divas dateless. Lack of sex or sex appeal are on the front stage. Nina learns that the most important person in Pegah's life is her mother, to a remarkable degree. When Morgan asks Debbie the last time she had sex, Debbie says in affected camp tones, "I'm a lady. I don't answer questions like that." Morgan responds, "Well, I'm a lady, and I DO answer questions like that." Again, different visions of "lady" are highlighted here. Morgan suggests that Debbie is a virgin, and announces to Debbie, "We're gonna turn you from the virgin to the vamp." Clearly, too much time spent with Mom or presumed virginity are problems the professors will try to solve. In her interview with Lenae, Raven cuts to the chase. Lenae replies to the question of when she last had sex by saying, "Over twenty years ago." Raven is incredulous. There is a sense that this is beyond anyone's understanding: "I'm surprised she's not ripping shit off the walls and beating people up, because that's what I would be doing." Ladies, girls, women, queens *need* sex, it is suggested—that's what defines success. Yet Lenae is cheerful and forthright, and makes it clear she is delighted to be on *Drag U*. Her enthusiasm is positioned in some ways as delusional, yet in comparison to the character Debbie in particular seems to adopt for the duration of the show, Lenae's presumed "realness" is key to her eventual win. Like with the girl fighters, Lenae is ready to work, ready to compete, ready to take a symbolic beating in order to win.

After the interviews, RuPaul summons "ladies and ladyboys" to the dragulator, a retro computer set-up that RuPaul calls a "highly sophisticated piece of technology." The dragulator is established as the authority on gender presentation, so there is in some ways less room for negotiation among team members than on *Drag Race*. The professors attempt to mold students into the form chosen by the dragulator. Each woman is made into a particular racialized, gendered stereotype.

RuPaul starts with Lenae. He types on the keyboard in an intentionally artificial and stereotypically limp-wristed way. A screen comes up with "readout" lines, a pink grid on black, and a computerized image of the contestant in unflattering undergarments. At RuPaul's command, the machine begins to "commence dragulatuion." In a moment, the machine presents tall, voluptuous African American Lenae as "Honey Boom." Lenae's "inner diva" is complete with glamorous makeup, chin-length wavy platinum hair, and a long draped gold evening gown showing off

Lenae's height and her bosom. Lenae says to the camera, "I said to myself, that's Marilyn Monroe. And she really is inside of me!"

Debbie and Pegah are less convinced about their computer-mandated alter egos. Debbie becomes "Moxie Mayhem," a bewigged, be-petticoated confection who the Asian-American contestant describes as "Memoirs of a Geisha meets Marie Antoinette." She claims to "love it," and asks Morgan to go "all out," but there is a sense of reserve or hesitancy we do not see in the effusive Lenae. Pegah becomes "Electra 21," a futuristic dominatrix. Nina is supportive, but Pegah is scared. She says, "It's that sexy, sex aspect of it that scares me." While Nina reassures Pegah about her fierceness, Pegah worries to the camera: "What is my mom gonna think, what is my grandma gonna think? You know I'm wearing leather, with the whip." Being a diva is heteronormative, and involves a particular type of sexual performance.

Marilyn Monroe, Geisha, Marie Antoinette, and dominatrix are all overtly sexual female archetypes, ripe for mocking as well as for (potentially) enjoying. The question, though, of whether the end goal of the transformations is a type of *jouissance*, female sexual empowerment, or male pleasure remains unclear. The theme of this episode is dating, which is a euphemism for sex. Flirting is taught, young hunky men are brought on stage, strawberries are eaten and fed lasciviously—in short, it's any dating reality show. Except it's not. Even with the swirl of racialized stereotypes, the light handling of the pain these women all seem to be looking to escape, and the university frame and classroom metaphors, it is the notion of the queen that shines through. When Lenae wins the flirting challenge, her prize includes makeup, shapewear (the modern euphemism for a girdle), and an online shopping spree. In many ways, this is another version of the TV show *Queen for a Day*, where women would compete with ever-increasing stories of misery and deprivation in order to be made "queen" and win a new refrigerator or other desperately-needed household appliance. The consumer goods on *Drag U* emphasize conventional aspects of "girl stuff": shopping, makeup, girdles, equally a symbol of desperation, and the use of female misery for material gain.

The contest hinges on performance. The final battle is the drag staple, the lip sync. Honey Boom, Moxie Mayhem, and Electra 21 perform Chaka Khan's "I'm Every Woman." Again, Lenae's enthusiasm makes her a clear winner. As she has done before in this episode, Asian-American Debbie employs black vernacular, saying, "I love me some Chaka," bringing up problematic elements of drag and cultural appropriation that resonate throughout the show. As the women react positively to the thought of dancing to Chaka Khan, however, the professors express concern. The girls are not physically up to par—their female bodies are trouble. Lenae is over 6'1" in heels, and Raven is concerned with how she will dance on stage in full costume. Nina is typically sympathetic about Pegah's sense of discomfort onstage, while Morgan, bluntly, says, "I'm looking at Debbie and I'm thinking 'horse on ice skates.'" During rehearsal, the queens join the women onstage. Morgan explains, "These dateless divas don't know anything about sexy. It's time for the real drag divas to show them how it's done." Typical for a reality show, the dateless divas are novices, where their mentors are experts, but even in moments of distress or frustration, there are moments of connection. Pegah and Debbie are both very concerned about their families' reaction to their onstage personae, while Lenae waxes philosophical, saying, "It felt amazing for everyone to be finally paying attention to me. I feel like I've always been Honey Boom; she's just been hiding deep down inside me." The narrative of true self is an interesting one in contrast to the artifice surrounding the show, the makeover, and the performance of another identity.

Debbie and Pegah come to embrace their inner divas, but it's Lenae who makes the honor roll. Named the winner, Lenae-as-Honey-Boom smolders in an orange and purple boa: "I never thought in a million years I would be the head pupil here at *Drag U!*" Raven acknowledges, "This experience changed Lenae's life, and I was honored that I was part of it." While Lenae approached the entire show with a willing attitude, there is a sense that perhaps for her, this is less of an experience in exercising the imagination than for the other two contestants. Lenae's grown son embraces Honey Boom, and says, "I want my mother to incorporate her new look and her new attitude every single day. The sky's the limit for my mother." His embodiment of pride and support is important, and one of the few times we see a heterotypical male body onstage. At the end, collecting her accolades, Lenae is a mother, a queen, a diva, and Honey Boom. More than "every woman," she is many women. Her prize includes make-up, a diet meal delivery plan, and a two-night Palm Springs getaway. She also, perhaps, "wins" a particular kind of middle-class white identity, linked to college graduation as well as the image of the vulnerable outsider Marilyn as pawn in games of male power.

Conclusion: Women, Queens and Princesses

Drag Race and *Drag U* draw on camp humor and inversions, presenting drag as a Carnival.[19] That includes moments of discomfort, and of reinforcing or eliding stereotypes. So invoking Lake Titicaca, the home of the fictional *Drag U* is presumed to be "funny," because the word contains slang for breasts and feces, but it's also racialized, pointing to an ostensibly hilarious "other" whose very language is full of unintentional double-entendre. *Drag U* has particular racialized visions of each woman, making her into a caricature of race, class, and ethnicity. It's consistent with mainstream drag culture, but it says something tired about identity. Race and class are thick in the air at the "Drag School of Charm," too. Tempele's a "bulldog," the women are "butch" and "manly," and Tempele herself remarks, "It's hard to be a girl."

Gender is WERK and work. The girls know it. The queens know it. The audience knows it. As much as gender and sex are decoupled, and new norms are created, recreated, and challenged, the specter of appropriate femininity lurks. *Drag Race* and *Drag U* certainly do symbolic damage as much as they entertain, and the strategic moments of trans inclusion that come in later seasons of *Drag Race* (particularly Monica Beverly Hillz's emotional coming out moment, where she reveals that she is not a drag queen, but a trans woman) do not negate the criticisms of transphobia and misogyny levied at the show and at mainstream drag. *Drag Race* contestants must be "drag queens," not trans women, drag kings, or other gender illusionists and performance. It's an odd combination of expanding and fixing unstable gender categories, and reinscribes some mainstream notions of who or what a successful queen may be. But *Drag Race* and *Drag U* have reach. The shows reach a broader cross-section of the viewing public than anyone would've guessed even following the brief public flirtation with drag queens in the 1990s.

Man, boy, girl, woman, butch, femme, queen, diva: over and over, viewers get the sense that gender's kind of a drag. None of the labels really fit any of the contestants, which is a source of delight for some, a problem for others, and revelation for more of the contestants than one might assume. And so we end where we begin, in a candy-colored girls' playdate, as Manila Luzon in heels towers over the child Joselyn Molina, approaching one another in friendship and imagination.

After coloring together on the beach, Manila coos to Joselyn, "Let me teach you to walk like a drag queen." That means "with confidence." On a wooden playground structure, the two take turns strutting and sashaying across a curved wooden bridge, with the ocean in the background. But Joselyn is already a successful public performer. She knows how to walk with confidence. Is she then "naturally" a drag queen? Or is it that the register of drag and existence of queens have become another category or frame of reference for girls and women? Here, the category of Drag Queen is one option available as role model. The only one? No. But the media reports recast this in a glib light—queens are better women than women, and better role models for girls. Not Queens are better than Princesses, but … it's confusing. It's complicated. Manila and Joselyn indulge in many of the Princess tropes: tiaras, shopping, high heels, being objects of attention. And they both are objects, knowing objects, as well as stars in their own right, on TV shows reaching international audiences.

Drag has become another familiar landscape for adults and children alike. In the drag club, Joselyn comments, "it's familiar to a disco-restaurant," although she acknowledges never having been to a disco. Onstage with Manila and a chorus of other drag queens, it "cheered me up to just be myself and dance and have fun and just let go." So: is she a mini-me, or "just me?" Again, authenticity and binaries are too easy. Manila is serving shades of Cruella DeVille, with her skunk-stripe hair and severe tailoring as another alternative to the Disney Princess: the villain. But she is sweet and tender and supportive, saying, "Joselyn is a natural drag queen. She probably did a better job at my song than I did." The element of support is a not-so-secret side or backstage of the drag runway. Professional actor Joselyn says being onstage with drag queens is "a good feeling, because you have a whole bunch of people that support you." *Drag Race* and *Drag U* show the unstable ground between support and sabotage, judgment and acceptance, but drag is invoked as an ideal-typical family, too.

Support is neither unproblematic nor automatic, but part of conscious negotiation of gendered agendas. We see this throughout *Drag Race* seasons, albeit not always intentionally. The "Drag School of Charm" is framed as a competition, but binaries are ruptured. It is particularly interesting to note that Ongina, "the queen who could have won it all," is eliminated here because of her genderqueer take on gender as well as her lack of effort in collaboration with her cis teammate.

Each season there are *Drag Race* contestants who are genderqueer, genderfuck, genderblur, and more and more, trans. With the exception of Monica Beverly Hillz, trans contestants like Sonique Love, Carmen Carrera, and Kenya Michaels have waited to come out until after the season wrapped. This is partly enforced by the show, which specifies that trans women contestants are not welcome. While this may reinforce some stereotypes, it shatters others, and emphasizes gender diversity and negotiation. *Drag Race* has rightly been criticized for taking an anti-trans and gender essentialist stand, and yet, in an interview, Precious Jewel, a trans woman, comments on the increasing visibility of trans contestants on and off the set, saying that Monica's coming out as a trans woman during the competition "shows us a loving and affirming RuPaul who dotes on Monica and proclaims, 'I brought you here because you are fierce,' although she deftly sidesteps the actual word transgender."[20] While Precious Jewel points to the "groundbreaking" aspect of Monica Beverly Hillz's coming out as trans during the competition, she acknowledges that, like any mass media production, the moment is strategic. Sometimes RuPaul seems to support trans identities and a range of gender identities in and out of drag. Sometimes she doesn't. Precious Jewel does not speak for all trans women any more than any of the queens, girls, and women on *Drag Race* or *Drag U* speak for anyone besides themselves. And particularly in earlier seasons, the notion of being trans, or of being anything other than a drag queen, is heavily contested.

In the makeup chair on *Drag Race*, girl fighter Michelle brings up the blurry line between personal authenticity—just being "yourself"—and public notions of authentic gender—the "real" woman, in an uncomfortable question and answer session with BeBe. Michelle, while getting her makeup, asks BeBe, "has anyone ever actually mistaken you to be a full, like a real woman?" BeBe answers, "It happens in the club, especially. All the time." Michelle is incredulous. "Really?" To a camera, in an interview, BeBe emphasizes, "I do not live my life as a woman. It's not my lifestyle." But the camera cuts back to the girls and queens in front of the makeup mirrors, with Michelle asking, "When that happens, what do you do? Do you tell them, like, the truth?" Busy with makeup brushes, eyes down, BeBe says, "I tell them the truth. I tell them that it's an illusion." BeBe elaborates, telling the camera she develops a character, so that people, "when they look at us performing, they don't necessarily say, 'oh, they are dressed up like this because they want to live like this.' No. That is just such a misconception." This is BeBe's story, but it also lends credence to the reading of *Drag Race* as an exercise in transphobia. BeBe continues, "I don't live my life like this, I don't go out like this," to which Ongina quips, "unless you're cleaning the house." So being trans is a different "lifestyle," and a punchline. Or as Pozner writes, reality TV,

> has the power to influence our notions of normalcy versus difference, convince us that certain behaviors are "innate" for different groups of people, and present culturally constructed norms of gender, race, class, and sexuality as "natural," rather than performances we've learned to adopt through societal education and expectation.[21]

What we see through the proliferation of mainstream drag in mainstream media might be a reminder not just that any gender's a drag, in the words of Patti Smith, but that making the invisible work of gender visible enable relationships, collaboration, and negotiation across social identities. Many more little girls are exposed to Disney Princesses than Drag Queens, but flesh and blood, though flawed, beat plastic hands-down. Other than that, competition may not be the only framework for relationships among women and queens.

Notes

1. The author wishes to acknowledge Dr. Melissa White and her early collaboration in shaping this essay.

2. Throughout the essay and the source material, there is slippage, intentional and otherwise, among terms like queen, girl, and woman.

3. Joy Martin-Malone, "Why Drag Queens Are Better Role Models Than Disney Princesses," *Huffington Post*, September 29, 2013, http://www.huffingtonpost.com/joy-martinmalone/drag-queens_b_4006697.html (accessed February 4, 2014).

4. Characters, including those who are "real people," will be referred to by their first names in this essay, in keeping with the familiarity and iconic status bestowed upon queens in *Drag Race* and popular culture.

5. I use "cis woman" to refer to cisgender women throughout the essay, as well as "girl" and "woman" when those terms are used in the source material.

6. Joshua Gamson, "Reality Queens," *Contexts* 12, no. 2 (2013): 52.

7. Gamson, 53.

8. Martin-Malone.

9. For examples, see Bronson and Merryman, *Natureshock*; Ornstein, *Cinderella*.

10. On January 28, 2014, the online video "Once Upon a Crime: Episode 5: Cinderella vs Snow White" was released, featuring Willem and Manila Luzon as Disney Princesses (Todrick Hall: http://www.youtube.com/watch?v=FOIMbhtosqk, part of a series of Disney parodies). The two basically hurl sexual insults at one another in this parody of "The People's Court"; the ubiquity of Disney Princesses and drag queens is notable in this example, even if the five-minute video is otherwise formulaic.

11. The 1990s were bracketed by Madonna's 1990 *Vogue* song, video, and MTV Music Video Awards show based on the drag ball culture, the 1991 documentary *Paris Is Burning*, focused on the drag ball culture of New York City, and the widespread success of the TV show *Will and Grace*, which did not focus on drag but did focus on the lives of gay men.

12. *RuPaul's Drag Race*, season 1, episode 5, Logo TV, 2009.

13. *Drag U*, season 1, episode 2, Logo TV, 2010.

14. Joshua Gamson, *Freaks Talk Back: Tabloid Talk Shows and Sexual Nonconformity* (Chicago: University of Chicago Press, 2008).

15. Ann Swidler, "Culture in Action: Symbols and Strategies," *American Sociological Review* 51, no. 2 (1986): 273–286.

16. The "She-Mail" concept (where RuPaul delivers a challenge to the queens in the form of a video e-mail) is one readily criticized by trans advocates and allies as continuing to marginalize or degrade trans women, for whom "she-male" is a slur, often invoked as hate speech along with other terms RuPaul and her queens readily use like "ladyboy."

17. Edward W. Said, *Orientalism* (New York: Vintage, 1978).

18. Chandra T. Mohanty, "Under Western Eyes: Feminist Scholarship and Colonial Discourses," in *Third World Women and the Politics of Feminism*, ed. Chandra T. Mohanty, Ann Russo, and Lourdes Torres (Bloomington: Indiana University Press, 1991), 55.

19. Mikhail Bakhtin, *Rabelais and His World* (Bloomington: Indiana University Press, 2009).

20. Nico Lang, "Breaking Ground: An Interview with Precious Jewel on RuPaul's Drag Race," WBEZ, http://www.wbez.org/blogs/nico-lang/2013–02/breaking-ground-interview-precious-jewel-rupauls-drag-race-105658 (accessed February 4, 2013).

21. Jennifer L. Pozner, *Reality Bites Back: The Troubling Truth About Guilty Pleasure TV* (Berkeley: Seal Press, 2010), 98.

The Prime of Miss RuPaul Charles

Allusion, Betrayal and Charismatic Pedagogy

DAVID J. FINE *and*
EMILY SHREVE

In the opening credits for *RuPaul's Drag U*, the *Drag Race* spin-off establishes one of its foundational references. While Pandora Boxx types away at a computer, RuPaul's voiceover announces that "we here at Drag U are in the business of putting drag-queen heads on women's shoulders."[1] RuPaul's mission statement paraphrases a line from *The Prime of Miss Jean Brodie*, a 1961 novel by Muriel Spark, adapted into a 1969 film of the same title starring Maggie Smith. The novel and the film recount the story of a charismatic teacher beset by criticism and, ultimately, betrayed by one of her acolytes. The allusion may seem trivial at first, but this essay argues for its interpretive centrality in RuPaul's drag queendom. In fact, RuPaul's self-identification with that teacher extraordinaire makes RuPaul's now-closed "school for girls"—*Drag U*—an unsurprising spin-off of *Drag Race*. But the references to the Scottish Miss Brodie permeate much more than *Drag U*. We argue that, despite its unpopularity, *Drag U* invites viewers to read *Drag Race* pedagogically.

Our contention is that one must consider *both* shows as part of a larger pedagogical project—one both fiercely traditional and quietly progressive—made visible through the allusions to Spark. Placing *Drag Race* into conversation with *The Prime of Miss Jean Brodie* allows one to understand the dynamics among RuPaul, her girls, and her critics. For RuPaul's school for girls is prone to the tensions that threaten all forms of education:

to maintain tradition is oftentimes to stifle the new; to engender her story is already to circumscribe it; to teach with charisma, uniqueness, nerve, and talent truly is to open oneself to unflattering readings. The critiques leveled against Jean Brodie are strikingly similar to those hurled against RuPaul Charles: she narcissistically reproduces herself in the queens who win her favor; she plays favorites; she dictates; she commingles reality and fantasy in order to manufacture drama. This transfiguration of reality into ratings creates each season's champion; thus, the success of each queen is both a product of RuPaul's pedagogy and the very factor which threatens RuPaul's reign. And yet, RuPaul's allusions to Spark's text purposefully enable the critiques that will, ultimately, destabilize her authority. With no rupaulogies, we argue that the allusions to Sparks' novel and its subsequent film adaptation help tease out the tensions between RuPaul and her girls, revealing the show's conservative center as well as its radical remainder. This is RuPaul's primetime, after all, and one must attend its influences carefully.

Given reading's fundamentality, we, as good students of RuPaul, practice our ABCs. First, we establish the richness of the Allusions to *The Prime of Miss Jean Brodie* within *Drag Race*. In this dilation, we analyze RuPaul's similarities to Jean Brodie and the educational theory of *RuPaul's Drag Race*. Second, we explore how Miss Brodie and RuPaul's shared teaching style makes them vulnerable to Betrayal. We outline external criticisms and demonstrate how they become internal to the contestants, as RuPaul's girls react against her self-propagating agenda. This betrayal extends the reach of RuPaul's Charismatic pedagogy, an expansion which we discuss in our third and final section. Ultimately, this investigation articulates education's ambivalent impulse to engender the new and conserve the old.

Allusion: RuPaul's Schools for Girls

On 25 August 2012, as students across the country prepared to return to school, RuPaul tweeted the following message from deep in the Lake Titicaca Valley: "Match Quote w/Movie: 'Little girls, I am in the business of putting old heads on young shoulders.'"[2] Like a good teacher, RuPaul's tweet quizzes her followers to see if they've been paying attention. The correct answer is, of course, *The Prime of Miss Jean Brodie*. In the movie, Maggie Smith loudly proclaims, "Little girls, I am in the business of putting old heads on young shoulders, and all my pupils are the crème de la crème. Give me a girl at an impressionable age, and she is mine for life."[3] To understand RuPaul's vocation, one must understand her references to Miss

Jean Brodie. RuPaul's self-conscious tweet asks viewers to remember that what might seem like a throwaway camp-gesture, similar to a flippant Cher hair toss, is actually a key text for the development of RuPaul's primetime television.

For this tweet teaches us at least two things: (1) RuPaul is deliberately referencing Spark's text and its film adaptation throughout her canon, and (2) she understands herself as performing a didactic role for both her queens and the larger viewing public. She sends this tweet, interestingly enough, in August 2012 during the promotion for *RuPaul's All Stars Drag Race*. Having just wrapped up her tenure as the president of *Drag U*, RuPaul nevertheless continues to see herself as engaged with the problematics of the Scottish pedagogue.[4] In fact, *All Stars'* tagline—"Bring back my girls"—has its roots in earlier references to Miss Brodie. The Scottish lilt RuPaul gives to the word "gurrrls" as she brings the drag queen competitors back to the judges' table has become a catchphrase, concretizing the show's intertextual play. Airing between seasons four and five, *All Stars'* tagline also signals a growing self-consciousness as to the show's premise. The series has now begun to reference itself and to intensify the work of containing its critics.

A similar interplay among criticism, community, and containment structures Spark's *The Prime of Miss Jean Brodie*. The text imagines a magnetic teacher under fire and narrates her fall from self-elected grace. In the narrative, Jean Brodie selects six students to form her special set. These pupils remain under Miss Brodie's influence while they study at the Marcia Blaine School for Girls in Edinburgh, Scotland. The year is 1930, and Miss Brodie has officially launched her prime. "It is important to recognize the years of one's prime," Miss Brodie opines, because one's "prime is elusive. You little girls, when you grow up, must be on the alert to recognize your prime at whatever time of your life it may occur. You must then live it to the full."[5] Miss Brodie directs her little girls to a full life, and, from the beginning, weaves politics into her pedagogy. "This is Stanley Baldwin who got in as Prime Minister and got out again ere long," she teaches, indicating a poster. "Miss Mackay retains him on the wall because she believes in the slogan 'Safety First.' But Safety does not come first. Goodness, Truth and Beauty come first. Follow me" (7). Miss Brodie's romanticism leads her students to risk—and, sometimes, lose—their lives. Eventually, Sandy Stranger revolts. As a result of this betrayal, Miss Brodie is dismissed "on the grounds that she had been teaching Fascism" (134). Taking her treason a step further, Sandy's converts to Catholicism and becomes a nun.[6]

The allusive connection between *The Prime of Miss Jean Brodie* and *RuPaul's Drag Race* takes root in season two, the season airing immediately before the summer 2010 premiere of *Drag U*. RuPaul's famous "Bring back my gurrrls!" wasn't formulated until the second season's fourth episode.[7] Previously, RuPaul had commanded, "Let's bring the girls back in" or "Bring back the girls," but the particular Scottish trill and that important "my" do not appear until the first "Snatch Game" challenge. This timing is fitting, because RuPaul here deploys her own celebrity impression (Miss Brodie à la Maggie Smith). The "my" stuck, sticking hard enough to become, as mentioned, one of RuPaul's signature catchphrases. But season two produces even more references to Miss Brodie. In "The Main Event Clip Show," RuPaul, chatting with three of her former girls, uses the same Brodiean inflection to announce, "Now, everybody knows, my girls are the crème de la crème."[8] With these allusions, RuPaul has consolidated the extent to which this is *her* queendom, and it is supreme. These are *her* hand-chosen queens, and like Miss Brodie's girls, they are a superlative set; even when Miss Brodie's students moved up to the fourth form, her girls "remained unmistakably Brodie, and were all famous in the school" (2). Likewise, RuPaul's queens, each famous for a particular contribution to the show, are also recognizable as having been shaped by the challenges of, and attention given to, *RuPaul's Drag Race*.

The references we've highlighted thus far are largely concerned with the coterie created by a charismatic leader—without specific reference to schooling. The educational element is introduced in a discussion during the first judging panel of the second season. Here, the judges debate the central purpose of *Drag Race*, sparking the proliferation of Brodiean allusions. In "Gone with the Window," the judges dissect the very raw potential of Shangela, who had only been performing in drag for five months prior to filming. When Kathy Griffin suggests, "she definitely can really *learn* how to perform" (emphasis ours), Mike Ruiz bursts out with an enthusiastic rebuttal: "We're not judging potential a year down the line; we're picking a drag superstar *today*." Chiming in on Ruiz's "today," RuPaul's next comment crystallizes the two sides of the debate; with Maggie Smith—like intonation, RuPaul remarks, "This is *RuPaul's Drag Race* not *RuPaul's School for Gurrrls*."[9] While RuPaul brings up the possibility of the reality competition's pedagogical opportunity, she contains it. Still, the moment puts pressure on the show's self-understanding. What does it mean to imagine *RuPaul's Drag Race* as *RuPaul's School for Girls*? One can picture season two, in its entirety, as a reflection on this question's implications.

Certainly the contestants themselves are able to picture the series as an educational resource. Morgan McMichaels, in "The Main Event Clip Show," comments: "Granted this is a competition; it's also a learning experience."[10] Although she foregrounds the competitive element, Morgan's insight into the show's ability to teach others suggests that contestants are learning as they move through the challenges. In the same episode, RuPaul surprisingly announces her role as drag educator. "At the end of the day," RuPaul hopes, "I'm less of a judge and more of a teacher. And the best way to teach, of course, is by example."[11] If RuPaul rejects an educational purpose in the first episode, by the tenth she has blurred the labor of the teacher with the work of a judge; in fact, she has *prioritized* the educational. Her "more of a teacher," however, is still a bit tongue-in-cheek; the clips which follow specify the somewhat absurd lessons engendered by RuPaul's example. She instructs Mystique to be, like her, "the MacGyver of drag"; she unpacks "popping a nut" with Raven; and she informs her girls that she has gotten a fifth facelift, because she, like Miss Brodie, is "*dedicated* to this, children."[12] RuPaul's unorthodox curriculum resonates with Miss Brodie's similarly esoteric subjects, as her twelve-year-old students had been schooled on, like

> the advantages to the skin of cleansing cream and witch-hazel over honest soap and water, and the word "menarche"; the interior decoration of the London house of the author of Winnie the Pooh had been described to them, as had the love lives of Charlotte Brontë and of Miss Brodie herself [2].

Miss Brodie's lessons depart from the standard educational fare, a mix of beauty tips *cum* lady lessons which culminate in knowledge of Miss Brodie herself. She leads by example, children.

So, too, does RuPaul. Looking beyond the moments cherry-picked for the clip show, we can see that RuPaul teaches through enchanting influence, personal biography, tête-à-tête tutorials, and professional challenges. The series' curriculum includes a general history of the drag arts and the specific story of RuPaul in her prime. For instance, the series designs many of its tests to inculcate LGBTQ herstory, with a concentration in drag. From Stonewall to Lady Gaga, RuPaul reminds her girls that they stand on the shoulderpads of giants. In season one, the queens film a MAC Viva Glam commercial directed toward those living with HIV; they also have a *Paris Is Burning*–style vogue battle and drag ball, with Swimsuit, Executive Realness, and Eveningwear categories. The second season includes the first reading mini-challenge and asks the competitors to make over veterans of the Stonewall riots. The girls of season four hold their own pride parade, with boat-shaped floats in all the colors of the rainbow. By season five, with *RuPaul's Drag Race* firmly an LGBTQ-institution, the second challenge requires the queens to recreate famous scenes from *Untucked!* The fabulous past instructs contestants and the public on issues central to the LGBTQ community and its struggle for civil rights. Beyond the challenges, the guest judges and the songs used for the lip sync battles provide a crash-course in gay cultural iconography, including guests like Charo, La Toya Jackson, the Pointer Sisters, and Chaz Bono, with songs by Donna Summer, Britney Spears, Madonna, and Cher.[13]

RuPaul herself is, of course, part of this broad history, yet the curricular emphasis on RuPaul also serves to shape the style of drag superstar created over the course of each season. Like Miss Brodie, RuPaul teaches about herself both to inspire the queens and to maintain her preeminence. After all, creating a true superstar is risky business, because it threatens the historical narratives, personal and social, in which the program is deeply rooted. The future generation's ability to disrupt the past's narrative is an anxiety written into *RuPaul's Drag Race* and the process of education alike. If this is one tension within education, which we'll discuss further below, a second concern involves modes of instruction and the responsibilities of an educator. The teacher's decisions in the classroom rest on value-laden assumptions about how students learn. RuPaul's particular pedagogical predilections can be investigated through the series' didactic allusions.

In the novel and film, Miss Brodie is forced, when questioned by the conservative headmistress, Miss Mackay, to outline her teaching methods. "To me," Miss Brodie explains, "education is a leading out. The word education comes from the root *ex*, meaning out, and *duco*, I lead. To me education is simply a leading out of what is already there." In response to this Platonic idealism, Miss Mackay rejoins: "I had hoped that my thoughts would be accepted about putting in." This pragmatic suggestion does not gain credence with Miss Brodie, who dismissively laughs before she responds to her colleague. "That would not be education but intrusion: the root prefix *in*, meaning in, and the stem *trudo*, I thrust; ergo, to thrust a lot of information into a pupil's head."[14] This "leading out" model of education is exactly the potential-focused process imagined, and rejected, for Shangela; it is a pedagogy practiced, however, throughout the bulk of the reality competition. RuPaul encourages each queen to draw from their own inner divas. At each episode's conclusion, RuPaul takes the runway first, literally leading out her girls. She calls them from their interior illusions to face the Truth.

While Miss Brodie and RuPaul share lofty educational goals, in their attempts to draw out they often thrust in. In fact, Miss Brodie's gloss of Socratic education merely emphasizes the extent to which she imposes facts and regulations on her little girls. When describing her encounter with Miss Mackay, she warns: "'Never let it be said that I put ideas into your heads. What is the meaning of education, Sandy?' 'To lead out,'" echoes Sandy (37). Beyond the definition of key terms, strict rules dictate even the most basic classroom conduct: "Whoever has opened the window has opened it too wide," she wails. "Six inches is perfectly adequate. More is vulgar" (47). Although RuPaul may allow for a little more fresh air, Miss Brodie's rules are meant to be followed. She attempts to teach Goodness, Truth, and Beauty. "'Who is the greatest Italian painter?'" she asks. One girl hazards a response: "'Leonardo da Vinci, Miss Brodie.' 'That is incorrect,'" Miss Brodie instructs. "'The answer is Giotto, he is my favourite'" (7–8). One notices, in this response, the extent to which Miss Brodie teaches her favorites: subjects and pupils. Far from pursuing Goodness alone, she lectures from personal preference. The promises behind Miss Brodie's preferences are fame and exceptionality. She exhorts, "If only you small girls would listen to me I would make of you the crème de la crème" (11). Good cream is never far from RuPaul's mind, either; she hopes her soon-to-be-famous-for-something students will rise to the top as seasoned professionals in the art of drag.

In case you still skeptically wonder at the didactic affinity RuPaul and Miss Brodie share, consider this quotation from a BET.com interview with Clay Cane. Post-Bush, RuPaul knew,

> there was a need for this show, especially after so many years of fear and hysteria that our country was involved in after 9/11. We just needed to laugh and have fun again, to see beauty and not take ourselves too seriously. But, listen, those windows where beauty and light shine through are very few and far between. We're enjoying the sunlight of the spirit now but the window can close up just as quickly. Our culture loves fear-based energy, it just does.[15]

This energy from the properly-opened window, one of "beauty and light," suggests RuPaul's idealism as well as her willingness to think politically. Fear—of terrorists and fascists, of Bush and Baldwin—does not justify closed windows or locked doors. Like Miss Brodie, RuPaul requires openness to life and beauty. Indeed, in an earlier BET.com interview with Cane, RuPaul described her show as part of a "new wave of hope, beauty, love and truth."[16] RuPaul's repeated emphasis on beauty, spirit, light, hope, and truth echoes the Goodness, Truth, and Beauty of Miss Jean Brodie. For both fearless instructors, safety does not come first.

Betrayal: Bring Back My Girls

What does it take to become America's next drag superstar? Given the philosophies espoused above, it seems like *RuPaul's Drag Race* would reward the unique contestant's risk-taking and self-fashioning. Nevertheless, in a dynamic common to many reality shows, safety often comes first: contestants who adhere closely to a particular challenge's requirements remain safe from weekly eliminations. This is not to say that the contestants are not encouraged to take chances, but the risks rewarded are the ones that mirror RuPaul's own career choices. Like Miss Brodie, her instruction looks more like a thrusting-in of knowledge than a leading-out of "what is already there." For example, Tyra Sanchez begins putting together a boldly-colored, boldly-textured fur dress as her red-carpet look for season two's Diva Awards. She explains her rationale to RuPaul as a desire for uniqueness: "I want to be in a gown, but I want to stand out." RuPaul's reaction to Tyra's idiosyncratic choice is one of concern. Tyra "may" want to consider something else; it "might" not work out.[17] Ultimately, Tyra makes a benign choice, choosing a pre-made, conventionally-glamorous evening gown, much like the ones RuPaul wears. She is extravagantly praised for this decision during the judge's comments. Uniqueness and nerve are sacrificed for safe beauty.

This highly-controlled reproduction of RuPaul's specific tastes underscores the two criticisms leveled at both Miss Brodie and RuPaul: (1) they narcissistically reproduce clones of themselves; and (2) they use others as pawns in their own self-serving fantasies. These two actions work together: it is narcissism that sanctions these charismatic leaders to treat their students as pawns and, as a result, manhandling the pawns shapes them into clones. Their egoism ennobles their manipulation, as it were. In this section, we look at how these two separate threads of criticism—the self-seeking and the other-using—wind throughout responses to both Miss Brodie and *RuPaul's Drag Race*.

As Miss Brodie's know-it-all resistance to Miss Mackay suggests, Miss Brodie believes her teaching methods are best. She believes she is special. In the book, Sandy posits that Miss Brodie mistakes herself for a god: "She thinks she is Providence, thought Sandy, she thinks she is the God of Calvin, she sees the beginning and the end" (129). Miss Brodie elects herself to predetermined grace. She acts like the God of Calvin and constructs a beautiful world of her own. And, like God, she makes pupils in her image. Her extraordinariness spills over and fills up her girls. To her, the art master shows interest in them, "'because you are mine,' said Miss

Brodie. 'I mean of my stamp and cut, and I am in my prime'" (103). They are fashioned a cut above the rest. She imbues her students with her sense of special election as well as her favorite painters. The girls each become "famous" for something, and they are "immediately recognizable as Miss Brodie's pupils" (1). In fact, she goes so far as to encourage Rose—"who was famous for sex-appeal" (6)—to take the art master, Teddy Lloyd, for her lover: he, who was Miss Brodie's own "true love" (120). Spark scholar Dorothea Walker sums up the darker side of Miss Brodie's pedagogy: "Her wish to broaden the vision of the youngsters is certainly a laudable one; but the determination to broaden it with her distorted version of reality suggests both her authoritarian nature and her desire to control. Her greatest wish is really to reproduce clones of herself."[18] A broadened vision results in a narrow carbon-copy. Miss Brodie's desire to reproduce infects even Teddy Lloyd who paints Miss Brodie although the model is Sandy, his own family, or, in the film's comic reveal, his dog, who shares Maggie Smith's heavy-lidded, seductive eyes.

If Miss Brodie's visage appears in the most unlikely spaces, RuPaul's face pervades the show's design—from the title credits to the workroom's walls. In addition, critics have accused RuPaul of Xeroxing herself in her selection of the next drag superstar. RuPaul's reincarnation begins with extensive lessons on her career. The girls learn about RuPaul as they lip sync to her songs, perform in her music videos, and participate in challenges inspired by her career. In the second season, contestants make over a RuPaul doll for the mini-challenge; the main challenge that episode is a strip show inspired by RuPaul's 2007 film, *Starrbooty*. Later in the race, the queens must create and promote autobiographies, a nod to 1995's *Lettin' It All Hang Out*. A third season mini-challenge is titled "Sh*t RuPaul Says," but the tenth episode, "RuPaul-a-Palooza," immerses the girls in RuPaul's music. Here, racers fill in RuPaul's song lyrics for a game of "Rusical chairs" and perform a genre-based cover of "Superstar." In the fourth season, the queens create infomercials for RuPaul's recent albums *Glamazon* and *Champion*. The fifth season moves beyond knowledge of RuPaul's music to knowledge of RuPaul's biography. In "Black Swan: Why It Gotta Be Black?," the contestants perform a ballet of RuPaul's life story, and, three episodes later, they roast RuPaul. Inundated as they are in RuPaul's puns, music, and legacy, perhaps the decor of the Interior Illusions Lounge best demonstrates the extent to which RuPaul demands influence over her girls' inner lives; their charismatic leader watches them, even as they untuck.

RuPaul is most authoritarian, however, in her choice of winners.

While many were disappointed by BeBe's win, Tyra's victory in season two cemented suspicions of RuPaul's desire to clone. Both of these queens, like RuPaul herself, were tall, glamorous, black queens with a classic hourglass figure. While passing over the edgy Nina Flowers was somewhat understandable, many thought Raven or Jujubee were better suited for the second crown. Fans turned to internet forums to express displeasure, vociferously enough to generate a post on queertywww from 29 April 2010 entitled "The Terribly Stupid Claim That RuPaul Is a Racist for Choosing 2 Black Winners." One viewer commented on the post that "the show is not looking for the Next Drag Superstar but someone that Ru feels is most like her." In a 27 April 2010 comment on a *courant.com* announcement of Tyra's win, another fan used Walker's exact language to complain about the choice: "Please … for the second season, Ru Paul [*sic*] Charles has decided that the next drag superstar is an African-descended long-legged *clone* of the icon's drag personna [*sic*—emphasis ours]." The RuPauline silhouette appears in each contestant with the same persistency with which Miss Brodie's face haunts the artist's canvases.

While season three's more androgynous winner, Raja, seemed to break from RuPaul's mold, rumors swirled that her "close friendship" with RuPaul guaranteed her the crown. Thus, even when escaping the charge of cloning, RuPaul seemed to be, like Miss Brodie, manipulating results and playing favorites: using the queens as pawns to garner reality show drama. Although Raja dismissed these incriminations, accusations of favoritism, especially for fishy queens, abound.[19] Michelle Visage and Santino Rice often bear the brunt of these accusations, but RuPaul makes the final decisions. Increasing gimmicks—the return of previously-eliminated queens, frenemies cast on the same season, lip sync pairings for maximum tears—pull back a curtain on the machinations necessary to create good television. It becomes difficult to imagine queens have won through merit and skill. Many have suggested that Willam's disqualification was a result of this same orchestration. Popular gossip bloggers Tom and Lorenzo point the finger in their recap of season four's reunion. They suggest, provocatively, that "Willam's whole story line was planned out. She was never going to win and in exchange for that, she got a highly visible exit from the show which is only going to help her career. You know it's true. She was a ringer. It's not the first time the show's used them."[20] Willam was not a competitor, but a performer—not a clone, but a co-conspirator.

Miss Brodie is no stranger to playing favorites or plotting story lines. The choice of a set is, from the beginning, an act of both favoritism and control; she "selected her favourites, or rather those whom she could trust;

or rather those whose parents she could trust not to lodge complaints about the more advanced and seditious aspects of her educational policy" (25). Turning her favorites into actors in her fantasies, she preordains Rose's first lover and, with dramatic flair, expects that Sandy will report on the affair's fruition. Her now bigger girls become chess-pieces in her attempt to love a married man by proxy: "It was plain that Miss Brodie wanted Rose with her instinct to start preparing to be Teddy Lloyd's lover, and Sandy with her insight to act as informant on the affair. It was to this end that Rose and Sandy had been chosen as the crème de la crème" (116). This romance requires manipulation as well as blanket pronouncements: "Sandy will make an excellent Secret Service agent, a great spy [...]. Rose will be a great lover" (116–117). Miss Brodie's totalitarian intervention into the lives of her students opens up the space for her betrayal. It comes, "in the event," from Sandy, "who slept with Teddy Lloyd and Rose who carried back the information" (117). Sandy, with her insight, disrupts Miss Brodie's plot. What used to be critiques from outside have become internal to her girls.

Sandy Stranger explains much later to Monica, famous for division, that it is "only possible to betray where loyalty is due" (136). Loyalty is no longer owed to Miss Jean Brodie. Sandy therefore acts decisively and stops Miss Brodie in her tracks. She tells Miss Mackay to examine Miss Brodie's politics more closely, and this investigation leads to Miss Brodie's termination on charges of fascism. In the film, this betrayal ends with Miss Brodie calling Sandy, "assassin!" In the book, the betrayal initiates a series of events terminating in Sandy's conversion to Catholicism—a backstab that cuts against Miss Brodie's individualist Calvinism. In both film and print, the student becomes the plot's author. Nevertheless, the texts present different rationales for the motivations behind, and the justification for, Sandy's betrayal. The film explicitly paints Sandy as jealous; she longs for the undivided devotion of Teddy Lloyd. But, in the book, Sandy expresses more of an anxiety about self-appointed grace and controlling leadership, which, seemingly, inspires her Catholic conversion; here, Sandy censures the good pedagogical intentions that result in hyper-controlling actions. Of course, Sandy betrays her own desire to play God, as she takes Miss Brodie's life into her hands. *The Prime of Miss Jean Brodie* oscillates, therefore, between different motivations: jealousy, on the one hand, honesty, on the other. In either case, Spark invites readers to think carefully about the ethics of betrayal and its consequences.

RuPaul's Drag Race plots its own narratives of betrayal again and again. In the "Main Event Clip Show," BeBe suggests that she should take over

RuPaul's job introducing the top ten moments of season two. When BeBe says, "I think it's time I take over," RuPaul fakes offense and huffs, "You may be the next drag superstar, but it's still *my* show."[21] BeBe's potential to be a usurper is quickly dissipated, as BeBe uses her interruption to introduce the number one slot: RuPaul's runway looks. In season two's final challenge, the top three queens act out a *Dynasty*-like confrontation, which ends with a slap from RuPaul. Season four's final three act out an elaborate attempt to overthrow a villainous RuPaul hell-bent on world domination. These betrayals, however, are like Miss Brodie's plan for Rose to love Teddy Lloyd. RuPaul writes them herself, and they serve to muffle mutiny.

The most acute threat arises in response to the *All Stars* season, when RuPaul most definitively identifies a "set." Just before, season four broke from form in response to the criticisms of the first three seasons. Macabre Sharon Needles, bolstered by fan support, took the title. Many believed RuPaul preferred the professional and polished Chad Michaels, a queen who, like RuPaul herself, built a legacy through hard-work and class. Thus, it was no surprise that Chad was included in the *All Stars* cast. In fact, some have suggested that *All Stars* itself was created for the express purpose of getting Chad a crown and a place among the former queens of *RuPaul's Drag Race*.[22] In the end, *All Stars* recreates the drama of the second, most Brodean, season as Raven again is left without a crown, still not quite able to become the RuPaul clone necessary for success.

It isn't Raven, though, who betrays RuPaul. Rather, Willam, famous for conjugal visits, exposes RuPaul's fascist control over her empire. Willam's song "RuPaulogize" shifts from the agreed-upon narrative, exposing her allegedly-revoked invitation for *All Stars*, and adding more fuel to the fire of those who imagine Chad was guaranteed a win. Willam here claims the Sandy spot, refusing to play the game. Like the twin Sandys of book and film, Willam's motivations are Janus-faced, a jealous competition for airtime *and* a thoughtful critique of RuPaul's serial machinations. As Willam points out, RuPaul's decisions have real career consequences for the queens. Perhaps RuPaul willingly signed off on the song, just like she play acts taking offense at BeBe. But, even if she did approve of the release, her absence from the video marks her girls' increased power. RuPaul does not appear at the end to reassert her dominance as supermodel of the world. It's no longer RuPaul's controlling joke, but a former student teaching a new lesson that exceeds RuPaul's curriculum.

Willam's song, released as RuPaul was about to crown a fifth queen, asks the public, as a surrogate headmistress, to acknowledge RuPaul's fascist practices. Sharon Needles' eerily-accurate portrayal of RuPaul in the "RuPaulogize" music video (her make-up even painted by RuPaul's long-time makeup artist, Mathu Anderson) intensifies the claims of Willam's lyrics. Delivered by Sharon, RuPaul's "consider that stolen," now seems a threat rather than an inside joke.[23] Reminding us that RuPaul can kill careers as well as make them, Sharon's RuPaul has contestants save themselves from "extermination" rather than elimination. Willam, however, grudgingly acknowledges the one silver-lining of the situation, as she draws attention to Sharon's win in the song's final moments: "But Ms. Needles sure did earn the crown."[24] As the song slows down and Willam draws out the note on "earn," we remember that Sharon's win was the first affected by popular acclaim. If the first three seasons and *All Stars* are marred by cloning, favoritism, and manipulation, then Willam's recognition that Sharon's win was beyond the boundaries of RuPaul's control speaks to hope for a new type of drag superstar. And yet, Sharon, famous for spookiness and originally the queen most distinct from RuPaul, is now able almost perfectly to inhabit RuPaul's persona, simply by virtue of her crowning. As both the book and film versions of Sandy Stranger make clear, caring enough to betray is, paradoxically, learning enough to recreate the very behavior one is condemning.

Charismatic Pedagogy: Crème de la Crème

As many teachers know, instructors with charisma are more likely to develop invested students, the very pupils who care enough to rebel. Jean Brodie and RuPaul Charles have charisma in spades. This charisma creates the conditions for their betrayal. There is a key difference, however, between Miss Brodie and RuPaul: RuPaul is parodying Maggie Smith's incarnation of the Scottish schoolmarm. With her intentional allusions to Miss Jean Brodie, students of Judith Butler's prime will read RuPaul as parodying Miss Brodie in order to acknowledge her own implication in "oppressive regimes of power."[25] Going a step further, we claim RuPaul's embodiment of Miss Jean Brodie engages parody as a mode of instruction. Quite simply, RuPaul actualizes a radical pedagogy through her engagement with Spark's text. RuPaul mocks the authoritarian schoolmistress as she creates space for an inevitable betrayal. Her allusions, caught as they are in the cultural imaginary, establish the expectation for rebellion, for the new. Thus, we are not arguing that RuPaul is a fascist teacher or a negative role model; rather, we argue that, by using Miss Brodie's narrative,

RuPaul is a radical teacher in the only way she can be given education's inherent conservatism and her own established legacy.

While Sandy's betrayal surprises and bewilders Miss Brodie, RuPaul knowingly plays the master-and-servant game. Doing so, she acknowledges a tension between authority and freedom. This tension sits at the center of Hannah Arendt's analysis of modern education. Indeed, Spark's contemporary gives scholars a language with which to approach RuPaul's radical pedagogy. In "The Crisis in Education" (1954), Arendt insists that education is, by its very nature, conservative and depends on the teacher's manifest authority. In post-war America, authority is, however, held in suspicion—especially in the classroom. For Arendt, the crisis provoked by this disconnect opens a window of opportunity through which to investigate the root experience of education:

> Our hope always hangs on the new which every generation brings; but precisely because we can base our hope only on this, we destroy everything if we try to control the new so that we, the old, can dictate how it will look. Exactly for the sake of what is new and revolutionary in every child, education must be conservative; it must preserve this newness and introduce it as a new thing into an old world.[26]

One must shield the new generation's ability to make the world anew. Education is therefore conservative, according to Arendt, "in the sense of conservation."[27] The modern pedagogical impasse "lies in the fact that by [education's] very nature it cannot forgo either authority or tradition, and yet must proceed in a world that is neither structured by authority nor held together by tradition."[28] Schooling must protect the traditions in need of transfer; the teacher's authority aids her in the transmission of this information. The world is changing, but teachers must preserve and transmit the old if they are to promote freedom.

Arendt's essay on pedagogical crisis, arguably as relevant today as when she published it, contextualizes *RuPaul's Drag Race*'s conservative impulses. Furthermore, Arendt's essay clarifies why progressive gender politics remain complicated by the conventional functions of education and reality television. In Arendt's words, "the function of school is to teach children what the world is like and not to instruct them in the art of living."[29] RuPaul spends so much time discussing LGBTQ history and foregrounding her authority in order to teach her girls about the world they are soon to inherit. RuPaul shows them the world as it is and thus exercises her students' capacity to serve newness. She is not in the business of "putting old heads on your young shoulders" (5), like Miss Brodie; rather, she *protects* the young heads on her drag queens' shoulders. If RuPaul herself must remain conservative, continuing her legacy and imprinting a queer herstory on her students, *The Prime of Miss Jean Brodie* reminds us that this conservatism also gives birth to betrayal, to rebellion where what is new or radically other in drag and queer identity can come to light. And so, Arendt contends that

> education is the point at which we decide whether we love the world enough to assume responsibility for it and by the same token save it from ruin which, except for renewal, except for the coming of the new and the young, would be inevitable. And education, too, is where we love our children enough not to expel them from our world and leave them to their own devices, nor to strike from their hands their chance of undertaking something new, something unforeseen by us, but to prepare them in advance for the task of renewing a common world.[30]

Teachers are called upon to love the world and to make room for their students to love and shape it differently—even when they argue that da Vinci is better than Giotto or that Lady Gaga is superior to Madonna. As Arendt's comments suggest to us, RuPaul and *RuPaul's Drag Race* are radical precisely because they engender critique and invite re-formation, however painful this might be for the teacher.

This invitation to reformation is exactly what *Drag U* promises its learners. This school "formed by drag queens" pledges itself to serve "biological women" and help them "unleash their inner diva and let the world have it."[31] These girls need all the help they can get; they are desperate, fat, lonely, worse yet, butch. *Drag U's* crash course will, with any luck, put "drag queen heads on women's shoulders." At the chapter's outset, *Drag U's* creation and its allusive title credits helped us to see the educational work of *Drag Race* as they also underscored the extent to which RuPaul views herself as an instructor. Now, after an investigation of true education as defined by Miss Brodie and RuPaul, we can shift gears and spin back to *Drag U's* troubled politics. On the one hand, fans excoriate *Drag U* for exemplifying a conservative self-involvement and an investment in traditional femininity. On the other hand, we suggest viewers can also see how RuPaul continues her charismatic education. Ultimately, she prepares her students, like in *Drag Race*, "for the task of renewing a common world" in sisterly solidarity. This feat is no small miracle.

Some viewers are quite disenchanted with this second school for girls. On 22 August 2010, Joelle Ruby Ryan posted an analysis on the Transmeditation blog concerning *Drag U* and another reality show on VH1, *TRANSform Me*. The critique has many layers, but it comes down to this comment: "Perhaps most troubling about these shows is the fact that they all reinscribe body and beauty *fascism* for trans and cis women alike" (emphasis ours).[32] Just as Miss Brodie's teaching style has her labeled "a born Fascist" (134), one finds the shade thrown at RuPaul apropos: she dictates women's beauty. Reality shows like *Drag U* censure women, the critique goes, for failing to reiterate their anatomical destiny while rewarding those who adhere seamlessly to norms. In addition to the reinscription of gender normativity, *Drag U* encourages narcissistic reproduction. Like the makeover episodes from *Drag Race*, which explicitly call for a "family resemblance" between contestant and partner, the drag professors often transform the "biological women" into their mirrored reflections. The professors only follow RuPaul's lead; as we have demonstrated, she first transforms them into her familiar image. Of course, as university president, RuPaul still maintains a strong presence on the show. Quotations from her work plaster the main stage; they are written in stone like the Ten Commandments. More importantly, her one-on-one conferences with each week's three contestants form the emotional heart and didactic center of the program. On a first reading, then, *Drag U* can appear to be a pure distillation of all of the most conservative and self-centered impulses behind *Drag Race*. RuPaul has graduated her former queens into the same fascist business she herself practices. As a consequence, the conventions of reality television—gender normativity, competitive aggression, and peacocky narcissism—recreate troubled hierarchies and introduce schisms in marginalized communities that critics believe should be united.

In line with our main argument, however, we suggest that this line of thinking misses how RuPaul, as in *Drag Race*, instills the potential for radical change. We don't want to whitewash the very real and troubling dynamics of *Drag U* but to suggest that its ambivalence works in its favor as much as against it. To claim the show successfully reinscribes gender norms both exaggerates and limits teaching's efficacy. First, even the most magnetic of teachers is unable to shape students as completely as they'd like; students very much have a will of their own. For a two-day reality television show, no matter the depths of despair in which the women are sunk, the power of their daily habits will likely win out over the immediate spectacle of their glamazon. Second, to see teaching's power as only one of reproduction misses its ability, as Arendt describes, to create situations where the students may deviate in unknown and unexpected ways. RuPaul and her drag professors can pass on the lady lessons of traditional femininity—some cucumber on the eyes here, a nip and tuck there—but it is up to the biological women to implement them. More often than not, the episodes highlight the messiness surrounding gender performance, the inability of natural women to get it right.[33] In fact, the lessons are so impractical as to demand, almost by force, their betrayal. Most women will hesitate, for instance, to stuff foam around their posterior before heading off for an otherwise humdrum day in the office. What they learn, instead, is the sheer outrageousness of femininity, its impossible practice. Critics are missing the point when they read the show as the professors teaching these women how to live; rather, they teach, as Arendt reminds us, a lesson about the world as it *is* and not as it should be. The world as it *should be* exists only in the unforeseen, in the new. Like RuPaul's girls, some draguates will recreate; others will deviate. The latter will branch off onto their own radical path.[34]

Miss Brodie herself has thoughts on what is "radical." In the novel, she tells her impressionable girls,

> So I intend simply to point out to Miss Mackay that there is a radical difference in our principles of education. Radical is a word pertaining to roots—Latin *radix*, a root. We differ at root, the headmistress and I, upon the question whether we are employed to education the minds of girls or to intrude upon them [38].

As we've shown above, the line between educating and intruding on the minds of girls is more blurred than Miss Brodie can admit. The very etymology she provides speaks to how the conservative and progressive in education remained intertwined. "Roots" are the foundation for the radical; the new and different grows, and branches off from, these grounded origins. In this paradoxical way, Miss Brodie and RuPaul both have radical power, even if their practice can look staunchly conservative. Education, then, is like drag itself: a site of ambivalence, "one which," to quote Judith Butler, "reflects the more general situation of being implicated in the regimes of power by which one is constituted and, hence, of being implicated in the very regimes of power that one opposes."[35] Drag does not necessarily empower. It remains always implicated in the powers-that-be but has the potential to make oneself and others more cognizant concerning the roots of those social forces. Likewise, Miss Brodie's classroom and RuPaul's reality shows do not necessarily empower in the sentimental sense, but these charismatic teachers instill lessons that inspire and enable life-giving extirpation.

RuPaul's deliberate use of allusions to Miss Brodie suggests that she is aware of her status as a charismatic leader. While her jokes about being displaced may reveal real anxiety about her long-lasting legacy, when RuPaul aligns herself with Jean Brodie, she invites her students into the role of Sandy. As a nun, Sandy later writes about "The Transfiguration of the Commonplace." As a draguate from RuPaul's school, each queen has the potential to transfigure the commonplaces of drag and gender performance. Many queens may, like mockingbirds, choose to chantey and stay in the style and form of femininity and drag superstardom modeled by RuPaul; they will respond to the part of RuPaul's charismatic pedagogy that forms students in her image. Others, however, will take the opportunity to sashay away, to depart from the roots that have nourished them. It is in these exits and departures that we see radical potential and the true fruition of RuPaul's charismatic pedagogy.[36]

Notes

1. *RuPaul's Drag U*, "Tomboy Meets Girl," Logo TV, 19 July 2010. Our own schooling has profoundly shaped this project. Kate Crassons' medieval miracle seminar transformed our *Drag Race* fandom into scholarship. Lehigh University's 2010 Feminism in Practice Conference and the Duquesne University's Echoes Conference provided us with forums for early versions of this essay. Katie Burton has been our welcome canary in the coal mine during the drafting phase. Finally, this essay would not have been possible without Carolyn Laubender in her prime.

2. RuPaul, Twitter post, August 25, 2012, 9:14 a.m., https://twitter.com/RuPaul (22 February 2014).

3. *The Prime of Miss Jean Brodie*, directed by Ronald Neame (1969; Beverly Hills, CA: 20th Century–Fox, 2004), DVD.

4. The final episode of *Drag U* aired 6 August 2012.

5. Muriel Spark, *The Prime of Miss Jean Brodie* (1961; rpt., New York: HarperCollins, 2009), 6, 8. Hereafter cited in-text by page number alone.

6. Sandy's conversion is never mentioned in the film adaptation. Because the film is, with the exception of the theological issues, a largely-accurate adaptation of the book, we use quotations from the film and novel interchangeably when discussing Miss Brodie's pedagogical style. However, our second section on Sandy's betrayal highlights the differences between the two texts.

7. *RuPaul's Drag Race*, "The Snatch Game," Logo TV, 22 February 2010.

8. *RuPaul's Drag Race*, "The Main Event Clip Show," Logo TV, 19 April 2010.

9. *RuPaul's Drag Race*, "Gone with the Window," Logo TV, 1 February 2010.

10. "Main Event."

11. "Main Event."

12. "Main Event."

13. Eir-Anne Edgar has also noted *Drag Race*'s use of "historically situated drag icons and practices," arguing that RuPaul "situates her show in the context of a long and complex queer historical record" (136). Edgar questions, however, whether *Drag Race* is radical enough to merit inclusion in this tradition. See her "*Xtravaganza!* Drag Representation and Articulation in *RuPaul's Drag Race*," *Studies in Popular Culture* 34, no. 1 (2011): 133–146.

14. *Prime*, DVD.

15. "Return of the Queen: RuPaul," by Clay Cane, BETwww, 1 February 2011, http://www.bet.com/news/celebrities/2011/02/01/rtrnqueenrupaul.html (22 February 2014).

16. Accessed 6 November 2010; since removed.

17. *RuPaul's Drag Race*, "The Diva Awards," Logo TV, 12 April 2010.

18. Dorothea Walker, *Muriel Spark* (Boston: Twayne, 1988), 41.

19. See Raja's interview by Jethro Nededog, zap2itwww, 26 April 2011, http://blog.zap2it.com/frominsidethebox/2011/04/rupauls-drag-race-raja-on-her-controversial-win-i-dont-mind-the-criticism.html (22 February 2014).

20. Tom and Lorenzo, "*RuPaul's Drag Race* Reunion," *Tom + Lorenzo: Fabulous & Opinionated*, 1 May 2012, http://tomandlorenzo.com/2012/05/rupauls-drag-race-reunion/ (22 February 2014).

21. "Main Event."

22. On 5 April 2013, Mat Crawford posted on *Untuckable*, "I believe that the whole All-Stars season was rigged for Chad Michaels to win, but that's a whole other story." http://untuckable.wordpress.com/2013/04/05/rupaulogize/ (22 February 2014).

23. During the season four finale, Willam coins the term "rupaulogize." RuPaul quickly responds, "consider that stolen." *RuPaul's Drag Race*, "Reunion," Logo TV, 30 April 2012.

24. Willam Belli, "RuPaulogize" (19 April 2013) 4 min. 10 sec.; video clip; from *YouTube*, http://www.youtube.com/watch?v=JKbHCi5rBpI (1 February 2014).

25. Judith Butler, "Gender Is Burning," in *Bodies That Matter* (New York: Routledge, 1993), 123.

26. Hannah Arendt, "The Crisis in Education," in *Between Past and Future* (1961; rpt., New York: Penguin, 2006), 189.

27. Arendt, 188.

28. Arendt, 191.

29. Arendt, 192.

30. Arendt, 193.

31. "Tomboy Meets Girl."

32. Accessed 6 November 2010; since removed.

33. Viewers have expressed dissatisfaction with the quality of *Drag U's* makeovers. Zack Bunker on the *Fierce & Nerdy* website claims that the show is "transforming perfectly nice women into creepy, messy transvestites." Critiques like these put pressure on the show to provide more practical solutions and streamlined makeovers. See Bunker's full review on his blogumn, "Tall Glass of Shame," 19 August 2012, http://fierceandnerdy.com/tall-glass-of-shame-drag-u-ruuuuupaul (22 February 2014).

34. In response to critics like Zack Bunker who thought RuPaul was hurting these women by providing impractical advice, *Drag U* became increasingly more realistic in its lessons. By the third season, the women were even receiving outfits to wear at home. The potential for betrayal and divergence became increasingly foreclosed. Perhaps this pragmatism contributed to the series' cancelation.

35. Butler, "Gender," 125.

36. As we make our exit, we have one last allusion to highlight. We celebrated the final,proofread draft of this essay by watching season six's Snatch Game episode. Here, to our great surprise and pleasure, BenDeLaCreme performed as Maggie Smith à la *Downton Abbey*. To announce BenDeLaCreme's victory in the challenge, RuPaul proclaimed, "Tonight … it's *The Prime of Miss* BenDeLaCreme!" Never one to be outdone, RuPaul invoked her own classic Maggie Smith impersonation, giving a Scottish enunciation to her famous, "Bring back my gurrrls." And, before we sashay away, there's just one more narcissistic thing: each queen must embody RuPaul in her runway look for "The Night of A Thousand Rus." Again, references to *The Prime of Miss Jean Brodie* call attention to RuPaul's charismatic presence and just how she nurtures the crème DeLaCreme. *RuPaul's Drag Race*, "Snatch Game," LogoTV, 24 March 2014.

About the Contributors

Libby **Anthony** is an assistant professor at the University of Cincinnati Blue Ash with research and teaching interests in international speakers of English, first-year writing, and writing center theory and pedagogy. Her work has appeared in *Reflections: A Journal of Writing, Service-Learning, and Community Literacy*, and she has presented at various national and international conferences.

Carolyn **Chernoff** is a visiting assistant professor of sociology at Skidmore College. Her research focuses on cities, arts, and social change, particularly on the level of social interaction and the production of "community." She investigates the role of culture in reproducing and transforming social inequality, and researches conflict around diversity and difference.

Jim **Daems** teaches in the English Department at the University of the Fraser Valley in British Columbia, Canada. His work focuses primarily on sixteenth- and seventeenth-century English representations of Ireland and queer theory. He has published books and articles on a range of early modern writers, as well as the Canadian multi-media artist and poet bill bissett, *Harry Potter*, Hank Williams and Chuck Berry.

David J. **Fine** teaches at Lehigh University in Bethlehem, Pennsylvania. He explores ethics and religion in the late modernist novel, believing that the sacred plays a central role in the articulation of ethical possibility. He has collaborated on projects with Emily Shreve relating to *RuPaul's Drag Race*, pedagogy, and the intersection of religion, literature and social justice.

Kai **Kohlsdorf** is completing his dissertation work in feminist studies at the University of Washington, Seattle. While he is interested in *RuPaul's Drag Race* as a capitalizing queer force, he is primarily focused on the creation of erotic care networks through in-community produced trans* and queer pornography. His work is analyzed through the lenses of feminist theory, queer theory, trans* studies, cultural studies and cultural geography.

Mary **Marcel** teaches communications at Bentley University and is the co-author, with Gordene MacKenzie, of "From Sensationalism to Education: Media Coverage of the Murder of U.S. Transgender Women of Color" in *Local Violence, Global Media: Feminist Analyses of Gendered Representations* (Peter Lang, 2009). She has worked closely with the founders of the Transgender International Day of Remembrance.

R. Gabriel **Mayora** is a Ph.D. candidate in the English Department at the University of Florida, where he also teaches. His main research focus is on representations of queer Latino masculinities in American literature, theater, TV and film. His dissertation is on Stonewall-era queer figures Holly Woodlawn and Sylvia Rivera.

Josh **Morrison** is a Ph.D. student in the Screen Arts & Cultures program at the University of Michigan. His research interests include camp and kitsch studies, queer media studies, feminist and queer theory, and drag queens on screen.

Laurie **Norris** is a doctoral student at the University of Georgia working in rhetoric and pop culture studies. She has presented on topics ranging from the rhetoric of electronic portfolio mark-up software to early modern drama, and gender dynamics in genres from hip-hop to children's cartoons. Her dissertation focuses on the rhetorical strategies of gender construction in media.

Fernando Gabriel **Pagnoni Berns** of the Universidad de Buenos Aires, Facultad de Filosofía y Letras, is a graduate teaching assistant of "Estética del Cine y Teorías Cinematográficas." He teaches seminars on American horror cinema and Euro horror. He is a member of the Art-Kiné research group on cinema, and he has published articles on Argentinian and international cinema, literature, comics and drama.

Emily **Shreve** teaches at Lehigh University in Bethlehem, Pennsylvania. She investigates how English literary texts in the late medieval period discerned between anger's wrathful potential to destroy community versus its righteous power to correct social ills. She has collaborated with David J. Fine on projects relating to *RuPaul's Drag Race*, pedagogy, and the intersection of religion, literature and social justice.

Bibliography

Abramovitch, Seth. "RuPaul, Inc.: Advice from a Business-Savvy Drag Queen." holly woodreporter.com, April 3, 2013. http://www.lexis.com (accessed February 19, 2014).

Arendt, Hannah. "The Crisis in Education." In *Between Past and Future*, 170–193. Rpt. New York: Penguin, 2006.

Aslinger, Ben. "Creating a Network for Queer Audiences at Logo TV." *Popular Communication* 7, no. 2 (April 2009): 107–21.

Babuscio, Jack. "The Cinema of Camp (AKA Camp and the Gay Sensibility)." In *Camp: Queer Aesthetics and the Performing Subject: A Reader*, edited by Fabio Cleto, 117–35. Ann Arbor: University of Michigan Press, 2002.

Badash, David. "United for Marriage Coalition Apologizes for Mistreatment of Trans and Undocumented Activists—HRC Signs on, Then Denies." The New Civil Rights Movement, March 29, 2013, http://thenewcivilrightsmovement.com/united-for-marriage-coalition-apologizes-for-mistreatment-of-trans-and-undocumented-activists-hrc-signs-on-then-denies/politics/2013/03/29/63826#. Uwja816N-4c (accessed February 22, 2014).

Bailey, Marlon M. "Gender/Racial Realness: Theorizing the Gender System in Ballroom Culture." *Feminist Studies* 37, no. 2 (2011): 365–386.

Baker, Katie J. M. "'A Graveyard for Homosexuals.'" *Newsweek Global Edition*, December 13, 2013. http://www.proquest.com/ (accessed February 16, 2014).

Bakhtin, Mikhail. *Rabelais and His World*. Bloomington: Indiana University Press, 2009.

Balzer, Caster. "The Great Drag Queen Hype: Thoughts on Cultural Globalisation and Autochthony." *Paideuma* 51 (2005): 111–131.

Barrett, Rusty. "Markedness and Styleswitching in Performances by African American Drag Queens." In *Codes and Consequences: Choosing Linguistic Varieties*, edited by Carol Myers-Scotton, 139–161. New York: Oxford University Press, 1998.

Battles, Kathleen, and Wendy Hilton-Morrow. "Gay Characters in Conventional Spaces: Will and Grace and the Situation Comedy Genre." *Critical Studies in Media Communication* 19, no. 1 (2002): 87–105.

Belli, Willam. "RuPaulogize." 19 April 2013; 4 min. 10 sec.; video clip. From *YouTube*, http://www.youtube.com/watch?v=JKbHCi5rBpI (accessed 1 February 2014).

Bennett-Smith, Meredith. "Human Rights Campaign Apologizes for Censoring

Undocumented, Trans Activists at Marriage Protests." *Huffington Post*, April 2, 2013, http://www.huffingtonpost.com/2013/04/02/human-rights-campaign-apol ogizes_n_2994939.html (accessed February 22, 2014).

Bersani, Leo. "Is the Rectum a Grave?" *October* 43 (Winter 1987): 187–222.

Bristow, Gillian. *Critical Reflections on Regional Competitiveness: Theory, Policy, Practice.* New York: Routledge, 2010.

Bronson, Po, and Ashley Merryman. *Nurtureshock: New Thinking About Children.* New York: Twelve, 2011.

Brower, Alison, and Stacey Wilson. "The Reality Heat List." *Hollywood Reporter* 419 (2013): 44–51. http://www.proquest.com/ (accessed February 16, 2014).

Brown, Gavin. "Homonormativity: A Metropolitan Concept That Denigrates 'Ordinary' Gay Lives." *Journal of Homosexuality* 59, no. 7 (2012): 1065–72.

Buchanan, Kyle. "RuPaul on *Drag Race, Hannah Montana*, and 'Those Bitches' Who Stole Annette Bening's Oscar." *Vulture*, April 4, 2011. http://www.vulture.com/ 2011/04/rupaul_on_drag_race_hannah_mon.html (accessed January 30, 2014).

Butler, Judith. *Bodies That Matter: On the Discursive Limits of "Sex."* New York: Routledge, 1993.

_____. *Gender Trouble: Feminism and the Subversion of Identity.* New York: Routledge, 1990.

Camerer, Colin, Teck-Hua Ho, and Juin-Kuan Chong, "A Cognitive Hierarchy Model of Games." *The Quarterly Journal of Economics* 119, no. 3 (2004): 861–898.

Canagarajah, A. Suresh. "Introduction." In *Literacy as Translingual Practice: Between Communities and Classrooms*, edited by Suresh Canagarajah, 1–10. New York: Routledge, 2013.

Cane, Clay. "BET.com: RuPaul on LL CoolJ, Shirley Q. Liquor and more..." *Clay Cane Blog.* Retrieved from http://claycane.net/2009/01/28/bet-com-rupaul-on-ll-cool-j-shirley-q-liquor-and-more/ (accessed November 18, 2013).

Carrera, Carmen. "carmencarrerafans." *Facebook.* July 21, 2013. https://www.facebook. com/carmencarrerafans, Web.

_____. "carmencarrerafans." *Facebook.* July 7, 2012. https://www.facebook.com/ carmencarrerafans, Web.

_____. "carmencarrerafans." *Facebook.* October 12, 2012. https://www.facebook.com/ carmencarrerafans, Web.

Caulfield, Keith. "'Drag' Divas make Splash." *Billboard* 125, no. 6 (2013): 73. http:// www.proquest.com/ (accessed February 16, 2014).

Cefai, Sarah, and Maria Elena Indelicato. "No Such This as Standard Beauty: Intersectionality and Embodied Feeling on *America's Next Top Model.*" *Outskirts: Feminisms Along the Edge* 24 (2011): 10.

Centeno, Miguel, and Joseph Cohen. *Global Capitalism: A Sociological Perspective.* Cambridge: Polity Press, 2010.

Cerna, Antonio. "Rebecca Glasscock Lip Syncs for Her Life." *New York Press.* http:// www.nypress.com/blog-3836-rebecca-glasscock-lip-syncs-for-her-life.html (accessed June 23, 2010).

Chance, Katy. "He Ain't Heavy—She's My Sister." *Business Day* (South Africa), February 7, 2013 Arts, Culture and Entertainment Section. http://www.lexisnexis. com (accessed February 19, 2014).

Clark, Cedric. "Television and Social Control: Some Observations of the Portrayal of Ethnic Minorities." *Television Quarterly* 9, no. 2 (1969): 18–22.

Cox, Michelle, Jay Jordan, Christina Ortmeier-Hooper, and Gwen Gray Schwartz. *Reinventing Identities in Second Language Writing*. Urbana: National Council of Teachers of Writing, 2010.

Daley, Lauren. "Dragged into Debate: Reality-TV Fame Puts Spotlight on Sharon Needles' Controversial Act." *Pittsburgh City Paper*. http://m.pghcitypaper.com/ pittsburgh/dragged-into-debate-reality-tv-fame-puts-spotlight-on-sharon-needles-controversial-act/Content?oid=1535799 (accessed June 20, 2012).

Davis, Precious. "What I Learned Auditioning for RuPaul's Drag Race." *We Happy Trans*, February 13, 2013. http://wehappytrans.com/news-media/rupaulsdrag race/ (accessed February 21, 2014).

Drushel, Bruce. "Performing Race, Class, and Gender: The Tangled History of Drag." *Reconstruction: Studies in Contemporary Culture* 13, no. 2 (2013). http://ehis. ebscohost.com.proxy.ufv.ca:2048/eds/detail?vid=11&sid=1c89b3de-6284–4a2c-bf9b-9cd1afe2a9e8%40sessionmgr110&hid=16&bdata=JnNpdGU9ZWRzLW-xpdmU%3d#db=hus&AN=90487034) (accessed November 2, 2013).

Duggan, Lisa. "The New Homonormativity: The Sexual Politics of Neoliberalism." In *Materializing Democracy: Toward a Revitalized Cultural Politics*, edited by Dana D Nelson and Russ Castronovo, 175–94. Durham: Duke University Press, 2002.

_____. *The Twilight of Equality? Neoliberalism, Cultural Politics, and the Attack on Democracy*. Boston: Beacon Press, 2003.

Dunbar, Michele D. "Dennis Rodman—'Barbie Doll Gone Horribly Wrong': Marginalized Masculinity, Cross-Dressing, and the Limitations of Commodity Culture." *Journal of Men's Studies* 7, no. 3 (April 30, 1999): 317–336. http://www.pro quest.com/ (accessed February 19, 2014).

Duthel, Heinz. *Kathoey Ladyboy: Thailand's Got Talent*. BoD, 2013.

Dyer, Richard, *The Matter of Images: Essays on Representation*. New York: Routledge, 2002.

Edgar, Eir-Anne, "Xtravaganza: Drag Representation and Articulation in *RuPaul's Drag Race*." *Studies in Popular Culture* 34, no. 1 (2011): 133–146 http://www. pcasacas.org/SiPC (accessed January 15, 2014).

Etkin, Jaimie. "RuPaul's Drag Race Dictionary." *Newsweek Web Exclusives*, April 24, 2011. http://www.proquest.com/ (accessed February 16, 2014).

Ferguson, Kathy. *The Feminist Case Against Bureaucracy: Women in the Political Economy*. Philadelphia: Temple University Press, 1984.

Fiske, John. *Television Culture*. Rpt. London: Routledge, 1990.

Fitzgerald, Christine. "Meet the Queens of RuPaul's Drag Race—Raja." *Socialite Life*. http://socialitelife.com/meet-the-queens-of-rupauls-drag-race-raja-01–2011 (accessed March 20, 2012).

Flinn, Caryl. "The Deaths of Camp." In *Camp: Queer Aesthetics and the Performing Subject: A Reader*, edited by Fabio Cleto, 431–57. Ann Arbor: University of Michigan Press, 2002.

Flóki, Björn. "Drag Dad." http://www.dragdad.com/about-the-film/ (accessed January 30, 2014).

Gamson, Joshua. *Freaks Talk Back: Tabloid Talk Shows and Sexual Nonconformity.* Chicago: University of Chicago Press, 2008.

_____. "Reality Queens." *Contexts* (Spring 2013): 52–54. http://www.proquest.com (accessed February 16, 2014).

Gan, Jessi. "Still at the Back of the Bus: Sylvia Rivera's Struggle." *Centro Journal* 19, no. 1 (2007): 124–239.

Garber, Marjorie. *Vested Interests: Cross-Dressing and Cultural Anxiety.* New York: Routledge, 1992.

Gerbner, George, and Larry Gross. "Living with Television: The Violence Profile." *The Journal of Communication* 26, no. 2 (1976): 173–199.

GLAAD. "Video: Jinkx Monsoon Performs Sondheim at the #glaadawards." glaad. org, last modified May 14, 2013, http://www.glaad.org/blog/video-jinkx-monsoon-performs-sondheim-glaadawards (accessed January 28, 2014).

Gorlée, Dinda. *Semiotics and the Problem of Translation: With Special Reference to the Semiotics of Charles S. Peirce.* Atlanta: Rodopi, 1994.

Graff, E. J. "What's Next?" *Newsweek*, September 27, 2013: 1. http://www.proquest.com/ (accessed February 16, 2014).

Grundmann, Roy. *Andy Warhol's Blow Job.* Philadelphia: Temple University Press, 2003.

Guha, Rohin. "On Gay Male Privilege: Excuse Me Sir, Your Privilege Is Showing." *Medium: Gender, Justice, Feminism.* January 18, 2014. https://medium.com/gender-justice-feminism/59fc5490b223.

Halberstam, Judith. "Drag Queens at the 801 Cabaret." *Journal of the History of Sexuality* 13, no. 1 (2004): 124–126. http://www.proquest.com/ (accessed February 19, 2014).

Hall, Stuart. *Policing the Crisis: Mugging, the State, and Law and Order.* New York: Holmes & Meier, 1978.

_____. *Representation: Cultural Representations and Signifying Practices.* London: Sage, 1997.

Harris, Daniel. "The Aesthetic of Drag." *Salmagundi* 108 (1995): 62–74.

Harvard Business Essentials: Business Communication. Cambridge: Harvard Business School Publishing Corporation, 2003.

Harvie, Jen. *Fair Play: Art, Performance and Neoliberalism.* New York: Palgrave Macmillan, 2013.

Hermosillo, Maribel. "Human Rights Campaign Fails to Advocate for Minorities." PolicyMic, March 29, 2013, http://www.policymic.com/articles/31563/human-rights-campaign-fails-to-advocate-for-minorities/424007 (accessed February 22, 2014).

Herzog, Amy, and Joe Rollins. "Editors' Note." *Women's Studies Quarterly* 41, no. 1 & 2 (2013): 9–13.

Hicks, Jessica. "Can I Get an 'Amen?'" In *Queer Love in Film and Television: Critical Essays*, edited by Pamela Demory and Christopher Pullen, 153–160. New York: Palgrave Macmillan, 2013.

Hilton, Perez. "The Search for America's Next Tranny." Perezhilton.com, May 14, 2008. http://perezhilton.com/2008-05-14-ru-paul#sthash.sYrZ4VSe.dpuf (accessed November 10, 2013).

Horner, Bruce, Min-Zhan Lu, Jacqueline Jones Royster, and John Trimbur. "Opinion: Language Difference in Writing: Toward a Translingual Approach." *College English* 73.3 (2011): 303–321.

Horner, Bruce, Samantha NeCamp, and Christiane Donahue. "Toward a Multilingual Composition Scholarship: From English Only to a Translingual Norm." *College Composition and Communication* 63.2 (2011): 269–300.

"How Are Gays Being Represented on TV?" *National Public Radio*, Washington, D.C., Morning Edition, January 2, 2013. http://www.proquest.com/ (accessed February 17, 2014).

Hudson, William. *American Democracy in Peril: Eight Challenges to America's Future*, 7th Ed. London: Sage, 2013.

Jackson, Isaac. "Reading Madonna: The Lessons of Truth or Dare Offer a Challenge to the Lesbian and Gay Community." *Gay Community News*, June 1, 1991, 20. http://www.proquest.com/ (accessed February 18, 2014).

Johnson, Karlee. "Equality for Some: A Critique of the Human Rights Campaign." *Daily Sundial*, October 10, 2011, http://sundial.csun.edu/2011/10/equality-for-some-a-critique-of-the-human-rights-campaign/ (accessed February 22, 2014).

Joseph, Ralina L. "Recursive Racial Transformation: Selling the Exceptional Multiracial." In *Transcending Blackness: From the New Millennium Mulatta to the Exceptional Multiracial, 1998–2008*, 188–224. Durham: Duke University Press, 2012.

_____. "Tyra Banks Is Fat: Reading (Post-)Racism and (Post-)Feminism in the New Millennium." *Critical Studies in Media Communication* 26, no. 3 (2009): 237–54.

Joyrich, Lynne. "Queer Television Studies: Currents, Flows, and (Main)Streams." *Cinema Journal* 53, no. 2 (2014): 133–139 http://www.muse.jhu.edu (accessed January 31, 2014).

Kent, Sharmin. "How 'Drag Race' Gave RuPaul a Comeback—and Made Him a Next-Generation Oprah." Thinkprogress, October 11, 2013. http://thinkprogress.org/alyssa/2013/10/11/2771461/rupaul-drag-race/ (accessed November 2, 2013).

Kirk, Mary. "Kind of a Drag: Gender, Race, and Ambivalence in *The Birdcage* and *To Wong Foo Thanks for Everything! Julie Newmar*." *Journal of Homosexuality*, 46 (2004): 169–180.

Kraszewski, John. "Country Hicks and Urban Cliques: Mediating Race, Reality, and Liberalism on MTV's *The Real World*." In *TV: Remaking Television Culture*, edited by Susan Murray and Laurie Ouellette, 179–196. New York: New York University Press, 2004.

LaFountain-Stokes, Lawrence. "Gay Shame, Latina- and Latino-Style: A Critique of White Queer Performativity." In *Gay Latino Studies: A Critical Reader*, edited by Michael Hames-García and Ernesto Javier Martínez, 55–80. Durham: Duke University Press, 2011.

Lang, Nico. "Breaking Ground: An Interview with Precious Jewel on *RuPaul's Drag Race*." WBEZ 91.5 Chicago, February 22, 2013. http://www.wbez.org/blogs/nico-lang/2013-02/breaking-ground-interview-precious-jewel-rupauls-drag-race-105658 (accessed January 30, 2014).

Levitt, Lauren. "Reality Realness: *Paris is Burning* and *RuPaul's Drag Race.*" *Interventions Journal*, November 7, 2013. http://interventionsjournal.net/2013/11/07/reality-realness-paris-is-burning-and-rupauls-drag-race/ (accessed February 19, 2014).

MacKenzie, Gordene, and Mary Marcel. "From Sensationalism to Education: Media Coverage of Murder of US Transgender Women of Color." In *Local Violence, Global Media: Feminist Analyses of Gendered Representations*, edited by Lisa Cuklanz and Sujata Moorti, 79–106. New York: Peter Lang, 2009.

Madger, Ted. "The End of TV 101: Reality Programs, Formats, and the New Business of Television." In *TV: Remaking Television Culture*, edited by Susan Murray and Laurie Ouellette, 137–156. New York: New York University Press, 2004.

Manalansan IV, Martin F. "Queering the Chain of Care Paradigm." *The Scholar & Feminist Online* 6, no. 3 (2008). http://www.barnard.edu/sfonline/immigration/manalansan_01.htm (accessed March 22, 2013).

Mann, Stephen L. "Drag Queens' Use of Language and the Performance of Blurred Gendered and Racial Identities." *Journal of Homosexuality* 58 (2011): 793–811.

Mao, LuMing. "Why Don't We Speak with an Accent? Practicing Interdependence-in-Difference." In *Cross-Language Relations in Composition*, edited by Bruce Horner, Min-Zhan Lu, and Paul Kei Matsuda, 189–195. Carbondale: Southern Illinois University Press, 2010.

Martin-Malone, Joy. "Why Drag Queens Are Better Role Models Than Disney Princesses." *Huffington Post*, http://www.huffingtonpost.com/joy-martinmalone/drag-queens_b_4006697.html (accessed February 4, 2013).

McClelland, Mac. "RuPaul: The King of Queens: How RuPaul Became America's Sweetheart." *Rolling Stone*, October 4, 2013, http://www.rollingstone.com/movies/news/rupaul-the-king-of-queens-20131004 (accessed January 28, 2014).

McNeal, Keith. "Behind the Make-Up: Gender Ambivalence and the Double-Bind of Gay Selfhood in Drag Performance." *Ethos* 27, no. 3 (1999): 344–378.

Michelson, Noah. "Monica Beverly Hillz, 'RuPaul's Drag Race' Contestant, Discusses Coming Out as Transgender." *Huffington Post*. http://www.huffingtonpost.com/2013/02/05/monica-beverly-hillz-transgender_n_2617975.html (accessed November 3, 2013).

Mitchell, Koritha. "Love in Action: Noting Similarities Between Lynching Then and Anti-LGBT Violence Now." *Callaloo* 36, no. 3 (2013): 688–717. http://www.proquest.com/ (accessed February 16, 2014).

Mittell, Jason. *Genre and Television: From Cop Shows to Cartoons in America Culture.* New York: Routledge, 2004.

Mohanty, Chandra T., "Under Western Eyes: Feminist Scholarship and Colonial Discourses." In *Third World Women and the Politics of Feminism*, edited by Chandra T. Mohanty, Ann Russo, and Lourdes Torres, 51–80. Bloomington: Indiana University Press, 1991.

Monforte, Ivan. "House and Ball Culture Goes Wide." *The Gay & Lesbian Review Worldwide* 17, no. 5 (2010): 28–30. http://www.proquest.com/ (accessed February 17, 2014).

Muñoz, José Esteban. *Cruising Utopia: The Then and There of Queer Futurity.* New York: New York University Press, 2009.

_____. *Disidentifications: Queers of Color and the Performance of Politics*. Minneapolis: University of Minnesota Press, 1999.

_____. "Toward a Methexic Queer Media." *GLQ: A Journal of Lesbian and Gay Studies* 4 (2013): 564.

Murphy, Tim, Ryan Wenzel, and Andrea James. "Gay vs. Trans in America." *The Advocate*, December 18, 2007, 39. http://www.proquest.com/ (accessed February 17, 2014).

Negrón-Muntaner, Frances. *Boricua Pop: Puerto Rico and the Latinization of American Culture*. New York: New York University Press, 2004.

Nero, Shondel J. "Discourse Tensions, Englishes, and the Composition Classroom." In *Cross-Language Relations in Composition*, edited by Bruce Horner, Min-Zhan Lu, and Paul Kei Matsuda, 142–157. Carbondale: Southern Illinois University Press, 2010.

Newton, Esther. *Mother Camp: Female Impersonators in America*. Englewood Cliffs, NJ: Prentice-Hall, 1972.

Ng, Eve. "A 'Post-Gay' Era? Media Gaystreaming, Homonormativity, and the Politics of LGBT Integration." *Communication, Culture & Critique* 6, no. 2 (June 2013): 258–83.

Niedzvieck, Hal. *Hello, I'm Special: How Individuality Became the New Conformity*. San Francisco: City Lights, 2006.

Nussbaum, Emily. "Camptown Races." *The New Yorker*, April 23, 2012. http://www.newyorker.com/arts/critics/notebook/2012/04/23/120423gonb_GOAT_notebook_nussbaum (accessed November 15, 2013).

Ornstein, Peggy. *Cinderella Ate My Daughter: Dispatches from the Front Lines of the New Girlie-Girl Culture*. New York: Harper Paperbacks, 2012.

Pardee, Thomas. "Is Gay Too Mainstream for Its Own Media?" *Advertising Age* 83, no. 11 (2012): 1,8. http://www.proquest.com/ (accessed February 16, 2014).

Paris Is Burning. DVD, Directed by Jennie Livingston. Distributed by Orion Home Video, 1990.

Parpat, Jane. "Deconstructing the Development 'Expert': Gender, Development, and the Vulnerable Groups." In *Feminism/Postmodernism/Development*, edited by Marianne Marchand and Jane Parpart, 221–243. New York: Routledge, 1995.

Patton, Tracey Owens, and Julie Snyder-Yuly. "Roles, Rules, and Rebellions: Creating the Carnivalesque Through the Judges' Behaviors on *America's Next Top Model*." *Communication Studies* 63, no. 3 (2012): 364–84.

Perez, Hiram. "You Can Have My Brown Body and Eat It Too!" *Social Text* 23, no. 3–4 (2005): 171–192.

Peters, Wendy. "Pink Dollars, White Collars: Queer as Folk, Valuable Viewers, and the Price of Gay TV." *Critical Studies in Media Communication*, 28, no. 3 (2011): 193–212.

Phillips II, Gregory, James Peterson, Diane Binson, Julia Hidalgo, and Manya Magnus. "House/Ball Culture and Adolescent African-American Transgender Persons and Men Who Have Sex with Men: A Synthesis of the Literature." *AIDS Care* 23, no. 4 (2011): 515–520.

Pozner, Jennifer L. *Reality Bites Back: The Troubling Truth About Guilty Pleasure TV*. Berkeley: Seal Press, 2010.

The Prime of Miss Jean Brodie, directed by Ronald Neame. 1969; Beverly Hills: 20th
    Century–Fox, 2004. DVD.
Puar, Jasbir. *Terrorist Assemblages: Homonationalism in Queer Times.* Durham: Duke
    University Press, 2007.
Pullen, Christopher. *Documenting Gay Men: Identity and Performance in Reality Tel-
    evision and Documentary Film.* Jefferson, NC: McFarland, 2007.
Rhyne, Ragan. "Racializing White Drag." *Journal of Homosexuality* 46, no. 3/4 (2004):
    181–94.
Rickman, Cheryl. *The Digital Business Start-Up Workbook: The Ultimate Step-by-
    Step Guide to Succeeding Online from Start-Up to Exit.* Chichester: Wiley, 2012.
Robinson, Lisa. "Lady Gaga's Cultural Revolution." *Vanity Fair* 9 (2010): 280. http://
    www.proquest.com/ (accessed February 18, 2014).
Rogin, Michael P. *Blackface, White Noise: Jewish Immigrants in the Hollywood Melting
    Pot.* Berkeley: University of California Press, 1996.
Ross, Andrew. *No Respect: Intellectuals & Popular Culture.* New York: Routledge, 1989.
_____. "Uses of Camp." In *Camp: Queer Aesthetics and the Performing Subject: A
    Reader,* edited by Fabio Cleto, 308–29. Ann Arbor: University of Michigan Press,
    2002.
RuPaul. *Lettin It All Hang Out: An Autobiography.* New York: Hyperion, 1995.
_____. *Workin' It! RuPaul's Guide to Life, Liberty, and the Pursuit of Style.* New York:
    It Books, 2010.
RuPaul's Drag Race Crowns a Drag Princess. Fusion TV, 2013. http://fusion.net/
    Alicia_Menendez_Tonight/video/rupauls-drag-race-drag-queen-crowns-drag-
    princess-215307 (accessed Feb. 4, 2014).
Russell, Thaddeus. "The Color of Discipline: Civil Rights and Black Sexuality." *Amer-
    ican Quarterly* 60, no. 1 (2008): 101–128, 231. http://www.proquest.com/ (accessed
    February 17, 2014).
Ryan, Hugh. "TV's Transformative Moment." *Newsweek,* July 17, 2013, 1. http://www.
    proquest.com/ (accessed February 16, 2014).
Said, Edward W. *Orientalism.* New York: Vintage, 1978.
Schacht, Steven P. "Lesbian Drag Kings and the Feminine Embodiment of the Mas-
    culine." *Journal of Homosexuality* 43, no. 3/4 (2002): 75–99, Print.
Schewe, Elizabeth. "Controversial 'RuPaul's Drag Race' Queen Willam Explains Dis-
    qualification: 'My Husband Was Coming to Bang Me Out.'" *Entertainment
    Weekly* May 1, 2012 1:22 a.m. http://popwatch.ew.com/2012/05/01/rupauls-drag-
    race-willam-disqualified-banged-out/ (accessed January 21, 2014).
_____. "Serious Play: Drag, Transgender, and the Relationship Between Performance
    and Identity in the Life Writing of RuPaul and Kate Bornstein." *Biography: An
    Interdisciplinary Quarterly* 32, no. 4 (2009): 670–695. Academic Search Premier
    (accessed February 17, 2014).
Schlenker, Barry, and Thomas V. Bonoma. "Fun and Games: The Validity of Games
    for the Study of Conflict." *The Journal of Conflict Resolution* 22, no. 1 (1978): 7–
    38.
Sciullo, Maria. "Shrimp Toss Ward for Loss in Semifinals of 'Cook-off.'" *Pittsburgh
    Post-Gazette,* February 9, 2013. http://www.lexis.com (accessed February 21,
    2014).

Sedgwick, Eve Kosofsky. "Some Binarisms (II)." In *Epistemology of the Closet*, 131–81. Berkeley: University of California Press, 2008.

Sende, Katherine. *Business, Not Politics: The Making of the Gay Market*. New York: Columbia University Press, 2004.

Shanikka. "Facts Belie the Scapegoating of Black People for Proposition 8." *Daily Kos*, November 7, 2008, http://www.dailykos.com/story/2008/11/07/656272/-Facts-Belie-the-Scapegoating-of-Black-People-for-Proposition-8# (accessed February 22, 2014).

Shapiro, Eve. "Drag Kinging and the Transformation of Gender Identities." *Gender and Society* 21, no. 2 (April 2007): 250–271.

Signorile, Michelangelo. *Queer in America: Sex, the Media, and the Closets of Power*. New York: Random House, 1993.

_____. "RuPaul Sounds Off on New Season of 'RuPaul's Drag Race,' Obama, the Word 'Tranny,' and More." *Huffington Post*. http://www.huffingtonpost.com/2012/01/13/rupaul-on-rupauls-drag-race-obama-tranny_n_1205203.html?ref=gay-voices (accessed November 2, 2013).

Sontag, Susan. "Notes on 'Camp.'" In *Camp: Queer Aesthetics and the Performing Subject: A Reader*, edited by Fabio Cleto, 53–65. Ann Arbor: University of Michigan Press, 2002.

Spade, Dean. "Resisting Medicine, Re/modeling Gender." *Berkeley Women's Law Journal* 18 (2003): 15–37.

Spark, Muriel. *The Prime of Miss Jean Brodie*. 1961. Reprint, New York: HarperCollins, 2009.

Spaulding, Pam. "The N-Bomb Is Dropped on Black Passersby at Prop 8 Protests." *Huffington Post*, November 10, 2008, http://www.huffingtonpost.com/pam-spaulding/the-n-bomb-is-dropped-on_b_142363.html (accessed February 22, 2014).

Stanley, Alessandra. "They Float Like the Clouds on Air Do, They Enjoy." *New York Times*, February 2, 2009.

Stevens, Quentin. *The Ludic City: Exploring the Potential of Public Spaces*. New York: Routledge, 2007.

Stransky, Tanner. "Kings of Queens." *Entertainment Weekly*, December 15, 2006, 28. http://www.proquest.com/ (accessed February 16, 2014).

_____. "RuPaul on 'Drag Race': Five Rules for a Killer Comeback." *Entertainment Weekly*. http://popwatch.ew.com/popwatch/2009/02/rupaul-on-drag.html (accessed on March 6, 2012).

_____. "'RuPaul's Drag Race' Disqualified Contestant Speaks Out: 'I wasn't caught doing anything.'" *Pop Watch Entertainment Weekly*. http://popwatch.ew.com/2012/03/20/rupauls-drag-race-willam-elimination/ (accessed on May 2, 2012).

Stryker, Susan. "Transgender History, Homonormativity, and Disciplinarity." *Radical History Review* 100 (Winter 2008): 144–57.

Swidler, Ann, "Culture in Action: Symbols and Strategies." *American Sociological Review* 51, no. 2 (1986): 273–286.

Taylor, Verta, and Leila J. Rupp. "When the Girls Are Men: Negotiating Gender and Sexual Dynamics in a Study of Drag Queens." *Signs: Journal of Women in Culture and Society* 30, no. 4 (Summer 2005): 2115–2139.

Tom and Lorenzo. "Cover Girl Put the Bass in Your Walk." http://tomandlorenzo.com/2012/03/rupauls-drag-race-cover-girl-put-the-bass-in-your-walk/ (accessed February 16, 2014).

Walker, Dorothea. *Muriel Spark*. Boston: Twayne, 1988.

Warner, Michael. *The Trouble with Normal: Sex, Politics and the Ethics of Queer Life.* Cambridge: Harvard University Press, 1999.

Weber, Brenda R. "Makeover as Takeover: Scenes of Affective Domination on Makeover TV." *Configurations* 15, no. 1 (2008): 77–99.

Wheaton, Ken. "ADAGES." *Advertising Age* 80, no. 3 (2009): 38. http://search.proquest.com/ (accessed February 17, 2014).

Whittington, Lew. "Latrice's Secret Weapon." *Huffington Post: The Blog.* Posted: 11/27/2012 2:13 p.m. http://www.huffingtonpost.com/lew-whittington/latrices-secret-weapon_b_2184520.html (accessed February 19, 2014).

Wierzbicka, Anna. *Semantics: Primes and Universals.* New York: Oxford University Press, 2004.

Wieselman, Jarett. "RuPaul Talks 'Drag Race' Hits—and Misses." ETonline, September 23, 2013, http://www.etonline.com/tv/138718_RuPaul_Lost_Drag_Race_Season_One_ Interview/ (accessed January 28, 2014).

Yoshino, Kenji. *Covering: The Hidden Assault on Our Civil Rights.* New York: Random House, 2006.

Index